BEFORE THE BELLS HAVE FADED

THE SINKING OF HMS FORMIDABLE
JANUARY 1, 1915 - THE FIRST BRITISH BATTLESHIP
TO BE SUNK BY A GERMAN U-BOAT

Mark Potts & Tony Marks

Printed and bound by CPI Antony Rowe, Eastbourne

*Every effort has been made to contact present
copyright owners to any pictures that appear in
the book which are not properly credited. We
will do our utmost to include any
acknowledgments to all parties involved
in subsequent reprints of this book.*

Previous page - The crest of HMS Formidable.

'Brave souls of the Formidable
the boats have gone away,
left all alone in the wind and rain
on a stormy New Year's Day.'

'Brave souls of the Formidable
your final hour has come,
no chance for fame or glory
or to see the morning sun.'

'Brave souls of the Formidable
made silent by the sea,
just hours before 500 men
had dreams of liberty.'

'Brave souls of the Formidable
you did not die in vain,
your names will live for evermore
to dull and ease the pain.'

'Brave souls of the Formidable
at home, your loss, our sorrow,
sacrificed for right and good
and England's tomorrow.'

'The introduction of vessels that swim under the water has, in my opinion, entirely done away with the utility of the ships that swim on top of the water' (Admiral Sir Percy Scott in *The Times*, June 5, 1914)

CONTENTS

ACKNOWLEDGMENTS

We would like to thank the following who helped us in the creation of this book. Peter John for his sterling work at the Public Record Office and for his proof reading skills. Jane Jones and the Medway Local Studies Centre who provided us with photographs of some of the casualties. The Dorchester Library, the Brixham Heritage Museum, and Brian Ogle for information on the dramatic rescue at sea of the survivors of HMS *Formidable* by the fishing vessel *Provident* and also Wendy Custerson, a great niece of the Skipper of *Provident,* who supplied us with photographs and other useful information. The Philpot Museum, Lyme Regis, especially Mike Cawte and Jo Draper, for allowing us access to photos and information regarding the *Formidable* tragedy. Maureen Annetts at the Enquiries Section, Commonwealth War Graves Commission who supplied the print-outs for the Roll of Honour and to Paul Darcy, who contributed data on the German submarine *U-24*. Nick Chipchase who has dived on the wreck of the *Formidable* and given us details of its condition and has loaned us several of his postcards of HMS *Formidable*. Tim Hughes & Associates, who researched the available war logs of HMS *Formidable* and also the Public Record Office (PRO) for formal permission to publish several photographs of the *Formidable*. To Edward Devine, Joan Booth and the late Colin Donaldson who were involved in the research regarding the story of Stanley Reed. Steve Cornes and Chris Cole who supplied details and maps pinpointing the exact location of the wreck of the *Formidable* and Sarah Thompson for her articles in the *Lyme Regis News* asking for photographs or local stories regarding the sinking. Jack Thomas of Uplyme, Dorset, for proof reading the script and helping in so many other ways in the production of this publication. Most of all, the relatives and descendants of the crew members of HMS *Formidable*, who kindly loaned photographs, supplied relevant information and provided ideas and encouragement towards this worthwhile project, especially Ray Booth, whose father served aboard *Formidable* and survived the sinking. He has dedicated his pastime to collecting everything to do with the *Formidable* and has contacted many relatives of the crew. We are indebted for his contribution to the book and for permission to publish his father's memoirs up to and including the sinking of HMS *Formidable*, which gives us an account of life in the Royal Navy in Edwardian times until 1915.

PREFACE

Of all the Royal Navy ships sunk during the Great War of 1914-18, the pre-dreadnought battleship HMS *Formidable* would figure in the top fifteen, in terms of men lost in a single action. Pick up any publication describing the naval actions of the Great War however, and the clashes at Jutland, Heligoland Bight, Coronel and the Falkland Islands are prominent in the pages which report, analyse and debate these sea battles between the Royal Navy and its German adversaries. To find an account of the sinking of HMS *Formidable*, the reader would find few words on the subject, or nothing at all. As examples, the highly respected *The War Illustrated*, published throughout the conflict and later released in a nine volume set, afforded just a few lines and three small photographs relating to the incident. In the popular six volume set *A Popular History Of The Great War*, edited by Sir J. A. Hammerton, the sinking and the rescue of the survivors cover just over half a page. We therefore hope to correct this maritime military oversight, by telling the story of events that saw the first British battleship of World War One sunk by an enemy submarine. It sank off the Dorset coast, joining the many other ships over the centuries, lost in these waters. This book is dedicated to the 547 officers and men who did not survive.

INTRODUCTION

The idea of writing this book was born on a snowy Sunday morning in December 1998, while I was researching the names on the local war memorial in my home town of Crewe in Cheshire, for another book project. While brushing away the snow from the iron cast tablets that list the names of the fallen of the Great War, I noticed that four men on the memorial were crew members of HMS *Formidable*. Immediately my thoughts were that the ship had been sunk in a famous battle during the war, but what type of ship was she, and what were the circumstances surrounding the deaths of the men listed? What intrigued me further was the fact that two of the men shared the same, but very unusual surname. Obviously they were related, but I wondered if they were in fact brothers. Realising I needed to know more about the names, HMS *Formidable,* and the task of piecing the story together, I enlisted the help of my long time friend and fellow local military historian, Tony Marks, to help gather the information needed to initially satisfy my inquisitive mind. A few months passed and with the help of the Commonwealth War Graves Commission and exhaustive periods spent in the local library studying the newspapers of the Great War period, the picture of events slowly started to come together. The surnames turned out, not only to be brothers, but twins! To my knowledge, very few twin brothers had died during the war in the same incident on the same day, so this made the story even more interesting. The other two names on the memorial turned out to be workmates of the twins, all of them employed in Crewe Railway Works. All four were members of the St. John's Ambulance Brigade attached to the Royal Navy Sick Berth Reserve, and were spending one week's training aboard HMS *Formidable* during their work's summer holiday. With war breaking out the very next day, they all volunteered to stay aboard, a decision which would cost them their lives. We also learnt that HMS *Formidable* was an old pre-dreadnought battleship in the 5th Battle Squadron, sunk by a U-boat off the coast of Lyme Regis on the first day of January, 1915.

During the next three months, through the power of the internet and letters written to newspapers in Dorset and Kent appealing for information, we managed to contact quite a few relatives and descendants of the crew. The story which was starting to emerge we thought was worthy of publication. We also spent several days in the picturesque town of Lyme Regis to study further information and photographs in the local museum and visit places relevant to the sinking and also to familiarise ourselves with the area where this sad event unfolded. After collating our information, what emerged was a story packed full of incidents, heroism, heartache, self-sacrifice, leadership, and survival. We hope we have done this fine battleship and her crew the justice they deserve.   *M. A. Potts*

THE BUILD UP TO WAR

As an island nation, Britain has always relied heavily on sea power to defend its shores. Not since October 21, 1805, when Admiral Horatio Nelson aboard HMS *Victory* had, at the cost of his life, inflicted a crushing defeat on the French and Spanish fleets off Trafalgar, had the Royal Navy been significantly threatened by another sea power. Until Nelson's death, the propulsion of men-of-war had been by wind and sail, but within a few years after the Battle of Trafalgar, some merchant ship owners began experimenting with the use of vessels propelled by paddles. These were iron hulled and viewed with interest by the Admiralty. In 1845, SS *Great Britain*, a screw propelled ship, successfully crossed the Atlantic Ocean and in 1859 HMS *Warrior*, a broadside ironclad ship, was constructed and commenced service with the Royal Navy in October 1861.

In the first few years of the 20th century, Germany, under the guiding hand of Alfred von Tirpitz (Secretary of the Navy), set about building a naval force to challenge Britain's command of the sea. For centuries, the strength of the Royal Navy was represented by her ships of the line, and in the 1890's, the design of the battleship was changed forever, with the introduction of the *Royal Sovereign* class to the Royal Navy, initiated and nurtured by William Henry White, who had become Director of Naval Construction in 1885.

War had been simmering in Europe for some time and both Britain and Germany realised if war was declared, then their sea-lanes would have to remain open for maintenance of overseas colonies. Britain had further reasons, as they were heavily reliant on imported food and raw materials, which would be so important if they were to maintain a sustained war effort. To continue as the dominant naval force, Britain would have to keep one step ahead of their rivals. Britain therefore met the challenge by stripping its overseas stations of ships and concentrated them in home waters. In 1904, the appointment of First Sea Lord John Fisher, transformed the Fleet, previously riddled with Victorian complacency, into a fighting machine, again with no equal. In a letter to reassure a worried public he wrote *'we will soon have in home waters two fleets, each of which is incomparably superior to the entire German fleet fully mobilised for war. So sleep easy in your beds.'* Comprehensive reforms of training followed and Fisher's ruthless retirement of incompetent senior officers made him an unpopular figure in some circles of the Royal Navy. His uncanny vision of future naval warfare was completely embodied in the transformation of the battleship design. In 1906 this transformation culminated in a new revolutionary battleship, which was faster, better protected and armed than all that had gone before. Such was her design, it made all earlier battleships virtually obsolete. The ship receiving all the plaudits was HMS *Dreadnought*. Its total concentration on heavy guns (10 x 12") made it the most powerfully armed ship of its time. Built at Portsmouth Dockyard in just 14 months, the vessel also boasted steam turbine machinery, which propelled the mighty battleship to speeds in excess of twenty knots. The commissioning of HMS *Dreadnought* triggered an international arms race and by the time war was declared in August 1914, Britain had constructed 24 dreadnoughts and battlecruisers ready for war, while Germany's total was just 16.

So on the outbreak, Britain went to war with a small but highly trained army, but the greatest navy the world had ever seen. Apart from the numerical advantage in big gun ships, Britain could also call on the naval strength of France. It was imperative for Britain that this naval advantage was maintained, because defeat of the Royal Navy and her naval Allies , would mean that Britain too would be open to invasion.

However after the excitement of a war with Germany had died down, not everybody at home was convinced that the Royal Navy could keep the enemy from the door. During the lead up to war, a naval revolution had been in silent progress, which could threaten the numerical advantage the Royal Navy possessed in terms of large fast 'man-o'-wars.' The revolution in question was the development of the mine and the submarine, an area in which Britain had sadly lagged behind, due to their concentration in building their "super battleships." Indeed when war was declared, Britain had no effective mines, properly fitted minesweepers, or any anti-submarine precautions.

Another problem with a war with Germany, lay in the fact that the Royal Navy's enemies in the past usually came from southward of the British Isles. Not since the Dutch War in the 17th century had they come across a first class naval power who were based north of Dover. This posed a huge problem for the Royal Navy of patrolling the vast expanse of the North Sea, especially the outlet between Scotland and Norway. Apart from patrolling, the protection of the east coast commercial ports would be paramount, as with no protection, these important ports would be vulnerable to attack. To combat this predicament therefore, the answer was simple. The Grand Fleet would have to be moved to Scottish waters so it could control the North Sea, just as the old Western Squadron controlled the Channel and its approaches. In Scotland there were two possible bases - one at Cromarty Firth and the other at Scapa Flow in the Orkney Islands, with the latter preferred after great debate (the Battle Cruiser Squadron of Admiral David Beatty then used Cromarty as their initial base). With the Grand

Fleet now positioned in the north, the Straits of Dover and the Channel were to be protected by torpedo boats, destroyers, supporting cruisers and pre-dreadnought battleships.

THE WAR AT SEA IN 1914 AND PRECAUTIONS IN HOME WATERS

The message from the Admiralty to "commence hostilities against Germany" was received by the ships and naval establishments of the Royal Navy at 11.00pm on August 4.

During the years leading up to the First World War, colonial lands provided Britain, France and their main enemy, Germany, with naval bases for supplies and repairs, a network of radio stations, vital to keep distant squadrons in touch with their home command, but above all coaling stations, the very lifeblood of a navy. Germany had acquired a colonial empire in the Pacific and Africa and one of the first tasks for the Allies was to take these colonial ports. In the Far East was the only other German naval force apart from the one in the North Sea. This was the German Asiatic Squadron commanded by Admiral Graf von Spee. This squadron alone defended Germany's Pacific colonies, so by taking away their bases, radio stations and coaling stations, would render this squadron totally helpless. The first port to be seized was Samoa, quickly followed by New Guinea and slowly but surely, all the islands flying the German flag fell, especially after the so-called impregnable port of Tsingtao fell after a nine week blockade. Von Spee had nowhere to go, and more importantly, no coaling stations to replenish his boilers.

Germany's African empire also began to crumble. In August Togoland fell, in September, the Cameroons and South Africa eventually fell with only East Africa holding out. Germany's empire had effectively disappeared from the map. Their merchant navy had also ceased to exist, due to the Royal Navy blockade imposed on the first few days of war. German merchant ships were penned up in neutral ports all over the world and neutral nations were prevented from bringing Germany any materials of war, which saw Britain initially clash with America because of these restrictions of trade.

Very few engagements or major incidents at sea were recorded in the first months of the war, as the German High Seas Fleet seemed reluctant to face the Royal Navy in open water. The first naval action took place on August 5, when HMS *Amphion* along with HMS *Lance*, *Laurel*, *Lark* and *Linnet* surrounded the German minelayer *Königin Luise* which had earlier laid a line of submarine mines off the Suffolk coast. The enemy vessel was duly sunk and the majority of survivors were taken aboard *Amphion*. However next day at 6.30am, *Amphion* ran into the very same mine field sewn by the *Königin Luise* and was badly crippled. When she hit a second mine, she sank with the loss of 148 of her crew and 20 German prisoners. The Admiralty suffered further anxiety when several ships reported sighting periscopes in the Channel, the North Sea and the Straits of Dover. They took some satisfaction though when *U-15* became the first U-boat of the war to be sunk, when on August 8, she was rammed by HMS *Birmingham* in Fair Island Channel.

On August 28, there was a morale boosting although fortuitous victory for the Royal Navy, during the Battle of the Heligoland Bight. This, the first major naval engagement of the war, was initiated by the Royal Navy. The daring plan was to attack German destroyers in Heligoland Bight using light cruisers, destroyers and submarines. Heligoland Bight was a stretch of water between the small heavily armed island fortress of Heligoland and the mouth of the Elbe, where the main German fleet were concentrated. The Germans were to be lured towards another group of submarines supported by the battlecruisers HMS *New Zealand* and *Invincible*. Unfortunately German naval intelligence were aware of the plan and the British ships were confronted by a strong cruiser force. However the day was saved with the arrival of Admiral Beatty's battlecruisers HMS *Lion*, *Queen Mary* and *Princess Royal*, who pounded their adversaries with their superior armaments. Three German light cruisers, *Köln*, *Mainz* and *Ariadne,* were sunk as well as a destroyer. Only the British cruiser *Arethusa* was damaged, but was towed safely to port. Although it was deemed a British victory, Admiral Beatty had indeed been fortunate in risking his battlecruisers in the mine infested waters of the Heligoland Bight. As for Germany, a defeat in their own backyard, brought home the realisation that in a fair fight, they were still no match for the Royal Navy, and that losses such as these could not be sustained. It left them no other alternative than to turn to a mine and submarine policy.

Germany's new policy soon saw positive results, when on September 5, the cruiser HMS *Pathfinder* was sunk by the German submarine *U-21* off St. Abb's Head, on the east coast of Scotland, although British submarines would have their say in the war when on September 13, the *E9* sank the old German cruiser *Hela* while it was steaming between Heligoland and the Elbe (in October the same submarine sank the destroyer *S126* off Emden).

On September 22, the full effect of the U-boat as a fighting machine was fully demonstrated with devastating loss of life for the Royal Navy. During the early months of the war, the Royal Navy had maintained a patrol of old *Cressy* class armoured cruisers known as Cruiser Force C, in an area in the North Sea known as the Broad Fourteens. Many senior officers, including Admiral Jellicoe, opposed this patrol as these old vessels were vulnerable to a raid by the more modern German surface ships. Such was the worry for the patrol, they were nicknamed "the live bait squadron." Kapitan Leutnant Otto Weddigen of the *U-9*, one of Germany's oldest submarines, was cruising off the coast of Holland and Belgium, when some sixteen miles north-west of the Hook of Holland, he spied Cruiser Force C, namely, HMS *Aboukir*, *Cressy* and *Hogue*, cruising in a single line without destroyer protection. This was an opportunity too good to miss and Weddigen positioned *U-9* into a favourable firing position and duly sank the *Aboukir* at around 6.55am. Thinking that the ship had hit a mine, the other two vessels came to her aid and assist in the rescue of the crew. The *Hogue* was next in the firing line and she quickly suffered the same fate as the *Aboukir*. HMS *Cressy* which was left to try and rescue the men, was now aware of the submarine attack, but was oblivious to its position. Incredibly *U-9* struck the *Cressy* with a torpedo at around 7.20am and within minutes she too had sunk. All three ships had been lost in around an hour. The cost of lives were 25 officers and 502 men from the *Aboukir*, 12 officers and 362 men from the *Hogue* and 25 officers and 536 men from the *Cressy*. Many of the dead were Reservists or Cadets. The survivors were picked up by Dutch (*Flora* and *Titan*) and British vessels (*JGC* and *Coriander*) and numbered only 917. Otto Weddigen returned to Germany and was given a hero's reception for his incredible feat of sinking three enemy ships "before breakfast."

On September 27, *U-18* became the first U-boat to enter the Dover Straits and while heading towards Calais, spotted and fired a torpedo at the light cruiser HMS *Attentive*. Fortunately the torpedo missed its target, but the surprise of the attack and the realisation that the cross-channel supply routes were in grave danger, prompted the Admiralty to act, by laying an enormous minefield across the entrance to the Dover Straits.

During October, 31,000 Canadian troops were safely transported over to France after leaving Halifax Nova Scotia. Their troop convoy, protected by HMS *Majestic* and the battlecruiser *Princess Royal*, was unmolested throughout the whole voyage. It was the biggest single troop convoy of the war.

On October 15, the effectiveness of the submarine was further realised, when *U-9,* again commanded by Otto Weddigen, sank the cruiser HMS *Hawke* off the east coast of Scotland with heavy loss of life (for the record Otto Weddigen was later killed in action on March 18, 1915, when aboard *U-29,* which was rammed and sunk in the North Sea, by HMS *Dreadnought*). Two days later on October 17, the *Hawke* sinking was somewhat avenged by the light cruiser HMS *Undaunted* and the destroyers *Lance*, *Lennox*, *Legion* and *Loyal*. They engaged four German destroyers, *S115, S117, S118* and *S119*, off the Belgian coast (Scheldt) and sank them all, in under half an hour

On October 20, the first attack on a British merchant ship was reported when the SS *Glitra*, with a cargo of oil and coal bound for Norway, was stopped near Stavanger. Members of the crew of *U-17* boarded the steamer and opened the Kingston valves after retrieving papers and charts. The crew were allowed to leave in lifeboats and after two hours the ship sank. This act was carried out under the terms of the 1909 Declaration of London, which was an international code of maritime law, especially as related to war. To summarise this declaration, any vessel at sea could be stopped, boarded and searched for war contraband.

On October 27, the Royal Navy suffered a severe loss as their numerical advantage in dreadnought and super dreadnought ships was reduced by one. A German minelayer had laid her cargo along the north coast of Ireland on the route taken by Atlantic liners. On the same day the 2nd Battle Squadron were engaged in gunnery practice off Tory Island, when at approximately 5.00pm, one of their units, HMS *Audacious*, one of the new breed of super dreadnoughts, struck one of the newly sewn mines. The stricken vessel was taken in tow, but at 9.00pm her magazine blew up and she sank. The only consolation for the Royal Navy was the fact that no casualties occurred.

As the year progressed, the protection of home waters was proving a harder and harder task. The Royal Navy had to be in total control of the waterways to freely move troops and stores. The escalation of mines and submarine presence further heightened tensions at Admiralty House, so to help with the patrolling, an Auxiliary Patrol was set up, initially using 150 trawlers and drifters as well as countless yachts and other small vessels. By September 1, around 250 vessels had been employed in this role. These craft were fitted with guns and explosive sweeps which were explosive charges on lines towed astern which could be electronically detonated when a submerged submarine was located. To remain disguised, these boats retained their peacetime colours and their fishing numbers, painted on their hulls. As the majority of the crews were either fisherman or experienced sailors, they proved invaluable to home water protection.

The growing submarine activity in and around the Channel called for increased protection for the transports crossing to France, especially when two further vessels were lost due to submarine attack in the space of a fortnight. On October 31, HMS *Hermes* was sunk by *U-27*, while eight miles off the coast of Calais, and HMS *Niger*, suffered the same fate at the hands of *U-12* while in the Downs on November 11.

However worse news had reached the Admiralty concerning actions off the coast of Chile. On November 1, Admiral Craddock's South American Squadron, consisting of the old armoured cruisers HMS *Good Hope*, *Monmouth*, the modern light cruiser *Glasgow* and the armed ex-liner *Otranto*, finally caught up with Admiral von Spee's German East Asiatic Squadron, which had been hunted by the Allies from the start of the war. Cut off from his colonies, von Spee had been steaming in the empty vastness of the Pacific, but following an intercepted radio message, the squadrons clashed in the Bay of Coronel off the Chilean coast. The British ships proved no match for their adversaries who were faster and easily out-gunned them. HMS *Good Hope* and HMS *Monmouth* were sunk with all hands, including Admiral Craddock. When the news finally reached the Admiralty and the British public, who had been reared on the legend of the unconquerable Royal Navy, it was greeted with disbelief.

Just days after the Coronel disaster, on November 3, a German force of three armoured cruisers and three battlecruisers bombarded Yarmouth from long range. Fortunately very little damage was done, but several British trawlers and a submarine were sunk, with the Germans losing an armoured cruiser when she hit a mine while returning to base. Therefore, as a counter-measure, from November 5 onwards, the Admiralty announced that the whole of the North Sea would be classed as a war zone. The announcement from First Sea Lord John Fisher read;

'All ships passing a line drawn from the northern point of the Hebrides through the Faroe Islands to Iceland do so at their own peril. Ships wishing to trade to and from Norway, the Baltic and Denmark are advised to come, if inward bound, by the English Channel and the Straits of Dover. There they will be given sailing directions which will pass them safely so far as Britain is concerned, up the east coast of England, whence a safe route will, if possible, be given to Lindesnaes Lighthouse. From this point they should turn north or south according to their destination, keeping as near to the coast as possible. The converse applies to vessels outward bound. By strict adherence to these routes the commerce of all countries will be able to reach its destination in safety, so far as Great Britain is concerned, but any straying, even for a few miles from the course indicated, may be followed by fatal consequences.'

On November 9, one of the great naval chases came to an end. The German light cruiser *Emden*, which had left a destructive trail in the busy sea-lanes of the Indian Ocean, was finally caught and destroyed. At the start of the war, she had been a unit of von Spee's East Asiatic Squadron, but had roamed freely and sunk seventeen merchant ships in the opening three months of the war. Hunted by virtually every Allied ship in the Indian Ocean, her luck finally ran out when she was surprised and rendered useless by HMAS *Sydney* at Cocos Islands. On November 14, the Fifth Battle Squadron of the Channel Fleet left their base at Portland and headed for Sheerness in case of possible invasion of the British Isles.

On November 21, a new plan for barring the Straits of Dover was instituted and the whole zone was divided into eight sections, with destroyers continuously patrolling each sector, while French submarines were on stand-by if and when the alarm was raised, along lines that extended from Cape Gris Nez to the Varne and from Calais to the Goodwin Sands. During November the continual build-up of the British Army in France saw 70,000 troops and over 16,000 horses transported over, which averaged at around 12 transports sailing daily. Also on November 21, the Royal Navy attacked the German submarine base at Zeebrugge, but little damage was done and the base remained operational.

Two other small incidents occurred on November 21, and five days later, which signalled the start of the enemy's attack on Army communications. On the same day as the Zeebrugge raid, the British steamer *Malachite*, operating from Liverpool, was stopped and then sunk by *U-21* after the crew were allowed to leave ship and on November 26, just north of Havre, the same submarine, although being hunted by French destroyers, sank the collier *Primo*. From these two incidents it was concluded that the precautions taken for the transports of men and supplies were inadequate so they were temporarily halted until destroyers were sent from Harwich to carry out the necessary escort duties.

On November 30, the British gained a significant advantage in the war at sea, when British intelligence broke the German codes, so could therefore read German enciphered radio signals. In a short time U-boat strength could be calculated and approximate locations were know by the Admiralty.

After the defeat at Coronel, it was imperative that the Royal Navy acted quickly, to restore some pride and public faith. Therefore a large force under the command of Admiral Sir Frederick Sturdee, set sail for the Falkland Islands on November 11. On December 8, the British force were in the process of coaling at Port Stanley, and unknown to each other, von Spee's squadron arrived in the same area. Among the Royal Navy's task force were the modern battlecruisers *Inflexible* and *Invincible* and in a straight fight there could be only one conclusion. After a titanic battle, the *Scharnhorst, Gneisenau, Nürnberg* and *Leipzig* were all sent to the bottom of the South Atlantic, with heavy loss of life in an action which was to become known as the Battle of the Falkland Islands. However, the fact that it taken over five hours for the inevitable result, raised disturbing questions about the ability of British gunnery. Coronel had been avenged and the Royal Navy's pride was, for the time being, partially restored.

The stark reality of a German invasion of Britain were further fuelled by the naval bombardment on December 16, of the north east coastal towns of Scarborough, Whitby and Hartlepool in a German reprisal to the defeat at the Falkland Islands. At 5.00pm on December 15, the German Battle Cruiser Fleet steamed out of Wilhelmshaven intent on attacking the Durham and Yorkshire coast unprotected by minefields. The Grand Fleet were soon aware of the raid and planned to confront them. At 8.00am the next day the German battlecruisers – *Seydlitz, Moltke, Blucher, Derfflinger* and *Von der Tann* – lying off the north east coast began the bombardment. At 8.00am Scarborough was hit with 500 shells in a 25 minute bombardment, with 18 fatalities. Between 8.03am and 8.52am the town of Hartlepool was pounded with 1,150 shells. Here six members of the Durham Light Infantry and 118 civilians were killed. However Hartlepool's two coastal batteries (Lighthouse and Heugh) fought back and inflicted serious damage to the battlecruiser fleet and also caused casualties among their crew. The final town to be attacked was Whitby with the attack commencing at 9.00am and lasting for eleven minutes. Here four more civilians were directly or indirectly to die during the incident. When the vessels of the German cruiser squadron steamed away from Whitby, part of the Grand Fleet were waiting for them. On one side of the German force was Sir David Beatty's battlecruisers and on the other was the 2nd Battle Squadron, consisting of eight super dreadnoughts. What was considered the perfect trap was then scuppered, when, just as the fire-control officers had marked the ranges and were about to open fire, the fog came down and the enemy disappeared from view.

Public and political outrage followed this savage attack. The Royal Navy were heavily criticised for allowing it to happen and also for allowing the enemy to escape. The bombardment on the east coast, in terms of war, was an inexcusable breach of the declared laws of maritime warfare, and only the attack on the lightly defended port of Hartlepool could be remotely justified. What enraged the nation further was the fact that innocent women and children were among the dead and wounded. Vice-Admiral Bayly who had recently taken charge of the Channel Fleet, begged the Admiralty to be allowed a crack on the enemy's coast as retaliation to the raid on the east coast, but because destroyers and fleet sweepers could not be spared, the plan was temporarily shelved.

On December 20, the Admiralty put into place plans which broke down the organisation of the defence of the whole coastline of the British Isles. They divided the coastline into 23 patrol areas, with each one under a separate command.

As the New Year approached all seemed quiet in the Channel and the Admiralty for the time being were content in the knowledge that their anti-submarine measures were starting to prove affective. New drafts of men and tons of stores poured across the Channel unmolested and for many days in a row, with no submarines spotted in the vicinity.

As the old year made way for the new, the bells, heralding a year of hope and victory had barely faded, when the Admiralty's optimism of their anti-submarine measures were quite literally blown out of the water when a U-boat operating off the English south coast, torpedoed the British pre-dreadnought battleship HMS *Formidable*. Two hours later, the ship would slip beneath the waves of the cold stormy waters of the English Channel, and 547 men would lose their lives.

This is the story of that sinking and of the officers and men who would survive and perish, in this most tragic of incidents during the Great War of 1914-18.

BATTLESHIP DESIGN

The improvement in battleship design had evolved through the late Victorian period of battleship construction, through the building of the *Royal Sovereign, Majestic* and *Canopus* classes. The strength in first-class battleships of all the great powers in 1897 saw Great Britain stand head and shoulders above their main rivals. A total of 24 had already been built with a further ten more under construction. Only France with 13 battleships and 5 under construction came anywhere near to challenging Britain's domination of the seas, with Russia, Italy, the USA and Germany lacking any significant numbers.

The general design of the battleship had taken a considerable step forward, when the seven ships of the *Royal Sovereign* class were built between 1892-1894. They were HMS *Royal Sovereign, Empress of India, Ramillies, Resolution, Revenge, Royal Oak* and the *Repulse*. They boasted four 13.5" breach-loading guns mounted on armoured barbettes (fixed circular steel platforms on which the main guns were mounted, that positioned the guns at a greater height above the sea), which were operated by hydraulic machinery. This barbette system became the accepted design for mounting the main armament of a man-of-war. Their armour consisted of a main belt of eighteen inches thick and two hundred and fifty feet long. The cost of this class of battleship was around £770,000.

The next major step in battleship design saw nine more under construction in the years 1894-1896 at a cost of around £1,000,000 each. The *Majestic* class formed the general design of the battleship which remained virtually unchanged for many years. The ships in this class were HMS *Majestic, Magnificent, Hannibal, Prince George, Victorious, Jupiter, Mars, Caesar* and *Illustrious*. Improvements included new 12" guns with greater penetrating power and accuracy with a higher rate of fire (this gun would remain as the standard British battleship weapon for the next sixteen years). This time the barbettes were hooded and became known as turrets.

The ship building period between 1897-1902 saw the *Canopus* class introduced. At a reduced cost of around £783,000 each, the class consisted of HMS *Canopus, Goliath, Albion, Ocean, Glory* and *Vengeance* which were around 2,000 tons less in displacement but were about two knots faster than the previous class. They were the first British battleships to be fitted with water-tube boilers, of a type known as the Belleville Economiser. These produced a greater heating surface, resulting in a substantial saving of fuel, as well as being easier to maintain and had the ability to raise steam much quicker. Their introduction thus ended the twin-funnel (side-by-side) disposition of previous battleships. The new design saw the funnels mounted fore and aft due to the disposition of the new Belleville boilers.

THE FORMIDABLE CLASS

The designs of the newer *Formidable* class, to be constructed under the 1897/98 Estimates, were first discussed on May 3, 1897, and it was concluded that a repeat of the *Canopus* class would be inadvisable due to the advance in the projected displacement of Japanese battleships already under construction. This new class improved upon previous designs with general improvements to the armour, inclusion of machinery and boilers first introduced in the *Canopus* class, and the fitting of a longer and heavier 12" gun with distinct curved turret faces, which made this class the most powerful European battleship model of her day. HMS *Formidable*, the first of the three ships built of this type, was laid down at Portsmouth on March 21, 1898. She was closely followed by HMS *Irresistible*, laid down at Chatham and HMS *Implacable* which completed the trio, when laid down at Devonport on July 13, 1898. HMS *Formidable* was launched on November 17, 1898, although not completed until September 1901, at a cost of £1,022,745 (guns £74,500). Completion of HMS *Formidable* and *Irresistible* were delayed due to the liquidation of their machinery manufacturers. Also strikes in the engineering shops, difficulties in the substitution of Krupp for Harvey armour, and the fitting of the Belleville boilers, became major concerns in the battleship building industry during the turn of the century. When completed, the *Formidable* class was considered a great improvement on the *Canopus* class, answered to the least touch of helm, and while travelling at 10 knots, boasted a radius of action of around 5,500 nmiles.

Displacement of HMS *Formidable* was 14,658 tons and 15,805 tons fully loaded. The overall length of the class was 431 feet, 9 inches, beam was 75 feet and maximum draught 29 feet. Complement of HMS *Formidable* according to the original legend was 758. Armament consisted of 4 x 12" Vickers guns (Mk.IX, 40cal., 80rpg), 12 x 6" (Mk.VII, 45cal., 200 rpg), 16 x 12pdrs. (12cwt., 300rpg), 2 x 12pdrs. (8cwt.), 6 x 3pdrs. (500rpg), 2 x Maxim machine guns, and 4 x 18" (submerged) torpedo tubes. The main 12" guns, weighing 50 tons, fired an 850lb round, and in terms of steel penetration, could pierce a 12" plate at 4,800yds. The armour fitted to the *Formidable* class consisted of a mixture of Harvey and Krupp plates. A 9" Krupp belt amidships, was 15ft wide by 218ft long. Thickness of the bulkheads ranged from 12-9". Side plating was 3" forward and 1½" aft. Gun protection included barbettes of 12-6", turrets of 10-8" and 6" casemates. The conning tower armour was in the form of 14-3" plates and the main deck armour measured at 1" thick, but was 3-2" middle deck and 2½-2" on the lower deck. Total weight of armour fitted was 4,335 tons, which contributed to nearly a third of total displacement. The class was powered by two sets of 3-cylinder vertical triple expansion engines (HMS *Formidable*'s manufactured by Earle) and twenty Belleville boilers (water-tube) and economizers, which drove the twin in-turning screws. The boilers were arranged in three compartments, with eight in the forward, eight in the midships, with the remaining four in the after section. The funnels on the *Formidable* were of unequal sizes with the larger second funnel athwartship. *Formidable* had no caging to her funnels but had heavy raised funnel caps. The designed Horse Power was 15,000 delivering 18 knots. The weight of the coal onboard ranged between 900-2,000 tons with 350 tons per day consumed at full power. The ship's boats included three steam pinnace (2 x 56ft, 1 x 36ft), one sail pinnace (36ft), one sail launch (40ft), three cutters (2 x 34ft, 1 x 30ft), one galley (32ft), three whalers (27ft), one gig (28ft), one skiff dinghy (16ft) and one balsa raft (13ft). Night lighting was provided by 6 x 24" searchlights (two on each bridge and one high on each mast). *Formidable* carried 3 x 115cwt anchors (2 x 115cwt Halls close-stowing and 1 x 115cwt Byers stockless).

HMS *Formidable* was commissioned at Portsmouth for service in the Mediterranean Fleet on October 10, 1901, under the command of Captain Alexander William Chisholm-Batten, with officers and crew turned over from HMS *Resolution*. She was the third Royal Navy ship to carry the name since the first in 1777. A refit was carried out while in Malta between December 1904 and April 1905 (which included the fitting of fire control and range finding equipment). On August 17, 1908 a further refit was carried out at Chatham Dockyards which was completed in April 1909. On April 20, 1909 she was commissioned at Chatham for service in the First Division, Home Fleet, Nore, until May 29 of the same year, when she was transferred to the Atlantic Fleet, in which she would serve until May 1912. During this spell she would undertake a further refit at Gibraltar. Between May 1912 and the outbreak of war in August 1914 (after being reduced to nucleus crew at Sheerness on May 13, 1912), HMS *Formidable*, along with her sister ships, formed part of the Fifth Battle Squadron, Channel Fleet. However between August and October 1912, she had developed serious defects in her boilers owing to hard and continuous steaming when operating with a nucleus crew. Such was the concern about her deterioration since her 1911 refit at Gibraltar, a Court of Inquiry was held to investigate the causes. In May and June 1914, *Formidable* undertook a further refit at Chatham Dockyard but was finished in time to take part in the great Spithead Review on July 20, which showed off the full might of the Royal Navy, just prior to the declaration of war with Germany.

THE CAPTAINS OF HMS FORMIDABLE

The following Captains served aboard HMS *Formidable* from 1901 until the ship was sunk on January 1, 1915.

1901 - 1904
(Alexander William Chisholm-Batten)
Born - September 28, 1851, Entered as a Naval Cadet - March 24, 1865, Midshipman - July 28, 1866, Sub Lieutenant - April 26, 1871, Lieutenant - April 15, 1875, Commander - January 1, 1886, Captain - June 30, 1893 (first known command was the cruiser HMS *Andromache*), Captain on HMS *Formidable* - October 10, 1901 until September 30, 1904.

1904 - 1906
(Thomas Philip Walker)
Born - September 16, 1858, Entered as a Naval Cadet - January 15, 1872, Midshipman - December 20, 1873, Sub Lieutenant - December 19, 1877, Lieutenant - August 30, 1879, Commander - January 1, 1893, Captain - June 30, 1898 (first known command was the armoured cruiser HMS *Warspite*), Captain on HMS *Formidable* - October 1, 1904 until March 21, 1906.

1906 - 1907
(Ernest Alfred Simons)
Born - September 3, 1856, Entered as a Naval Cadet - January 15, 1870, Midshipman - March 21, 1872, Sub Lieutenant - December 20,

1875, Lieutenant - May 24, 1877, Commander - January 1, 1890, Captain - December 31, 1896 (first known command was the cruiser HMS *Pomone*), Captain on HMS *Formidable* - March 15, 1906 until February 4, 1907.

1907 - 1908
(Herbert Lyon)
Entered as a Naval Cadet - January 15, 1870, Midshipman, Sub Lieutenant (unknown), Lieutenant - February 7, 1880, Commander - June 30, 1894, Captain - December 31, 1900, Captain on HMS *Formidable* - January 31, 1907 until August 18, 1908.

1909 - 1911
(Reginald A. Allenby)
Born - September 4, 1861, Entered as a Naval Cadet - January 15, 1875, Midshipman - March 23, 1877, Sub Lieutenant - March 23, 1881, Lieutenant - December 31, 1884, Commander - January 1, 1897, Captain - December 31, 1902 (first known command was the battleship HMS *Centurion*), Captain on HMS *Formidable* - April 20, 1909 until April 3, 1911.

1911 - 1912
(Philip Nelson-Ward)
Entered as a Naval Cadet - July 15, 1879, Midshipman - December 21, 1881, Sub Lieutenant - January 20, 1886, Lieutenant - April 1889, Commander - June 1900, Captain - January 1905 (first known command was the 1890 cruiser HMS *Indefatigable*), Captain on HMS *Formidable* - April 4, 1911 until December 11, 1912.

1912 - 1914
(Drury St. A. Wake)
Born - September 16, 1863, Entered as a Naval Cadet - July 15, 1876, Midshipman - July 25, 1878, Sub Lieutenant - September 16, 1882, Lieutenant - June 30, 1885, Commander - December 31, 1897, Captain - December 31, 1905 (first known command was the armoured cruiser

HMS *Bedford*), Captain on HMS *Formidable* - December 11, 1912 until September 4, 1914.

1914 - 1/1/1915
(Arthur Noel Loxley)
Born - October 31, 1874, Entered as a Naval Cadet - July 15, 1888, Midshipman - July 15, 1890, Sub Lieutenant - April 14, 1894, Lieutenant - April 14, 1895, Commander - January 1, 1905, Captain - June 22, 1911 (first known command was the battlecruiser HMS *Inflexible*), Captain of HMS *Formidable* - September 2, 1914 until it was sunk on January 1, 1915.

On the outbreak of war on August 4, 1914, the Channel Fleet, commanded by Vice-Admiral Sir Cecil Burney, comprised of pre-dreadnought battleships and a small number of light cruisers, which formed the Fifth, Sixth, Seventh and Eighth Battle Squadrons. Of these, the Fifth and Sixth were manned before mobilisation with nucleus crew.

THE FIFTH BATTLE SQUADRON, CHANNEL FLEET

The Fifth Battle Squadron comprised of the following units (*class according to *Conway's All the World's Fighting Ships 1860 - 1905*).

1. HMS *Prince of Wales* (flag) - launched March 25, 1902 (*London* *), commanded on the outbreak of war by Captain R. N. Bax.
2. HMS *Bulwark* - launched October 18, 1899 (*London**), commanded on the outbreak of war by Captain G. L. Sclater.
3. HMS *London* - launched October 18, 1899 (*London**), commanded on the outbreak of war by Captain J. G. Armstrong.
4. HMS *Venerable* - launched November 2, 1899 (*London**), commanded on the outbreak of war by Captain V. H. G. Bernard.
5. HMS *Queen* (2nd flag) - launched March 8, 1902 (*London**), commanded on the outbreak of war by Captain H. A. Adam.

6. HMS *Formidable* - launched November 17, 1898 (*Formidable**), commanded on the outbreak of war by Captain D. St. A. Wake.

7. HMS *Irresistible* - launched December 15, 1898 (*Formidable**), commanded on the outbreak of war by Captain The Hon. Stanhope Hawke.

8. HMS *Implacable* - launched March 11, 1899 (*Formidable**), commanded on the outbreak of war by Captain H. C. Lockyer.

Also attached was the light cruiser HMS *Topaze*, launched on July 23, 1903 and commanded on the outbreak of war by Captain W. J. B. Law. The *Gem* class light cruiser HMS *Diamond* (Commander L.L. Dundas) was also attached to the Channel Fleet. On August 7, 1914, following the suppression of the Sixth Battle Squadron, the *Lord Nelson* class battleships, HMS *Lord Nelson* and HMS *Agamemnon,* joined the Fifth Battle Squadron. The flagship of the Channel Fleet, HMS *Lord Nelson*, was laid down in 1905 and completed in October 1908. She was the last pre-dreadnought battleship built, as although she was launched before HMS *Dreadnought* on September 4, 1906, she was not completed until after *Dreadnought*, making her virtually obsolete in terms of battleship evolution. As well as having her 4 x 12" guns, *Lord Nelson* also boasted 10 x 9.2" guns mounted in turrets (replacing the standard 6" second armament, first introduced in the *Royal Sovereign* class). The *London* class units of the Fifth Battle Squadron, were generally repeats of the *Formidable* class with improved modifications to their armour.

The Fifth Battle Squadron came under the command of Rear-Admiral Bernard Currey and Rear-Admiral Cecil F. Thursby, and in the very early stages of the war was responsible for patrolling between the longitudes of Dungeness and the Owers (off Selsey Bill), which protected the Straits of Dover from a possible enemy breakthrough. On August 25, to protect the important Belgian port of Ostend, four Royal Marine battalions were transported across the Channel, with the Portsmouth battalions ferried across by units of the Fifth Battle Squadron, namely the *Prince of Wales, Venerable, Irresistible* and

Formidable. On September 3, the Fifth Battle Squadron departed from their Spithead base and arrived at Portland two days later. During their time here, HMS *Formidable* and other units of the squadron took part in target practice (September 8), and firing exercises (September 21 and 23). On November 14, the squadron was transferred to Sheerness, arriving there on November 16, in anticipation of a possible invasion attempt.

For the British Army to lead a successful campaign in France and Flanders, a smooth passage across the English Channel of men, supplies and hardware were imperative. The dangers to this supply route came in the form of mines, fast torpedo boats and the dreaded underwater scourge - the submarine. The plan was to land men and supplies in the north-west area of France. All the details had been worked out between the Army and Navy over a three year period leading up to the outbreak of war, with even the smallest details planned to perfection. The main port chosen for the embarkation of troops and horses in England was Southampton, with Havre and occasionally Boulogne chosen as the landing port. Units in Scotland would embark from Glasgow, while those stationed in Ireland would embark from Dublin, Queenstown and Belfast. For the transportation of the vast amount of supplies needed, the principal port of Newhaven was chosen, with mechanical transports sailing from Avonmouth and Liverpool. To minimize the risk of attack on the troop ships, no convoys were planned, but the transports were to sail singly or in pairs, without escorts. The preferred method of protection lay in the fact that both ends of the Channel were to be sealed off, by a combined force of British and French torpedo boats, destroyers and submarines who held the Dover Straits, and a joint British and French cruiser force who held the other end of the Channel, with the Channel Fleet commanding the centre. The Grand Fleet would then take up a position to strike out at the German High Seas Fleet, should they dare risk an attack on the transports. The initial crossings were originally postponed for two days, but commenced on August 9.

THE LOSS OF HMS BULWARK

During the opening throes of the war, the Royal Navy could ill-afford losing a vessel and a highly trained crew through incompetence and neglect, but unfortunately this is what happened in November 1914. During this time the Fifth Battle Squadron were in moorings off Sheerness, with the battleship HMS *Bulwark*, moored at Keyhole Reach on the Medway. The battleship, built at Devonport in response to France's shipbuilding programme, had been laid down on March 20, 1899 and launched on October 18, 1899, although not completed until March 1902 at a cost of just under one million pounds. It was one of the first to be fitted with a Marconi wireless telegraph. *Bulwark* served as the flagship in the Mediterranean Fleet from 1902 until 1907, but as a counterbalance to the emergence of the German High Seas Fleet, she returned to home waters as flagship in the Home Fleet until 1912, when she was transferred to the Fifth Battle Squadron of the Channel Fleet. Among the *Bulwark's* previous commanding officers was Captain Robert Falcon Scott, better known as the famous polar explorer "Scott of the Antarctic," who took command of the ship in 1908.

In the early hours of November 26, 1914 the *Bulwark's* crew were in the process of coaling ship. They were taking breakfast when at 7.53am a series of massive internal explosions ripped the battleship apart. Debris from the explosions rained down over four miles away, as well as causing damage to other units of the Fifth Battle Squadron, including the nearby HMS *Formidable* (Able Seaman W. F. Older, who had previously served aboard the *Bulwark*, had witnessed the explosion, and found the curtains from the Captain's cabin on the *Formidable's* deck). When the smoke eventually cleared the *Bulwark* had disappeared. In all 727 of the crew, including the Captain, Guy Lutley Sclater were killed, with the majority from the Portsmouth Port Division. Such was the force of the explosions, they were heard as far away as Whitstable and shook the pier at Southend. Only 12 of the crew survived. Rumours were rife in what had caused the explosions and initially sabotage was suspected. However at a subsequent Board of Inquiry, it was suggested that the most likely cause was the self-detonation of aged and deteriorating cordite, some of which was over twelve years old, stored in abnormally high temperatures.

Although the loss of the *Bulwark* reduced the strength of the Fifth Battle Squadron, a replacement was not drafted in to fill the gap.

During the opening period of the war, the Channel was constantly patrolled and light and navigation marks were extinguished or altered. The anti-submarine system seemed fully effective and drafts of men and stores poured across to France in an almost never-ending stream of merchant vessels. Day after day passed with the route unmolested. From the first week of December, transports were ordered to sail singly, each with a destroyer for company. The true test came when on December 19, the Twenty-Seventh Division was to begin crossing. Such was the size of the unit to be transported, the worry for all concerned was that the passage could not be completed under the cover of darkness due to the state of the tide, which made it impossible to enter the port of Havre until after daybreak. Thankfully the large force of attending destroyers ensured the crossing was made without mishap. Despite the success of this operation, the possibility of a U-boat attack in the Channel remained constantly in the minds of the relevant authorities. In December 1914, the submarine threat to Allied warships had been further realised when the French dreadnought *Jean Bart*, during a sweep of the Adriatic, was struck by a torpedo fired from an Austro-Hungarian submarine. Fortunately the well-designed hull compartments enabled the ship to stay afloat and reach port.

Re-organisation of commanders on December 17 saw Vice-Admiral Sir Lewis Bayly, originally in charge of the First Battle Squadron, exchange places with Vice-Admiral Sir Cecil Burney, and take command of the Channel Fleet.

HMS *Formidable*, minus her armour belt, being launched on November 17, 1898. (Below) Note the prominence of the bow ram. The role of the pre-dreadnought battleship would still be an active one during the war. They bore the brunt of the action during the Dardanelles campaign and undertook dangerous patrolling roles in the English Channel and the North Sea. Not surprisingly, of the 13 battleships sunk during WW1, 11 were pre-dreadnought vessels. (BRITISH BATTLESHIPS 1892-1957)

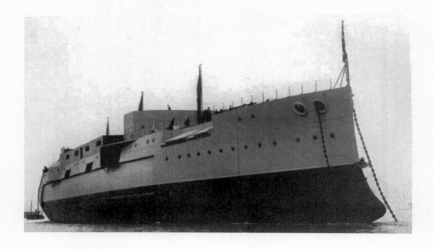

HMS *Formidable* after completion at Portsmouth, October 1901.

Commander of HMS *Formidable* 1904-1906, Captain Thomas Philip Walker.

Formidable at Malta c1905.

HMS *Formidable* coaling party c1912 and (below) a line drawing showing the main belt of armour (shaded) and a birds eye view of the armament layout. (JANE'S FIGHTING SHIPS OF WW1)

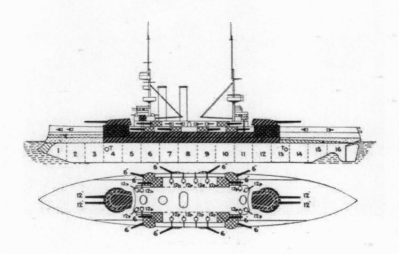

Sir Lewis Bayly

During the final days of 1914, the Sixth Battle Squadron (which had been reformed in November) had just completed firing exercises off Portland and in Vice-Admiral Bayly's opinion, his Fifth Battle Squadron required similar practice. On December 26, he was given permission to move from Sheerness to Portland. The normal practice for sailing through the Straits was to time the passage so the squadron passed through the narrows at night, or if this proved difficult, a daylight passage was carried out with destroyer protection. On December 28, Vice-Admiral Bayly informed the Admiralty that he wished to sail at 10.00am on December 30. An arrangement with Commodore Reginald Tyrwhitt, commanding the Harwich Destroyer Flotilla, was then made for six destroyers to be sent to the Nore to accompany the squadron as far as Folkestone. On the day of the sailing, the destroyers carried out their task without incident and at around 3.00pm left the squadron and returned to their Harwich base. From this point on, the only other protection the squadron had from possible torpedo attack was from the two attached light cruisers HMS *Topaze* and *Diamond*.

THE SINKING OF HMS FORMIDABLE

The squadron that day was headed by HMS *Lord Nelson,* with HMS *Formidable* bringing up the rear, in what was known as the "coffin position." A further mile astern were *Topaze* and *Diamond*. By 4.00pm on December 30, the squadron passed close to Dungeness and by 7.00pm were directly south of Beachy Head. As darkness fell, the squadron continued on a straight course and at 11.20pm, had reached a point south of Selsey Bill. At 1.30am on New Year's Eve, the line of battleships and cruisers were approximately ten miles south of St. Catherine's Point, on the Isle of Wight. At 4.10am, HMS *Lord Nelson* parted company with the rest of the squadron to secure hatches on her forecastle. She steamed towards St. Alban's Head, before rejoining the squadron - which had continued on a straight course - at 8.00am, twenty-five miles south of Lulworth Cove. Within an hour the Fifth Battle Squadron passed south of the Bill of Portland, where firing and steaming exercises were carried out. They then headed back on an eastward course towards St. Catherine's Point as Vice-Admiral Bayly decided to continue with exercises until Saturday morning, much to the disappointment of the crews, who were hopeful of spending New Year's Eve at Portland.

Fleet Orders stipulated where a submarine attack was possible, an alteration of course was to be executed just after dark. Although no submarine activity had been recorded in the Channel for the whole month, to comply with the order, a 16-point alteration of course at 7.00pm was made, when south of The Needles, thus the squadron went back to the westward, almost in their own wake. The night, although cloudy, was clear and visibility was around two miles. A stiff southward breeze however made the sea choppy, making the detection of a submarine in the area difficult. Despite this the squadron remained on a straight course at a speed of around 10 knots, with the ships in close formation approximately two cables (400 yards) apart. At 8.50pm they were south of Hengistbury Head and aimed to continue on a straight course for around six hours. Another change of course was planned at 3.00am where the squadron would be approximately 15 miles off Start Point. All seemed to be going to plan, until around 2.20am, as the squadron passed through a number of fishing vessels, HMS *Formidable* was seen to turn out of line. Commander W. J. B. Law of HMS *Topaze* investigated and found the battleship with a pronounced list to starboard and already in the process of lowering her boats.

Initial fears were that the battleship had struck a mine, but it soon became apparent that the vessel had been torpedoed. The torpedo which had struck the battleship had been fired at a range of 360m by a German U-boat operating from Flanders, which had been tracking the squadron all day. The *Formidable* had been struck abreast of the foremost funnel, with this devastating blow hitting the No.2 boiler, causing an almost immediate 20° list and the loss of all steam. At the time of the explosion,

Captain Loxley of the *Formidable*, together with Commander Ballard and his signalling officer were on the bridge. The first order given by the Captain was to close all watertight doors and in the same breath he ordered the crew to be piped to collision quarters. He then brought the wounded battleship up hard into the wind, to get her head to the rising sea. The weather seemed to worsen but perfect order reigned as the *Formidable's* launch and pinnace were lowered in complete darkness. Two barges full of men were also got out, but one capsized, tossing its occupants into the dark and angry seas. The U-boat commander meanwhile had remained in the area, patiently waiting for his prize to sink, but forty-five minutes after the first explosion (around 3.05am), his patience ran out and another torpedo was expended, which slammed into the side of the stricken vessel, fired from one of the bow tubes of the submarine at a distance of only 160m. This time it exploded abreast of the after funnel on the port side, hitting the No.1 boiler.

The effect of this was to bring the mortally wounded ship on an even keel. Debris from the explosion rained down on the men in the boats and on the fleeing U-boat, damaging the conning tower, preventing operation of the periscope. With no steam aboard *Formidable*, the boom boats could not be properly lowered, so orders were given for all available hands to bring up woodwork and also to break up the after shelter deck to aid the men who would soon have to jump clear and into the sea. This included the ship's piano, which some seemingly unconcerned jack tar had been playing ragtime on, until it too was thrown overboard. Everything was done to keep up morale and the chaplain of the ship, the Reverend George Brooke Robinson, showing great bravery, even venturing back down below to fetch cigarettes for the officers and crew, seemingly unconcerned that the ship could capsize at any moment.

The U-boat which had carried out the attack was *U-24*, commanded by Kapitanleutnant Rudolph Schneider. The type *"U-23"* boat was a patrol submarine built at Germaniawerft, Kiel (construction number

178) and was the first class of U-boat to be fitted with diesel engines. It was launched on May 24, 1913 and was 65m in length (beam was 6.32m), displacing 675 tons (870 tons submerged) and carried a crew of 4 officers and 31 ratings. She carried six torpedoes which could be fired from two 50cm bow or stern tubes. Submerged, the vessel could travel at nearly ten knots, but this improved to around sixteen when on the surface. The range of this class of submarine was around 8,000 nautical miles at 8 knots while on the surface, which was significantly reduced to around 80 nautical miles when submerged and travelling at 5 knots. Diving time was 133 seconds, compared with 85 seconds to surface. The vessel was powered by a 1,800 H.P. diesel engine while on the surface and a 1,200 H.P. electric motor which was operated while submerged.

Just four days after the start of the war, *U-24* was one of the submarines patrolling in the North Sea (Maas and Outer Gabbard line), for the purpose of attacking the British Expeditionary Force during their crossing over to France. After an unsuccessful patrol, *U-24* along with *U-19* and the light cruisers *Strassburg* and *Stralsund*, then took part in a reconnoitring sweep towards East Anglia which commenced on August 17, 1914, in the hope of ascertaining British naval strength north of a line joining Lowestoft and Ymuiden (Ijmuiden). This patrol lasted two days before they returned to Germany. On September 3, 1914, just days after the Battle of Heligoland Bight, *U-24* was one of four submarines sent to the Ems to afford Heligoland flank protection (westward of) in the event of further Royal naval operations in and around that area. When *U-19* returned to Germany for repairs after she was rammed by the destroyer HMS *Badger* off the Dutch coast, *U-24* took her place and two days later, on October 26, 1914, she was the first to attack an unarmed merchant ship without warning. The *Amiral Ganteaume,* carrying 2,000 Belgian refugees and mistaken for a troop ship, was steaming to France from Belgium and the Low Countries and was torpedoed by *U-24* off Cape Grisnez, but did not sink and was towed to Boulogne with the loss of life amounting to forty. In December

1914, *U-24* was transferred to the U-boat base at Zeebrugge and it was from here that she would attack the 5th Battle Squadron. *U-24* and her crew arrived at Bruges on Christmas Eve 1914 having navigated along the ship canal from Zeebrugge. Bruges, in December 1914, was being developed as an advance base for German operational submarines. The officers and men of *U-24* remained at base over the Christmas period and set sail on December 27. Their orders were to attack British and Allied shipping in the English Channel and the Western Approaches. *U-24* submerged shortly after clearing the Dutch coast and Schneider set a course which would take them towards the Dover Straits. He then surfaced in order to sail over the mined nets which were hung from buoys to prevent hostile craft from passing through the narrow channel. Shortly before midnight on the second day after leaving Zeebrugge, *U-24* was south of the Isle of Wight, when Schneider spotted two unescorted British battlecruisers heading towards Sheerness. After a great deal of consideration he decided against an attack and proceeded to the Plymouth area. It was the next day when the Fifth Battle Squadron was sighted. Schneider could hardly believe his luck.

The *U-24's* log on December 31 and January 1, shows the breakdown of the attack on HMS *Formidable* and the 5th Battle Squadron. Please note that German times are shown and differ slightly from British times recorded.

December 31

8.25am   *SW 3, sea 2, long stopped. Charged batteries. Swell, clear, good visibility.*

10.50am   *Dived, as various smoke clouds and later mastheads are in sight in NW. Tried with a general course 6 dg. To close in on a fleet formation, maybe a battle squadron of 5 or 6 ships, which are practising.*

14.30pm   *Gave up attack as there are 840 Amps only left in the battery and the squadron is steering E in athwart line. Although I am going all ahead, the distance is increasing. In front of the squadron a light cruiser is acting as repeater. The right flank escort is a battlecruiser with 3 funnels. On all ships of the line the aft topmast is missing. Course 180 dg. In order to get out of the steamer-route.*

16.40pm   *To the surface. Stopped. Charged batteries.*

18.30pm   *In direction 132 dg. a searchlight and in 154 dg. a flashing light in sight. It must be the French coast and I have drifted considerably to the E.*

23.30pm   *Course 290 dg. at 10 knots. I intend to approach Start Point in order to arrive near Plymouth during the night.*

January 1

01.55am   *SW 5, sea 4, overcast, clear, moonshine at times. Alarm as there are 3 vessels   without lights in sight 0 dg. When closing in it turned out to be big ships, bow-attack on last ship the only possibility.*

02.45am   *Launched torpedo tube No.1, very acute angle. No detonation. Distance about 700m. The 3 vessels run off. Shortly afterwards a bigger number about 5 ships, without lights on the same course, in sight. Attacked one.*

03.12am   *Launched torpedo tubes No.'s 3 and 4 with 6 second interval. Heavy detonation after 19 seconds. Ship starts listing to starboard. All other ships steam off quickly. No searchlights. The damaged ship is still under way. Can't attack a second time as the boat is too close.*

04.07am   *A third attack launching torpedo tube No.2. Detonation after 9 seconds. 5 seconds later 3 muffled detonations. Seems to be ammunition stores. Supports of the aft periscope are breaking, also a rivet of the conning tower. It is not possible to check the result of the attack as the periscopes cannot be moved any more. On the conning tower heavy shocks as if ship's parts are thrown against it.*

04.15am   *Course 140 dg. 3 knots submerged. The type of vessel could not be discerned. I guess it was a ship of the squadron which was practising in the forenoon. From my experience, vessels without lights will be always considered as destroyers at first sight. It is very difficult to estimate the distance through the periscope at night. I thought to be further off in each case, while the distance was 360 and 160 metres only according to the running times of the torpedoes. It was difficult to keep the boat submerged during the attack. It repeatedly surfaced and submerged. This made any observations very difficult. There must be a heavy sea on the surface.*

06.40am   *SE 8, sea 7, squalls. To the surface, stopped, charged batteries. When opening the conning tower hatch it was found out that the aft periscope and all the supports for mine deflection were bent to one side. It seemed as if a part of the ship's hull was thrown against the upper part of the conning tower. On the railing of the break water, which was destroyed as well, there was to be seen red paint of a ship's bottom.*

As the *Formidable* continued to sink, HMS *Topaze* circled around trying to get the men in the boats aboard, but the heavy seas made the job even more hazardous. She managed to rescue 43 men off a barge, when Captain Loxley ordered her to close down a passing liner and directed her to stand by, but although distress rockets were fired from the *Formidable*, the liner continued on its way. Fearful of a further submarine attack, Captain Loxley ordered the cruiser to clear away and try to get the attention of a nearby steamer, but this also proved a hopeless cause.

Captain Arthur Noel Loxley, who had been in command of the battlecruiser HMS *Inflexible* (from November 5, 1912 until August 28, 1914) when war was declared, was transferred to the *Formidable* on September 2, 1914. Before these appointments, he had been Flag Commander to Vice-Admiral Sir A. Berkeley Milne, commanding the Second Division, Home Fleet (March 24, 1909 - August 8, 1910) and performed the same role between August 9, 1910 - July 21, 1911 on HMS *King Edward VII* to Vice-Admiral Callaghan. He was the son of Alice Loxley of "The Little Cloisters," Gloucester and the late Reverend Arthur S. Loxley, the former curate of St. Mary's Church, Northchurch and husband of Gladys Maud Loxley (nee Brooke-Hunt) whom he married in December 1900. One son was born to the family, Peter, in June 1905. During the war the family would lose three sons. Captain Vere Duncombe Loxley, of the Royal Marine Light Infantry, would be killed in action on the Somme on November 13, 1916. He had been mentioned for distinguished and gallant services in Gallipoli during the period of General Sir Charles Munro's command of the MEF from October 1915 to the evacuation. His citation appeared in *The London Gazette* on July 12, 1916. Captain Reginald Victor Byron Loxley, of the Royal Air Force, would lose his life on October 18, 1918, just weeks before the Armistice.

The weather continued to worsen and it was now pitch black. Somehow the old battleship remained afloat and the men left onboard, with little or no chance of survival, stood on deck smoking and singing, until around 4.40am when the *Formidable* suddenly gave a lurch to starboard and began to heel over and settle by the bows. Captain Loxley gave the word for everyone to take to the water. Many were attired only in their "fearnoughts," a one piece flannel night garment. His final words were *"Lads, this is the last, all hands for themselves and may God bless you and guide you to safety.* " He then walked to the forebridge, lit a final cigarette and with his faithful and beloved terrier Bruce by his side, waited for the inevitable to happen in true Royal Naval tradition. He was never seen again. As men slid down the sides of the vessel, not all had cleared when she turned over and plunged down head foremost. In this position she remained for a minute or so with her screws and rudder clear of the water. Suddenly another lurch downwards and she was gone. Moments later, little evidence remained of her fight for survival, apart from a small area strewn with debris and men fighting in vain to stay alive.

In an interview with an Exeter newspaper, an unnamed survivor told of the final moments of the stricken ship. *'I was one of the last to be plucked from the sea, and when she had given up the struggle to stay afloat, she started to slip below the waves. I cannot describe the noises coming from the ship, it almost sounded as though she was in great pain. The creaks and groans of her sinking will stay with me forever. At one point she seemed to stop sinking, she must have hit the bottom, after all she was over 400 feet long. In this position she remained, rather undignified, with her screws and rudder sticking out of the stormy waters. Then her fight with the sea was concluded and with a final defiant lurch downwards she was gone. I wept uncontrollably.'*

The officers in the sea fared best due to their safety waistcoats, as the collars issued to the men proved of little use in the stormy seas. Those lucky enough to be aboard the boats still faced the prospect of the waves capsizing them at any moment. HMS *Diamond*, despite the conditions and threat of a further submarine attack, succeeded in rescuing 37 men (of whom 14 were officers), who, although suffering from the effects of the cold, were in good health apart from Engineer Commander C. J. M. Wallace who had suffered a broken rib and Stoker W. Hawkins with abdominal injuries. It would take ten hours for the *Diamond* to reach Portland due to the terrible weather conditions. An extract from the ship's log states that at 10.00am the ship was rolling very heavily and the foretopgallant mast and port sounding boom were carried away by the storm. The *Diamond* then hove to until the weather improved with crew members securing the boats and rigging sounding boom. The rest of the Fifth Battle Squadron also headed back to the safety of Portland and at 5.00am had reached the Empress Buoy, south of Lyme Regis, before changing course eastward and turning for the Bill at 7.00am off Worbarrow Bay. Lessons had obviously been learned from events that saw the *Aboukir*, *Hogue* and *Cressy* sunk in quick succession by a lone submarine.

The *Formidable's* launch which had got clear with 12 men aboard, was soon crowded with men plucked from the sea. With only eight useable oars, she drifted away as those onboard fought a desperate battle to stop her from sinking, by constantly bailing-out with every implement available. Thankfully at around 9.30am, she was spotted (after hoisting a piece of clothing tied to an oar) some 15 miles off Berry Head by the Brixham trawler *Provident (BM291)*, who herself had been lying-to in the gale waiting to make harbour. The trawler was directed towards the launch by the third hand John Clark, who had defied the stormy conditions by climbing the rigging. After three abortive attempts to pass her a line, the skipper Captain William Pillar risked his own life and that of his crew of four, by defying the full gale that was still blowing and the thirty foot high waves, by bringing his own boat alongside the sinking launch. Incredibly he managed to transfer all 71 half-frozen men, and not a second too soon, as the launch sank almost immediately the last man, Gunner Daniel Horrigan, was hauled aboard. All this was achieved without major mishap, apart from one sailor who crushed his hand during the transfer and another who was slightly injured. The shivering men were then accommodated in the engine room and fish holds where they were fed and given hot drinks. The daring manoeuvre to get alongside the launch and the transfer of men had taken some three hours. Even so, the danger wasn't over and the *Provident* and its crew battled the elements for a further six hours until the overloaded boat reached Brixham at around 7.00pm.

There it anchored in the outer harbour and Captain Pillar rowed ashore to report the events to the coastguard. Arrangements were made at once for the tug *Dencade* to pull the *Provident* alongside the landing stage. The men, waiting patiently onboard the trawler, were then removed in batches of four and five, wrapped in blankets and taken in waiting cabs to the Bolton Hotel, the Cafe and the Sailors Institute, where they were provided with hot food and warm clothing, kindly donated by local residents and the wife of the vicar of Paignton. Beds were then provided, either at these establishments or private homes thrown open to them.

HMS *Topaze's* log book entry for January 1, 1915 was as follows;

Position 1 mile astern of Formidable.

02.20am	*Observed explosion starboard side of Formidable – who fell out of line to port. Course and speed as required to stand by Formidable.*
02.55am	*Observed large volume black smoke from Formidable. Communicating with her.*
03.10am	*Closed Formidable - observed several boats and men in water. Stopped - let go both lifebuoys. Received onboard 43 men from water and boats.*
03.18am	*Proceeded 130 revs. Course as required to intercept strange vessel. Hands to action stations.*
03.45am	*Communicated with stranger - ordered her to stand by Formidable. Closed Formidable.*
04.15am	*Stopped. Informed by Captain of Formidable of presence of submarine.*
04.18am	*Proceeded full speed (150 revs) to intercept second strange steamer.*
04.25am	*Communicating with her. Hove her to and tried to hail her.*
04.30am	*Heard minute guns fired from Formidable.*

04.38am	*Firing ceased.*
04.40am	*Cruised around in vicinity of place where Formidable last seen altering course every 5 minutes. 120 revs.*
05.50am	*Sighted Diamond - cruising round looking for Diamond's boat and for survivors. Southerly wind now hurricane force and very heavy sea running.*
08.15am	*Abandoned search. Course east 130 revs.*
09.20am	*Lost overboard in heavy seas 1x30 foot cutter No. 3483 - Chatham with seaboats fittings complete.*
09.25am	*Hove to on southerly course - both top gallant masts carried away - taking wireless aerials with them.*
09.45am	*Resumed course East. 130 revs.*
10.15am	*Sighted Portland Bill. Lt N 10W. Course as required for entering Portland.*

The log of HMS *Diamond* has the *Formidable* sinking at 4.39am.

From the *Provident*'s log, Captain Pillar wrote on the day of the rescue;

'At 9.30am Friday January 1, 1915 - Blowing a heavy gale from south with a very high sea running. I was running ship for Torbay - we are shipping very heavy seas and I deemed it too dangerous to keep ship running and rounded ship too for safety. Whilst doing so sighted a large boat under our lee bow, she had an oar on end with a scarf or shirt on it as a signal of distress and was apparently full of men. Before we could manoeuvre for her, owing to the height of the gale, had to clew reef the mainsail and shift the jib and set storm jib. Whilst doing this we lost sight of the boat. Kept ship off in the direction in which I judged the boat had drifted and sent J. Clark (third hand) aloft to look out for her. Shortly after he reported sighting the boat bearing away on our lee bow. Then bore away for her. She was riding with a sea anchor and the men were bailing with boots and caps. I hailed to them to slip their sea anchor and drift down to us, but they were waving for

us to come to them. I at once trimmed sails to work up to them. After 3 attempts and having to jibe over once I succeeded on the 4th attempt in fitting a line on board the boat from my weather quarter. Ship then being hove up in the wind - passed the line to leeward and forward to our steam capstan. By this means and by very great care, succeeded in pulling the boat, a launch, alongside under our lee and safely got all her crew numbering 71 on board. Two of them being injured had to be lifted out of the boat - got all the men below deck and them as comfortable as possible - the boat, a launch, being half full of water and leaking badly, cut her adrift and at 1.00pm made sail for Brixham. Got alongside the pier there at 7.00pm when they were all landed and looked after. The whole of my crew, W. Carter, 2nd hand, J. Clark, 3rd hand and Dan Taylor, boy, assisted me and worked splendidly through the whole transaction.   *W. Pillar, Skipper*

The official report stated; *'The rescue was only effected by careful and splendid seamanship and not without danger to the smack. An error of half the ship's length would have swamped or crushed the boat which was already holed in several places and kept afloat by constant bailing with sea boots, while clothing and even legs and arms were stuffed into the holes. The small boat was cut adrift and sank almost immediately.'* For this outstanding and fearless piece of seamanship, Captain William Pillar and his crew were awarded silver gallantry medals for saving life at sea, conferred on them by King George V, at Buckingham Palace on February 5, 1915. The King told Captain Pillar: *"I congratulate you upon your gallant and heroic conduct. It is indeed a great feat to have saved 71 lives. I realise how difficult your task must have been, because I know myself how arduous it is to gybe a vessel in a heavy gale."* (the King had been a former naval officer and had frequently raced the huge yacht *Britannia*.) Captain Pillar (on the instigation of Winston Churchill, First Lord of the Admiralty) was also awarded a gratuity of £250 and £100 each went to his second and third hands William Carter and John Clark. A further £50 was awarded to the apprentice Daniel "Dan" Taylor (who had carried out life saving duties by ensuring the rescued men were fed and supplied with cups of coffee) and £25 to the Captain's nine year-old nephew, Leonard "Cher" Pillar, who in fact didn't receive a medal as he was on his school holidays and had sailed unofficially. The rescue was also recognised by the Shipwrecked Fishermen and Mariners' Royal Benevolent Society by the award of their gold medal and a purse of £5 to Captain Pillar, their silver medal and a purse of £3 each to Carter and Clark and a bronze medal and a purse of £3 to Daniel Taylor.

One of the fortunate survivors rescued by the *Provident* gave a short account of the ordeal in a local newspaper a few days later.

'The wind increased in velocity and we despaired of being rescued. The seas broke clean over us. It is a miracle that any of us are alive to tell the tale. The men stuck manfully to the oars, while others baled out with their caps and boots. Our boat was badly holed, and one man took off his trousers, stuffed them in the hole, and sat there to keep them from washing out. Towards daylight we sang "Its a long way to Tipperary" but in such awful weather we could not keep it up for long. The boat hook was used as the mast and a black silk muffler was fastened to the top. One man held on to this for several hours like grim death.'

On November 28, 1916, the *Provident* was ironically sunk, 24 miles W. by S. off Portland Bill, by a surface U-boat using an explosive charge. Captain Pillar and his crew were allowed to leave the *Provident* in an open boat prior to the sinking (a new *Provident (BM28)* was built in 1925 and was still sailing at the time of writing this book). In 1917, William Pillar was appointed Temporary Skipper in the Royal Naval Reserve and sent to the East Coast. After training in mine sweeping, he commanded the armed trawler *Concord II*, based at Grimsby, until 1919. Later he became a member of the crew of the R.N.L.I. lifeboat based at Brixham. On December 30, 1935 he was part of the crew that saved the lives of the crew of the French trawler *Satanicle* during a violent storm in the English Channel. For their actions they were presented with a medal by the French government. William Pillar received the Marine Marchande, Courage et Devoument medal. On December 16, 1939, the lifeboat saved the crew of the schooner *Henrietta* off Start Bay. Because of this rescue, the R.N.L.I. on February 8, 1940 awarded the crew further medals in recognition of their heroics. William Pillar went on to become the Chief of Brixham Lifeboat. In his old age, he would be a familiar figure on Brixham fish quay. On several occasions he was sought out by elderly Royal Marines and sailors who came to the town to shake his hand again, forty and fifty years after he had saved their lives when the *Formidable* had sunk. He died, aged 87, in 1970. A road in Brixham, "Pillar Avenue" perpetuates his name. In December 1990 his medals came up for auction at Sotheby's. Including his gallantry awards and the British War and Victory medals, the life-saving group fetched £3,960.

His nephew, Leonard "Cher" Pillar, would follow in his uncle's footsteps and become a trawler skipper in Cardiff. During WW2 he commanded minesweepers, but was discharged before the end of the war due to ill-health. Returning to fishing, his exploits continued when he shot down a German plane during one particular voyage.

Meanwhile in the other boats, the fight for life was just as desperate. A capsized cutter was found on the Chesil Beach near Abbotsbury along with four bodies by the destroyer HMS *Savage,* and the pinnace originally containing 71 men, was finally beached at Lyme Regis at 11 o'clock the following night, after a heroic struggle. The men had rowed without proper direction (as no compass was aboard) and had spotted a liner and eleven other craft during their perilous voyage, but due to the mountainous seas, had not been spotted themselves. Their salvation came when a Lyme Regis resident broke the blackout regulations and the light which shone from shore allowed the men to get their bearings and steer the boat to dry land (these lights could well have been from the Assembly Rooms cinema, when the projector broke and the operator shone it through the window for a few seconds). Fortunately Leading

Seaman Thomas Carroll, the coxswain, had kept the light to starboard. If he had steered them to port, the boat would have been smashed to pieces on the rocks and probably all hands lost.

The outline of the boat was first spotted some 400 yards off shore by Miss Gwen Harding and her parents, William and Annie, of Churnside, Lyme Regis. They had been returning home along the Marine Parade after dining out with friends. At first they thought the boat contained German raiders as no reply was heard from their hails. Within minutes the alarm was raised and the local constabulary notified, who duly arrived on the scene in the form of Police Sergeant James Stockley and his assistant Police Constable Rideout. As the pinnace drew near to the beach, one of the sailors threw Sergeant Stockley a line, who succeeded in grabbing hold. One sailor scrambled ashore, but another (Able Seaman John Cowan), so weak with exhaustion, fell into the raging surf. Sergeant Stockley at once ran into the foaming sea and pulled out the unconscious sailor and dragged him onto the beach. He also rescued Petty Officer Stoker Arthur Petts, who had tried in vain to rescue John Cowan, and Able Seaman Charles Stoakes, who had also fallen exhausted into the sea.

The pinnace was finally beached below the Cobb Gate. The survivors owed a massive debt of gratitude to fellow seamen Petty Officer Herbert Bing and especially Leading Seaman Thomas Carroll, for keeping morale so high during the ordeal, even when all seemed lost. Herbert Bing openly confessed to "bullying" the men to prevent them from falling asleep, which meant, under the circumstances, almost certain death. Thomas Carroll, a native of County Kerry, who had joined the Navy in 1893, acted as coxswain throughout the whole voyage and steered the boat through mountainous seas with the use of just an oar. Of the 57 men left onboard, 6 were dead and 3 would die while on shore. Fourteen bodies had been thrown overboard during the struggle, to help lighten the load.

In an interview with a local paper, Thomas Carroll and Herbert Bing explained how they prevented the pinnace from sinking. (Carroll) *'The boys tell me I saved them, but there was another Hand behind mine on that oar. Providence was with me, for I never would have believed that a boat of that size and so laden could have lived through such terrific seas, if I had not been in it. Once I did feel as if I was going to lose hope and thought all was up. That was when we shipped a big sea that swamped us and smashed several oars and carried away others. We were down in the water up to our thwarts. By all known records of the sea we should have sunk.'* (Bing) *'Yes, but then again you saved us. (referring to Carroll) He went dead against all the rules of the sea. He ordered the oars to be shipped and the popits to be replaced in the rowlocks while we baled the boat. That gave us another six inches above the water and then he let her run with the sea while we cleared the boat. The rest of the crew had the Lady Jellicoe blanket erected as a sail and then against the rules of seamanship, he let her run before the wind and sea instead of putting her head into it.'*

The response from the locals in Lyme Regis, when the alarm was raised, was magnificent. Many helped during the rescue of the pinnace (Mr. R. Battenbury, Mr. E. O. Yerbury and Harry Gush) and in assisting the men from the boat (Mrs Strapps, Miss A. H. Hill, A. A. Loud and A. Fowler). Others provided food, clothing and blankets in abundance, while homes were offered for recuperation and rest including that of Alderman Harris. Proper medical attention was soon provided by Doctors J. Spurr and H. J. Cooper. Other able assistance was rendered by Police Constables Meech and Stanley, Mayor A.J. Woodroffe and the coxswain of the lifeboat R.W. Abbott. Other survivors were taken to local hostelries (including the New Inn), many showing little or no sign of life. In the Pilot Boat Inn, which was only yards from the beached pinnace, a wood fire was soon lit in the large room as helpers attempted to revive and accelerate recovery with warm blankets, vigorous rubbing and hot beverages, cigarettes and brandy. The bodies of nine of the sailors, six who were dead at the bottom of the pinnace and three who could not be saved, were laid out in the Assembly Rooms. Among them lying side by side, were twin brothers who had been on the battleship for only five months. Master At Arms Albert Edward Cooper had the grim undertaking of identifying the bodies. The task was made even harder due to the fact that only one of the dead sailors wore an identification disc. What personal belongings they had, were gathered up to be sent on to their relatives.

However, among the stories of heartache and tragedy, one emerged that had a happy ending. "Tommy" Atkins the landlord of the Pilot Boat Inn had a a rough-haired cross-bred collie called Lassie, who took a particular interest in one of the men who lay lifeless on the Pilot Boat Inn floor. For around half-an-hour the dog continued to lick and nuzzle the body of Able Seaman John Cowan (Armourer on Admiralty survivor list) who originated from Lochgelly in Fifeshire, and was the sailor pulled from the surf by Police Sergeant Stockley. Incredibly he began to show signs of life and willing hands soon completed the recovery started by the dog. Before long he had recovered sufficiently to be transported to hospital. Canine intuition had undoubtedly contributed to saving his life (several sources state that Lassie had been trained to raise an alarm, as the landlord's wife was an epileptic). John William Spowert Cowan was born in Edinburgh on June 21, 1884 and worked as a wireman in a coal mine before joining the Navy on January 25, 1900. He had been discharged from the Navy at the end of his engagement on June 20, 1914, joining the Royal Naval Reserve a day later and was then called up on August 2, 1914 when war with Germany was inevitable. He had been posted to the *Formidable* on August 31, 1914.

While he recuperated, Cowan and the dog became inseparable and would spend many hours in front of the kitchen fire. Lassie was awarded two medals and the story of the dog's exploits was soon known all over the country, and culminated in her winning first place in the Canine Heroes and Heroines section at the 1915 Crufts Dog Show. According to local folklore, the story of Lassie eventually reached Hollywood and inspired the creation of the immortal sheepdog "Lassie" who would star in many films and become known the world over.

The inquest concerning the deaths of the nine men took place next day (Saturday, January 2) at 4.00pm in the Assembly Rooms, conducted by the coroner of West Dorset. Among the jury was Mayor A. J. Woodroffe and William J. Harding, whose family had first spotted the pinnace out at sea. After the sad task of viewing the bodies was performed in an adjoining room, Master At Arms Albert Edward Cooper gave evidence, followed by Petty Officer Herbert Bing, Leading Seaman Thomas Carroll, Police Sergeant Stockley and Doctor H. J. Cooper. After all the evidence was heard, the jury returned the verdict that the deceased *"died from exposure at sea in an open boat, following an accident having occurred to their ship."* The Mayor, speaking on behalf of the jury members, conveyed the great sorrow felt at the loss of these gallant men who had died carrying out their duty for King and country.

For his bravery, Police Sergeant James Stockley, was awarded in May 1915, the silver medal of the Board of Trade for Gallantry in saving life at sea and the Bronze Medal of the Royal Humane Society. Born at Corfe Castle, Dorset, he joined the Police force aged 19, on May 16, 1891. His first posting was Hazelbury Bryan (May 1891), followed by Charminster (June 1895), Puddletown (March 1898), Chickerell (March 1900), Cranborne (July 1908) and finally to Lyme Regis in March 1914. He was promoted to 2nd Class Sergeant on July 23, 1908 and gained 1st Class rank on March 1, 1914. He would retire from the force on September 25, 1919.

Mr William J. Harding, who had helped raise the alarm when spotting the pinnace from the Marine Parade, wrote an account for friends and family on January 4. At this early stage, many believed *Formidable* had struck a mine.

'The New Year was ushered in by a violent tempest, and the sea rolled in with terrific uproar. When the rain ceased, the Parade and Cobb were thronged with people watching the huge waves, and at one spot the beach was covered in foam waist high. Boys, racing through it, emerged as though they were covered with snow. While we were at tea an invitation came from our friends the Pattersons asking us to dine with them at the 'Royal Standard,' close to the Cobb. Dr. P. has a large practice in London, as a Dentist and he had just joined his family in Lyme. We went down in torrents of rain and spent a very jolly evening. It was almost 11 o'clock when we left, and as the rain had ceased and the tide was on the ebb, we decided to walk home by the shore. There was a moon over the sea, but its light was fitful and partially dimmed by black clouds. Gwen said she thought she saw a boat out at sea and her mother was inclined to believe she was right. But I was sceptical till we mounted the steps to the Bell Cliff at the foot of the main street of the town. I then distinctly saw a large pinnace and summoned a police sergeant, who is stationed at night at this point. He said he fancied he had heard voices too, but had seen nothing and did not know whence they came.

Another policeman was sent off to awaken the Life Boat coxswain and four of us hurried to the beach. No other people were about. The boat was now in the surf, but fortunately the sea was not very rough, the tide being on the ebb. I hailed the boat and only an indistinct voice replied. It was hopeless to attempt to direct them to the harbour, so we shouted to the crew to run straight on to the shore. The boat grounded a few yards from the spot where we stood, and a man clambered out with a line which he threw to us. We held it till one or two men arrived with a stronger cable. A few of the crew then staggered through the shallow water and one was nearly washed away. They were helped up to the beach and the steps and taken to the Pilot Inn about 50 yards from the sea. Annie and Gwen went with them, and roused the landlord from his bedroom. He and his wife seemed to think the men were Germans besetting their house, until they were told by Annie that they were survivors from the 'Formidable.' News of the disaster in the

Channel had appeared in the evening papers. Fires were rapidly made in a large room with a long table, which was subsequently laden with the unconscious wretches that we carried in. The ladies then visited the adjacent shops, the grocer's, baker's, butcher's, chemist's etc, and sent messages to the Hospital and Vicarage. The doctors had already been warned.

Annie implored them all to make up their fires and prepare hot water and blankets and to bring clothes of any description. The sailors were nearly all in their night dress, except those who were doing watch duty when the explosion occurred. Hot coffee and bread and butter were soon provided and one woman came to the shore with a bottle of brandy. Many of the poor fellows were too far gone to swallow anything, and we could only rub their lips. After the first dozen, they all had to be lifted out of the boat and carried to the adjacent houses, which, on the alarm being given, were thrown open to receive them. We did not know whether the men we carried were alive or dead : they were quite rigid and stone cold. About thirty were in this state of collapse and had to be rubbed and stripped and rolled in hot blankets. But nearly all of these were restored to consciousness in the course of two hours. Three doctors arrived on the scene about half an hour after the boat reached the land, and they devoted themselves to the worst cases. The Mayor arrived a little later and his motor car was most useful for conveying the men to various houses, where they were at once put to bed. As the boat was swamped with water, we had little hope for the last six that were lying at the bottom. They were all dead. Of the others all recovered except three, and they were too far gone. Everybody behaved splendidly. There was no noise, no fuss and women as well as men toiled ceaselessly, trying to restore circulation and respiration, and their efforts have been crowned with success. The crew had been through mountainous billows and storms of hail and sleet and drenching rain, with merely a vest and trousers to cover them, for 21 hours. They had no provisions and were obliged to bale constantly with the few boots they had amongst them. For a long time they could only keep their boat headed to the waves to avoid sinking.

During the first five or ten minutes we appeared to be almost alone, but a host of willing workers soon joined us. I was so intent upon the task of getting the men up the beach that I quite forgot to send for Dr. Patterson, whom we had just left, till all were safely landed and the coxswain had no time to send up the Life Rocket which usually arouses the whole town. The Life Boat house is a quarter of a mile away. Consequently most of the inhabitants slept peacefully not knowing anything of the occurrence. The 'Daily Chronicle' of today (Jan. 4) has an account of the whole affair. If I can get a copy, I will enclose a cutting. About 70 men started in the boat and 14 succumbed on the voyage and were dropped overboard to lighten the vessel. It was a terrible ordeal for the women helping. Gwen and her mother kept up wonderfully and the Mayor kindly brought us to the top of the hill in his motor.

On the next day (Saturday Jan. 2) I went down early to send off telegrams to the relatives of the sailors. I found all but five quite jolly. They received visitors all day and were pleased to have gifts of cigarettes and fruit and chocolate. Several ladies took a turn at the Cottage Hospital to relieve the nurses. In the afternoon I attended the Inquest. A few of the survivors were in church on Sunday evening. The funeral was fixed for today (Jan. 4) but I hear it is postponed till Wednesday, when sailors and soldiers will come over from Devonport. The satisfaction of seeing the grateful happy faces the next morning did much to alleviate the strain and shock of the previous night, but the scene was one which will not easily be effaced from our memories. Most of the survivors seemed to think the ship was torpedoed, as there were two explosions at an interval of half an hour. But I doubt whether a submarine could have aimed straight in such a violent storm. One of our own mines, perhaps from Portland or Plymouth was picked up near Sidmouth and it is at least possible that another mine, or mines, may have caused the catastrophe. The second explosion might be due to fire reaching the magazine. No theory as to the cause was suggested at the Inquest and the jury returned a verdict of death from exposure. I have hurried to write this brief account, as I thought our sisters, brothers and friends might be interested to have the version of an eye-witness.'

Mrs Annie Harding, William's wife, later wrote an essay on the events for a competition. In this small extract she gives her account of one sailor who sadly could not be saved (probably Boy 1st Class Bernard Arthur de Plumley Smythe).

'One nice fair-haired lad of eighteen was carried up and laid on the floor of a pretty drawing-room, close to where they landed; it was no good; his heart had ceased to beat. The coxswain told us afterwards of this lad's unfailing spirits: he had been cheery all through that awful night and day and had even made a joke as the boat came ashore, but it was his last effort. He lay there young and fair, with a smile on his lips, which seemed to bring comfort to the heart of his poor mother, who came many miles from an inland town for a last look at her boy.'

On Wednesday January 6, the burial of six of the men who died in the pinnace took place at Lyme Regis. During the morning of the burials, a firing party and gun crew arrived from the Devonport School of Musketry and also a detachment of the 11th (Service) Battalion, Devon Regiment commanded by Lieutenant Rule. On a gun carriage drawn by a crew of twenty men rested the body of Petty Officer William Feldon, while the remaining five coffins containing the bodies of Stokers Horace Bernthall, William Eley, William Fawkes, Henry Souter and Boy 1st Class Bernard Smythe carried by townspeople, with each coffin draped by the Union flag. At the entrance to the church, the cortege passed between a guard of honour formed by the local Boy Scouts. A crowd too large to count lined the funeral route through the town and up past the church to the cemetery. After the brief ceremony carried out by the Vicar Reverend Canon Jacob with an address delivered by the Bishop of Salisbury, Dr. Ridgeway, the cortege took the short journey from the church to the cemetery. After the chief mourners, there followed forty-six of the survivors, each carrying a floral tribute to their lost shipmates. These were followed by the Mayor with his mace-bearers carrying a wreath of white carnations and lilies, further followed by French and Belgian refugees carrying their own national flags. They were buried side by side in one large grave with volleys fired over the grave followed by the "Last Post." The remaining three bodies (Senior Reserve Attendants Henri and John Villiers Russell and Leading Stoker John William Pells) were sent to their home towns for burial.

Among those sent home were 29 year-old twins from the town of Crewe in Cheshire. The Villiers Russell brothers, Henri and John, along with their friends, Albert Kinlay and James Burnell, all worked for the great railway company at Crewe Works. John and Henri were employed as labourers in the Joiners Shop. All were members of the St. John's Ambulance Brigade and attached to the Naval Sick Berth Reserve. During the 1914 Crewe Works holidays, they travelled down south to serve their seven days training on the battleship HMS *Formidable,* joining the ship on August 3. Next day when war was declared, all four volunteered to stay aboard. They would never see loved ones or their home town again. The bodies of their friends, Kinlay and Burnell, were never found. The twins were transported back to Crewe by train for burial, paid for by Mr. C. J. Bowen Cooke, the chief mechanical engineer of the London and North-Western Railways. The funeral took place on Thursday afternoon, January 7, and was attended by thousands of local folk, who shared in the grief felt by the whole town and in particular Isabelina Villiers Russell, their widowed mother. The twins were buried in the family plot and their final resting place in Coppenhall Church Cemetery in Crewe was marked by an impressive Italian marble headstone and two anchors with the inscriptions *'Fast They Stood'* and *'For Right and Good'* paid for by friends and workmates.

In life and death the twins were inseparable and postcards printed to raise money for the twins' widowed mother contained a verse which summed up their lives together.

'Together they first saw the light of day,
Together at mother's breast they lay,
Together they smiled, together they cooed,
Together they settled their childish feud;
Together they toddled the self-same way,
Together they progressed day-by-day,
Together at school they learned to spell,
To reason and think and do all things well;
Together they worked, together they played,
By life's cares and worries they were ne'er dismayed,
Together they joined the Ambulance Corps,
Together they studied and came to the fore;
Together they answered their country's call,
To secure us victory or 'neath our flag fall,
Together they suffered, together they died,
Together embraced, brought home by the tide;
Together they traced their oft-beaten track,
Enshrouded in glory and our Union Jack,
Together by father they now lie at rest,
Numbered we know with those of the blest.'

The Villiers Russell twins are still remembered in the town today and are commemorated by a plaque hanging in the Municipal Buildings in Crewe and also in the form of a residential area in Crewe (Villiers Russell Close), built virtually on the site of the Methodist Chapel in which they worshipped and where they lay overnight before burial. The plaque in the Municipal Buildings states that after the sinking and the loss of the twins, a debate in parliament led to an Admiralty directive that no brothers should serve on the same Royal Navy vessel. Despite an exhaustive search on this matter, no evidence has been unearthed to substantiate these claims or any material found that this directive was issued or discussed.

Footnote. There were very few occasions during the Great War where twin brothers died in the same incident on the same day. On November

1, 1914, twin brothers Edward and Harry Turner, aged 33, from Cheltenham and both stokers on HMS *Good Hope,* were both killed in action during the Battle of Coronel. On June 30, 1916, Leonard and William Crossley were both killed in action serving with the 21st (Service) Battalion, The King's Royal Rifle Corps, near Ploegsteert. Their bodies are buried in adjacent graves in Berks Cemetery Extension. The only other known twins killed on the same day were Brighton men, Frank and Herbert Bindoff, aged 21, whilst serving with the 2nd Battalion, Royal Sussex Regiment.

In a letter to a friend written on December 9, 1914, Henri Villiers Russell writes about their trip down to Sheerness and their early experiences on the *Formidable*.

'After chatting with a Marine we learned that he was bound for the HMS Formidable. Our train arrived and we were very pleased to find another St. John's man. He was also for the HMS Formidable for a week's training. The Marine told us he had been recalled from leave. After much shunting, bumping and thumping we reached Sheerness (by sheer-luck) at 9.35 a.m. A short walk soon found us at the Dock Yard and after waiting for the steamer to take us to the HMS Formidable, we were politely informed that our ship had left a few days ago for Portland. We then separated ourselves at the Depot. Here we found more "Johnnies." As we sat down to an emergency meal which consisted of pig's trotters and pop, we were then handed a warrant for Portland. On changing at Chatham we arrived at Portland (Bill) about 12.10. On reporting at the Depot we were met by a naval officer who instructed us to proceed to the steamer. We were surprised to find on boarding her our other comrades who had left Sheerness some time before us. We saw three of them on to their ship, The Russell, then we proceeded to ours (the Formidable) leaving 3 others for the Lord Nelson. We did feel proud boarding a large man-of-war. We were escorted to the Sick Bay crouching under hammocks so that we may not disturb the slumbers of the Jolly Tars. Finally we reached the desired

Haven and as it was so late and rather early in the morning we sufficed to bed down on seats and couches. We were soon in the land of nod and would have remained there but for the sound of a bugle and later on came the call to "lash up and stow." Of course we had nothing to lash and stow so we simply got up, washed and had breakfast along with the chief steward and staff. The next day we were informed that England and Germany had declared war, we were also informed our brigades and reserves had mobilized. So we volunteered to stay aboard. Saw several hospital ships. Went ashore, attended a concert for servicemen. Had all night leave but could not get digs, so slept in a bathing tent on the beach. Next day inspection by the new captain. Then we had a new departure, took a cot case to hospital ashore. On one occasion John had the pleasure of a trip in rough seas on the picket boat. Have had several route marches. Have had the pleasure occasionally of attending Divine Worship at a Wesleyan church ashore. We met our St. John comrade off the Lord Nelson occasionally when ashore and a few others but no Crewe men. I was excused a route march through a sore heel obtained at the last one. Later John was in the same predicament. We had the honour of giving a turn at a concert on aft deck and were cordially applauded. We dressed in civvies for the occasion. Another route march, saw some Scottish Borderers off to the front with a splendid bagpipe band, also a number of wounded Belgians. We have been supplied with winter clothing and a swimming collar. Burnell took sick with a sore throat but is now well again. I suppose you read of the explosion of the Bulwark. We were close to at the time.'

An account of the sinking and the fight for survival was told by Leading Stoker J. H. Taplin who was among the 48 survivors landed at Lyme Regis.

'It was midnight – the ship was rolling heavily with the seas crashing over her bows with a noise like thunder. It had just struck 16 bells (8 for the old and 8 for the New Year) as the Fleet steamed down the

channel with the Formidable bringing up the rear. Many of the crew were awake to see the "Old Year" out and the "New Year" in, wishing one another the usual greetings. Little did we think it would be the last that many would hear. "I turned in" (a phrase sailors mean for getting into the hammock) when suddenly a heavy dull thud was heard forrard. At the time I thought it was a hatch being dropped, (forgetting we were already battened down). I settled down to try and snatch a few hours sleep prior to going on watch. A shout went up "We've been torpedoed." A few seconds after, the engines stopped and all lights went out. Everything was black. I jumped from my hammock feverishly fumbling for clothes, eager to get on deck as the ship was listing badly. I lost all sense of direction owing to the pitch darkness, running into staunchions, hammocks, bulkheads, in fact everything seemed to get in my way in my frantic endeavour to find a companion ladder.

At last I found it and scrambled up with what clothes I could find under my arm (on reaching the deck I found I had a pair of trousers and one sock). It was terribly cold and the ship was in a sorry plight rolling and heeling over. Two light cruisers were dodging and searching around us, dropping life-buoys and hoping to save some of the crew. They were almost as helpless as we were. They had to keep on the move in case they got torpedoed and it was impossible to get near us as the terrific seas were washing over us. Several men were in the water crying for help but we could do nothing.

An order came from the Captain (Capt. Loxley) "Remember lads we're British. Cheer up, be British and do your best." The order came "Out Boats" but owing to the list and the seas, much difficulty was experienced. Finally one boat was got out, but no sooner had she touched water than a sea caught her and smashed her to matchwood against the ship's side, killing all hands on her, some 40-60 men and boys. Two more boats were swung clear and managed to get away but another got stove in and sank.

Suddenly the ship gave a terrific lurch, throwing some into the water and the rest of us hanging on for dear life. The Captain shouted, "Well lads, this is the last. All hands for themselves and may God bless you and guide you to safety." He then walked to the bridge and stood there with his dog by his side waiting for the end. We were all wet through and shivering with the cold when the Chaplain served us out with cigarettes (he had gone below at the risk of his life for these). What a God send! There was no panic. Some were looking for wreckage to hang on to when the ship gave her final plunge. Some were singing and others were talking on topics as though the ship didn't concern them.

Out of the darkness one of the boats we launched came alongside as they had some room to spare (a very brave act as they had their full complement and were in danger of getting smashed against the ship). We put as many boys as the boat would safely carry. When she pushed off it seemed that we were then cut off from the last link. It would be hard for anybody to picture the scene unless having experienced something of the sort. The ship was sinking fast, heeled over to an angle of almost 45 degrees, freezing cold, while those of us left on board watching the two light cruisers circling around dropping life-buoys which were quickly swept away. Everything seemed hopeless. A scene of desolation. Not one of us 500 left on board ever thought of seeing land again.

Without warning a terrific explosion rent the ship. A second torpedo had caught us blowing the boilers up. I had a peculiar sensation of seeing the ship below me and with her nose well down. Another moment I was in the icy water struggling for life with the breath knocked out of me. At first I could not realise what had happened. Gradually my head cleared. I had a recollection of seeing the ship. It seemed a long way off. It looked as though she was turning over. I struck out. The seas kept breaking over me, choking me. I was gasping. I had a life saving collar around my neck (very nice in calm weather but in a rough sea "useless"). It was holding my head up enough to let the waves wash over and slowly drowning me. I fought hard to get it off (it was tied on with ribbons of cloth). I could not untie the knots as the water had swollen them tight (in a crisis like this people say keep calm. Let them try in a rough sea and half drowned!). I tore recklessly at it trying to break it but it would not give way. Each gasp I gave I sucked in water. Choking and spluttering, my hand touched the valve (I had forgotten this in my panic). I managed to turn it and so deflate the thing. I breathed a prayer. At last I was free.

I struck out using every ounce of energy to keep afloat. I tried to shout but could not hear my voice. I swam for dear life. I tried to float but the waves turned me over and over. I was getting feebler. Could I hold out? I was swimming mechanically. As I rose on a crest of a wave I saw something loom up in the darkness. A boat? Again I tried to shout. "Oh God can I hang out long enough? Was it a Boat? Had they seen me?" (it was a boat and they had seen me but it was some time before they found me). My limbs felt like lead. I had a feeling of being dragged down. A thought ran through my head, what a shock for my parents when they heard the news (my younger brother [Alfred Charles Taplin] lost his life on the "Good Hope" a few weeks before in the Falkland Battle). Dozens of such thoughts surged through my brain in those few minutes (or were they seconds?). I tried to swim – I must not give way. There was a rushing past my ears, I was sinking. I felt tired and sleepy. I thought I was lying on an ever so soft bed, sinking farther in, going to sleep. The noises went farther and farther away – then "oblivion."

How long I was unconscious I cannot say. I heard noises far away. "Where was I?" My arms were moving – I remembered – I must swim! I was in the water! Somebody said, "He's all right now." I stared about me. I was in a boat filled with survivors. How I got there I had no idea. Thank goodness I was out of the water. My arms were still moving. I found I had been propped up on a thwart (seat), an oar placed in my hands and double-banked by my Saviour at the side of me. The man behind was keeping me upright, thus it wasn't long before I had the blood coursing through my body again. I heard some groaning, hurt by the last explosion I thought. After some time I was feeling much better and was able to carry on by myself. I bent to the work with a will. They told me I had been in the water half to three quarters of an hour. My hands and feet were swollen with the cold. I think we were all so cold we did not feel it, until the boat shipped a big sea then with one accord we all gasped for breath. This happened every few minutes. The boat was getting swamped. She was nearly full of water. We had to stop several times to bale her out. Those who had boots used these or with anything we could lay our hands on. "Try to keep her nose on" Coxswain Carroll shouted. We all pulled and strained but no sooner had we got her nose on than another wave would wash us back again.

We had no food or fresh water and no tiller (the Coxswain using an oar for this purpose). The night wore on, but what a night. It would be impossible to describe it. Dawn came at last. We were up to our waists in water. "Bale, bale" Coxswain Carroll shouted. "We're sinking." We kept baling, pulling and baling. Once as we rose on the crest of a large wave we sighted a torpedo destroyer searching the seas. Had she seen us? We shouted until we were hoarse without avail. The destroyer disappeared. Our hopes dropped to zero. What a time! Never did time seem to drag so much. I looked round at the crew. What a sight! Blue with the cold, unshaven, any old clothes on; we must have all looked a sorry sight. Nobody would recognize the Royal Navy here. I think we all had given up hope. In the stern sheets two or three wounded were wrapped in a blanket. Now and again a groan issued from under it. Poor fellows how badly they were hurt nobody will know for they died shortly afterwards and their bodies put overboard.

The seas were still running high and showed no sign of abating. We were all by this time getting very weak. The men were dropping through exposure. The man alongside (my Saviour as I call him) suddenly fell forward. I tried to rouse him, it was no use. He had gone to his last sleep. This was the beginning as another went a few minutes after. A kind of frozen sleep. They just sighed and fell forward. A man in the bows shouted that a trawler was off the starboard bow. We shouted again and again. We tried to signal with a piece of blanket tied to an oar. It was as much as we could do to raise the oar. No good – the trawler vanished. Imagine our feelings. Not long after we saw a boat (bottom up). Somebody remarked "that's one of our boats" – "they've all gone" (we discovered later the trawler we had seen was from

Brixham and had picked up some survivors). To make matters worse, some of the men went out of their minds. One big chap must have gone mad. He started shouting out orders, then turned on those about him, biting right and left and then jumped overboard and sank. Several more expired, some passing peacefully away, others shouting incoherently. The scene was indescribable. Only those who went through the ordeal know what it was like. I firmly believe if it hadn't been for the coxswain (a Petty Officer) we would all have been lost. He cheered us on.

Time dragged on. We were getting despondent not caring what happened. The seas kept swamping us. We despaired. We couldn't bale it out. We were in it up to our waists and with the dead lying around, it was terrible. Some were talking of making a hole in the water (meaning to dive overboard). The men were dying fast. At last the coxswain said we would have to get rid of the bodies or the boat would be lost. With a prayer on our lips we struggled and rolled them overboard (some two dozen). This made the boat much lighter, enabling us to get her nose to the waves. Towards the end of the forenoon we sighted a steamer (or liner). She seemed to be making straight towards us. Had they seen us? Yes! We tried to cheer. There was no mistaking it. They had seen us. All was bright again. We got excited. My head was spinning. We were all hysterical with excitement. We were going to be saved.

Then – Oh God – she's altered her course. She's going away. Three times our hopes rose as she seemed to make straight for us, only to turn off just when we thought it was impossible for her to miss us (whether she had seen us or whether the seas were too heavy I cannot say). At last she disappeared leaving us parched with thirst, more dead than alive (perhaps it was our boat altering her course which made us think the steamer was). About noon the sun broke momentarily through the clouds. This enabled the coxswain to take a rough bearing. "Pull her nose around" he cried "we're heading to sea." We tugged and strained at the oars (of which 6 or 7 were left out of 16 owing to the waves breaking them).

More hands expired. The afternoon slowly dragged by. Everyone gave themselves up for lost. Not caring what happened. Darkness came.

Each hour took its toll. We put some more dead overboard. No one knew in what direction we were going (or cared). We did not know if we were moving at all. The seas were still running high. Black and angry. Not a star in the sky. What clothes we had on were threadbare and the waves and wind struck our bodies like the lash of a whip. The sea was waiting greedily for the rest of its victims. Some more poor fellows were pushed overboard. We were all more or less overcome by the intense cold. Our rowing was becoming erratic, our strength was ebbing fast. I felt drowsy; I fell forward scraping the skin off my nose and chin. This roused me. No, I mustn't give way or my fate would be like the others. I should never wake again. My mouth and throat felt terrible. Oh for a drink! Visions of hot soup, hot baths, anything hot came to me.

We were now pulling mechanically hardly knowing what we were doing. We thought every wave that came over would finish the boat and leave us to our fate. Then the rain came (or rather hail). Never was it so welcome as at that moment. We threw our heads back and opened our mouths to catch every drop we could. It tasted glorious. It pelted down. We felt revived. What a God send! A shout went up "Pull lads, there's a light. It must be the shore." What part of the coast it was or country we did not care. It was land and that was good enough. We tried hard to pull but were very feeble. We couldn't lift the oars from the water. Suddenly a bright light shone out showing us a rocky outline. Then as suddenly as it came it went out. That did not matter, we had seen land about 3 miles off and that was good enough. Some more men succumbed. We had no strength to pass them overboard. They lay under the water in the bottom of the boat. Slowly, (maybe it was a couple of hours) we crept nearer, near enough to discern a breakwater. Could we make it? No! The wind and tide were too strong for us. Only 6 oars were left.

We all shouted "Land Ahoy, Land Ahoy." We prayed somebody would hear us. Perhaps the people were asleep (we had no idea what time it was). We cried again and again. "Land Ahoy, Land Ahoy." It was futile. The seas were thundering against the rocks, drowning our voices. At last, with many a weary struggle, we felt the boat ground on the shingle. We were absolutely exhausted. The dead were strewn about, some floating, some under water which almost reached the gunwales. A Police Sergeant (Sgt Stockley) waded up to his waist and hung on to the boat. A number of people had gathered on the beach wondering who or what we were. Somebody cried out "push them out again, they are Germans. Look at the crest on the boat. A Spread Eagle." "We can easily attend to that when we get them out, for by the look of things they won't be able to do much damage" the Sergeant replied. I have a hazy recollection of having the oar knocked from my hand and lifted out and put on the beach. I staggered to my feet, gave a couple of steps and fell. I felt somebody help me up and half carry me. One lady thought we were drunk, but bless her how was she to know. When the people found out we were survivors from the "Formidable" they could not do enough. They carried us to an Inn and gave us hot soup, brandy, etc. and a good rub down. Last but not least, cigarettes. What a contrast in such a short time.

The place we landed was Lyme Regis on the Dorset Coast. I cannot dwell too much upon the kindness of its people. They were kindness itself. They did everything for our comfort. Nothing was too much trouble. We were billeted in the various Hotels and houses. Out of 72 or 3 who were in the boat, 33 survived. The majority being in a very sorry state. We had spent 22½ hours battling with the sea. The worst sea, a local fisherman stated, they had experienced in that part of the coast for many years.

It is interesting to relate how the people discovered we were arriving there. A gentleman and his daughter were going home after a Whist Drive when the daughter remarked "Hark, what is that? It's somebody calling?" The father listened but heard nothing remarking it was the rough sea. After a few moments the daughter cried, "hark, there it is again." They stopped and listened. "Yes," the father said. "I can hear it now." They rushed back and found the Police (Sergeant Stockley) who called for help. The news quickly spread and most of the village turned out and came to our aid. We afterwards told them about the bright light we saw and how we tried to make for the breakwater." Providence must have guided you" they remarked. "The bright light you saw was from the cinema. The machine had gone wrong and the operator in examining it had accidentally shone it through the window. As for the breakwater, you would never have landed for what with the heavy seas running and the treacherous rocks just below the surface, the boat would have been smashed to pieces and every soul lost. The only place to land was where you landed." There is a rough channel through the rocks where the fishing boats land and if we had been used to that part of the coast all our lives we couldn't have made a better landing.

We stayed at Lyme Regis some 9 or 10 days until the Doctor passed us as fit to travel to our respective depots. In the meantime we buried some of the poor fellows that were dead (9 of them, the others were claimed by their relatives who took them away for private burial). On the day of the funeral, people thronged the streets. Many coming long distances. The Bishop of Salisbury presided and the words he uttered I shall always remember. "Let any person ask me what our Navy is doing" he remarked "people go to bed in peace, get up, have their meals, go about their daily work thinking of nothing beyond themselves, least of all an invasion. That's what the Navy is doing. Allowing you to do this. And what a price to pay," he added pointing to the nine coffins along the aisle. "They pay toll with their lives without a murmur."

Not a dry eye was in that church. As for us survivors, we completely broke down. His words brought the scene vividly back to our minds. We slowly walked out of the Church up the hill following our comrades to their last resting place. The coffins were placed in a large grave, side by side. It was a big ordeal. When at sea when we tumbled them overboard we did not think much of it but on shore it seemed to take on a different aspect. With a prayer on our lips we left them, walking back with our relatives who had come down to see us. At last the day arrived to leave and with many a hearty cheer and handshakes the train steamed out with the band playing 'Should Old

Acquaintance.' I cannot conclude without paying tribute to "Lassie." The dog that saved a sailor's life. When we were brought ashore many were unconscious and artificial respiration was resorted to. Those dead were placed on one side. One lad was put aside as dead. While attending to the others he was forgotten for the moment until they found Lassie lying across him licking him. They couldn't get her away and eventually they found that her licking and her warm body had actually pulled him from the grave. Later they were able to remove him to Hospital, where I believe he recovered.' (J.H. Taplin).

A further 43 survivors were brought in by HMS *Topaze*, but the final casualty list made grim reading. Out of the *Formidable's* known complement of 747, a total of 34 officers and 513 ratings had died, either in the torpedo attack, of exposure or by drowning. The majority of these belonged to the Chatham Port Division and the rank of stoker made up over a quarter of the casualties. The actual ratios of men who died were stokers 85% compared to around 66% for seaman etc. The losses of the Royal Marine Light Infantry however were staggering. Around 90% of all members of the Regiment died during and after the sinking,* with the vast majority of these from the Chatham 'Grande' Barracks, which was the senior of the three divisions of the RMLI.

*No real reason has been properly explained why these casualty figures were so high in the RMLI.

Of the dead, only 18 bodies and the Captain's dog Bruce were recovered for burial. One body was washed ashore as far away as Dieppe, France (Able Seaman George Ashbee). Nine of the 18 were landed at Lyme Regis in the pinnace and 2 bodies were washed ashore at Burton Bradstock (Private Alfred Clapham and Stoker Frederick Mead). Only 6 further bodies were recovered, and of these, four were found close to a capsized cutter on the Chesil Beach near Abbotsbury. On February 6, 1915 - over a month after the sinking - the body of seventeen-year-old Signal Boy Frederick Norman was found on the shore at Portland. The sea laid claim to the other 529 bodies.

NOT AFRAID TO DIE

During the sinking there were many acts of heroism which could be told, but none more so than the unselfish act performed by Royal Marines bugler Stanley Christopher Reed, who was just 16 when he perished. He was born on June 21, 1898 in Chatham and prior to joining the Royal Marines at Chatham, seven days before his fourteenth birthday, he lived locally with his parents at 90, Dale Street (later at 45, Skinner Street). He was the youngest of four brothers; the eldest, William, drowned in Calais harbour in 1913 and the next eldest, Sydney, was killed in action in France in 1918. Young Stanley served aboard HMS *Aboukir*, *Falmouth* and *Queen* before joining the *Formidable* on July 1, 1914. The following account by Private Herbert Beal of the Royal Marine Light Infantry, describes the final moments of Stanley Reed's short but heroic life.

'On 1 January 1915 about 4.30am following the torpedoing of HMS Formidable, I was on the quarter deck of that vessel with others of the ship's company after all the boats had left. There I saw Bugler S. C. Reed, who I knew well through being a messmate of his. I enquired how he felt and very calmly he replied "all right." I then suggested that he should use his drum as a means of keeping afloat on the ship sinking. His reply to this that he had thought of it but he had given it to one of the bluejacket boys for the same purpose as the lad had nothing to keep him afloat in the heavy seas then prevailing and that he himself did not feel very nervous. I then parted from him and saw him no more.'

The bluejacket referred to was never identified and it is not known whether he survived or died. Stanley Reed, while the *Formidable* was sinking, was one of the volunteers assisting in launching the ship's boats. He also sounded the last bugle call "every man for himself." He was last seen floating on a piece of wood and he remarked to a survivor that the water was a bit cold but he was *"not afraid to die."*

On May 6, 1915 in the House of Commons, Mr. G. F. Hohler MP asked the First Lord of the Admiralty whether his attention had been called to the gallant conduct of CH/17153 Bugler S. C. Reed, RMLI and would he consider whether a medal or some other enduring record of the boy's fine example might be given to his parents. Dr. MacNamara, Financial Secretary of the Admiralty replied, *'There is no medal which could be given for an act of this sort, but the relations will get the War Medal. The Admiralty have already shown their appreciation of this boy's courage by sending to his father a special letter.'*

The contents of this letter, dated March 14, 1915, read;
'Sir, I am commanded by My Lords Commissioners of the Admiralty to inform you that they have received through General Sir Francis Thomas KCB, Royal Marine Light Infantry, the enclosed statement made by Private Herbert Beal, RMLI, of a gallant act performed by your son, the late Bugler S. C. Reed, RMLI, on the occasion of the sinking of HMS Formidable in the Channel on New Year's Day 1915 in which he unfortunately lost his life. My Lords desire me to convey to you their high appreciation of the courage and self-sacrifice displayed by your son and they trust that the knowledge of the facts may be some consolation to you in your bereavement.'

A verse about Stanley's exploits was sent anonymously to the parents of Stanley Reed and was published in many newspapers.

ENGLAND'S DRUM

'The Drum – the drum of England
How it stirs the laggard blood
How it surges through the Empire
Like a resistless flood!

There has not been, nor ever will
In ages yet to come.

A sound to equal in its power
The best of England's drum.

But another use the drum has,
Than to stir the world to strife:
A bugler boy has proved to use
'Twill save a human life.

'And 'twill do more than that,' he said
As he held it in his hand:
'Here, you take this, you little chap,
Mother will understand.'
When the gallant FORMIDABLE sank
Into the silent sea.
No doubt she carried many a one
As brave and bold as he.

But to this bugler lad alone
The golden chance has come
To add to the hidden mystery
That is held in England's drum.

The drum – the drum of England!
Oh it makes us very glad.
You parted with it to your friend,
Brave little bugler lad!'

As a footnote to the exploits of Stanley Reed, he was awarded the Royal Humane (Life Saving) Society's Certificate. Stanley, his parents and brothers are commemorated on a memorial stone in the cemetery in Maidstone Road, Chatham. As for Marine Herbert Beal, who submitted the report on Stanley Reed's actions, he remained in the RMLI until March 12, 1932 when he was discharged to pension with the rank of Colour Sergeant. He enlisted in the Royal Marine Police on May 2, 1932 and died on March 4, 1955.

THREE MEN LOST FROM SAME STREET IN CHATHAM

During the First World War around 750,000 men from the British Isles lost their lives - around one in eight who enlisted. Some towns, in terms of casualties, were left relatively unscathed and some villages lost no men at all. However at the other end of the casualty scale, towns and villages were left decimated by the men lost who enlisted, and it was not uncommon for many houses in the same street to have lost a loved one. In the British Army this was common as the "Pals" or "Chums" battalions were units of volunteers who shared close civilian ties. They were connected through schools, villages, places of employment, or sports clubs etc., and came from all classes of British society. The problem of these close knit units however was the fact that if they were involved in a battle or campaign where losses were high, then whole communities of enlisted men could effectively be wiped out. One famous example of this was the Accrington "Pals" (11th Battalion, East Lancashire Regiment), who on the first day of the Battle of the Somme, on July 1, 1916 were cut-to-pieces by German machine gunfire while attacking Serre. Of the 700 officers and men, drawn mainly from the towns of Accrington, Burnley, Chorley and Blackburn, who took part in the advance across "No Man's Land," over 600 were either killed, wounded or reported as missing. The effect on the towns was devastating. In the Royal Navy however, when a vessel was lost, generally the casualties were from a predominant port and this was no exception when the *Formidable* was sunk. The majority of the crew were from the Chatham Port Division (only about 10% of the casualties were from the Portsmouth and Plymouth Divisions), although the officers and men, were drawn from all corners of the Empire. Indeed if you study the addresses of the men who were lost from newspaper cuttings and the printout of the casualties from the Commonwealth War Graves Commission, London addresses are most prominent in the findings. Studying the addresses closer, are to be found three men from Chatham who were all from the same street. The town of Chatham, nicknamed "The Town of Tears" after the *Formidable* sinking had already suffered naval tragedy with the loss of HMS *Bulwark*. The men who died from the same street were Private Herbert Phillips (aged 31) of the Royal Marine Light Infantry, who had resided with his wife and three young children at 166, Castle Road and had completed nearly fourteen years in the service. Private Robert Walter Kemp (aged 28), also of the RMLI, lived at 232, Castle Road and had served eleven years and Able Seaman Albert Botley, just nineteen years of age, resided with his parents at 148, Castle Road. Albert had been transferred to the Navy from Greenwich School some three years previous and had served aboard the *Formidable* for around two years. His younger brother George, at the time of his death, was a bugler in the Royal Marines and his father was a First Class Petty Officer aboard HMS *Lancaster*.

On Monday January 4, around sixty of the survivors rescued by the *Provident* returned to their depot at Chatham. The train from Brixham departed at 10.15am but did not reach Chatham until 6.30pm. Six L.G. C. omnibuses, converted into ambulances, were in waiting to convey the men to the Royal Naval Barracks. Outside the station a large crowd had gathered, but only relatives of the men and a few privileged people were allowed access to the platform. When the survivors stepped from the train, many dressed in unfamiliar civilian caps and clothes, there were many fond embraces with wives and loved ones. Many hardened sailors openly wept. Others stood on the platform hoping the published survivors lists were wrong, but they were to be disappointed. The embraces however were swift and within five minutes the men were quickly ushered into the waiting ambulances and taken via Railway Street en route for the Naval Depot. On arrival the men were issued with new kit and granted a ten day leave.

On January 8, a memorial service was held in St. George's Chapel of the Royal Barracks in Chatham. Attending among the large congregation were the Mayors of Chatham and Gillingham and many other dignitaries, including Captain Loxley's widow, Gladys Maud, his son Peter, and his brothers. (Captain Loxley's son, Peter Noel Loxley, died during World War Two. He married Elizabeth Lavender

Dawnay on July 26, 1938. They resided at Mill House, Longparish, Andover. On February 1, 1945 he was killed in an air crash aged 39. He was in a British delegation as First Secretary to the Foreign Office representing His Majesty's Diplomatic Service on his way to the Yalta Conference held in the Crimea. The aircraft he was travelling aboard crashed into the sea en-route.)

THE AFTERMATH

An extract from a letter written by an eye witness aboard HMS *Prince of Wales* (Commander K. G. B. Dewar) to a fellow officer about events on January 1, summed up the feelings of many in the squadron that day. Commander Dewar's attack on Vice-Admiral Sir Lewis Bayly was particularly damning.

'During the whole of 31st December 1914 ships of the Fleet carried out manoeuvres in the vicinity of Portland. After sunset, we steamed to the eastward at 10 knots, five ships in single line ahead. There was a full moon and it was extraordinarily clear and bright until about 3am on 1st January. Visibility of a battleship probably about two or three miles. At 7pm the Fleet turned 16 points and returned back over the same ground still proceeding at 10 knots. At about 11.30pm Portland Bill was abeam 15 miles. Shortly after Formidable had been torpedoed at 2.15am (approximately) the Fleet turned 16 points and steamed back over the same ground passing within a mile of the same position occupied at 7pm. At 3am the Fleet moved and increased speed to the North East. No one minds taking risks when there is an adequate object in view, but our only object was Fleet exercises and gunnery. Surely we should have carried this out to the westward and out of sight of land. Portland is the Channel port where we have kept battleships throughout the war, and surely it is the place where hostile submarines might be expected to operate. The submarine probably followed us to the eastward and Formidable was the last ship in line. I do not think it would have been possible to take greater risks than were taken on that night. After Formidable was hit, the rest of the ships stayed on the

Captain Arthur Noel Loxley, the last commander of *Formidable*.
(CAPTAIN LOXLEY'S LITTLE DOG)

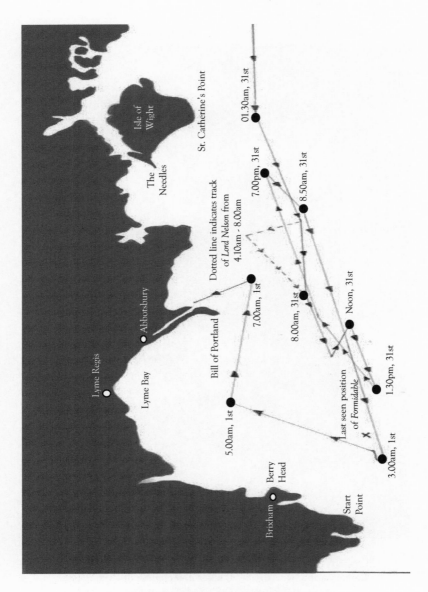

**Track chart of HMS *Lord Nelson*, after passing
St. Catherine's Point, December 31 - January 1.**

(Top) Captain Loxley's son Peter with Bruce and (left) Bruce's grave. He is buried in a small dog's cemetery in the Abbotsbury Sub-Tropical Gardens. His body was washed ashore below Abbotsbury Castle a few day after the sinking.
(CAPTAIN LOXLEY'S LITTLE DOG)

(Top) HMS *Diamond*, affectionately known as "The Old Dicky Di" pictured in Venice on February 1, 1919, just after the war's end.

HMS *Topaze*.

H.M.S. FORMIDABLE SUNK IN THE CHANNEL.

SUPPOSED WORK OF A GERMAN SUBMARINE.

CREW OF 790 OFFICERS AND MEN.

199 SAVED.

MANY LANDED AT LYME REGIS & BRIXHAM.

THRILLING NARRATIVES.

TERRIBLE EXPERIENCES OF SURVIVORS.

ALL NIGHT IN AN OPEN BOAT.

DEATHS FROM EXPOSURE.

INQUEST ON NINE BODIES AT LYME.

The Bridport News headlines on January 8, 1915, which offered it's readers a very full account of the sinking and (below) the beached pinnace on Lyme Regis beach.

(Top) Lassie with her awards and (below) impressive funeral scenes in Church Street, Lyme Regis on Wednesday January 6, 1915. (Top right) Able Seaman John Cowan with his saviour. (Bottom right) The funeral cortege outside the church.

**The grave in Lyme Regis Cemetery of six of the dead from
the pinnace beached at the Cobb Gate.**

Two of the heroes of the Lyme Regis landing. (Left) Leading Seaman Carroll and (right) Police Sergeant James Stockley. (Below) The plaque depicting the badge of HMS *Formidable*, which hangs in the Guild Hall, Lyme Regis.

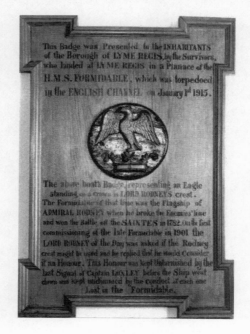

(Top) The Villiers Russell twins pose proudly, just prior to joining HMS *Formidable*. (Top right) Villiers Russell Close in Crewe, Cheshire and (bottom right) their grave in Coppenhall Cemetery, Crewe.

(Top) Proud Brixham fishermen (left to right) William Carter, William Pillar, John Clark and Daniel Taylor after their medal presentation. (Above) Leonard "Cher" Pillar and (left) the famous Brixham trawler BM291 *Provident*.

A plaque presented to Captain William Pillar by the London Devonian Association in recognition of his bravery and seamanship. (Below) Pillar Avenue in Brixham, named after William Pillar.

THE 'DAILY GRAPHIC, MONDAY, JANUARY 4, 1915.'

SEVENTY SAVED BY FIVE.

Survivors from H.M.S. Formidable grouped round the crew of the trawler Provident, which brought seventy of them into Brixham. Members of the crew: 1. John Clark. 2. Captain Pillar (the skipper). 3. W. Carter (mate). 4. Dan Taylor (cook). 5. L. Pillar (boy).

(Top) The crew of *Provident* and some of the rescued in *The Daily Graphic* Monday January 4, 1915. (Above) Survivors landed at Brixham pose with local children.

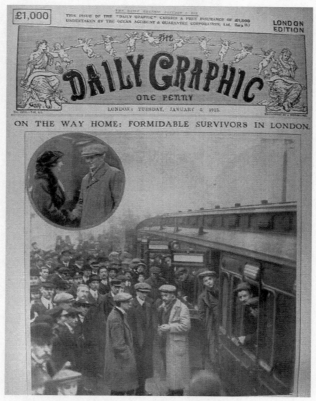

(Top) Captain William Pillar and his medals, which were sold at Sotheby's in December 1990. **(Above)** Brixham survivors on the way back to Chatham at Paddington Station. Pictured (inset) is J/8718 Norman Harford.

Bugler Stanley Reed (right) poses with his brother George.

same course until altering course 180 back to the Formidable's position. Still in a single line at slow speed (10 knots) was exceedingly difficult to understand. There is no doubt that the Formidable was sacrificed to the gross stupidity of a very ignorant man - and long before the incident occurred, both officers and men criticised the folly of taking such risks for no object whatsoever. One does not blame the Admiral (Sir L. Bayly) - he is God - the Navy made him - a thoroughly obstinate and stupid man. One blames only the system which makes it possible for such a man to command a Fleet. In peacetime, he has continually shown himself as ignorant of the personnel, as he is of the material. Every Fleet has been unhappy and thoroughly discontented. No one thought he would be employed again until Winston Churchill game him command of the 3rd Battle Squadron.'

In 1912, Commander Dewar, along with fellow colleagues, had formed a Naval Society which enabled officers to state their personal views without fear of reprisals. This society still continues to this day.

THE CONSPIRACY THEORY

So was it fate or just good luck on the part of the U-boat, that HMS *Formidable* was sunk on January 1, 1915, or were there spies operating from isolated areas on the south coast? This conspiracy theory continues to play a part in the sinking and there is some evidence that this could have been a pre-planned operation. Just after the start of the war, the Admiralty put several fishing trawlers in the English Channel manned by Royal Naval personnel disguised as fishermen. A few weeks before the *Formidable* was sunk, one of these trawler crews became suspicious about a house situated around Start Bay. Along this sheltered bay, ran a sandy shoal, protecting it from a swell from seaward, thus making it a perfect base for a submarine to operate and gain valuable information from shore. One night the crew of the trawler saw a series of coloured lights shining from the house under suspicion. Was this a signal to a U-boat in the area, or was it just an innocent occurrence? The trawler crew, rather than passing on their suspicions, kept watch on the house for several more days, in the hope of catching the submarine in the act, but nothing was reported until after the *Formidable* had been sunk. Within a few days of the sinking, the house was searched by members of the Military Police, but no evidence was found indicating that they had acted as spies or the occupants had housed spies in the days leading up to the sinking. On February 15, 1915, a debate in the House of Commons, instigated by Sir J. Lonsdale, asked if the Admiralty were aware that on the night of December 31, 1914, lights were observed at sea off Shoreham, and in a house on the sea-front at Hove, flashlights were seen. Although these claims were reported, no action by the police or the Coastguard resulted in any arrests or any investigating of yacht and boat ownership at Shoreham. These finding of course does not prove or disprove the conspiracy theory, or that *U-24* had gained an advantage, either through secret intelligence, or information passed on by a network of south coast spies. However, by studying the *U-24's* log record of events, it seems to indicate that their run in with the 5th Battle Squadron happened purely by chance and no hard evidence has come to light to substantiate the theory.

After the sinking another controversy surrounding events came to light after the survivors had time to reflect on events of January 1. Many who had been pulled from the water later complained that the Admiralty swimming collar that they had been issued with, was totally useless in the stormy waters, and were more of a hinderance than a life-saving piece of equipment. On February 8, 1915, the subject of the Admiralty swimming collar was raised in the House of Commons and was unfavourably compared to the German equivalent, which consisted of an efficient life-saving waistcoat. Certain critical statements had also appeared in the national press regarding the comparisons, but the swimming collar was defended in the Commons by the Parliamentary Secretary to the Admiralty, Dr. Macnamara, who stated that the collar could easily be carried by the user, did not encumber the wearer in the performance of his duty and was more than an effective aid to the swimmer. He also stated that the collar had saved many lives since its introduction in the Royal Navy. (The argument regarding the swimming collar again raised its ugly head following the sinking of HMS *Hampshire* on June 5, 1916. Many bodies washed ashore wearing the swimming collar were found to have broken their necks, probably caused when jumping from the sinking vessel.)

THE SURVIVORS

The following men listed below survived the sinking. Please note that names, ranks and service numbers, where known, are from the Admiralty survivors lists stored at the Public Record Office. Although fairly accurate, the list does contain errors and discrepancies. Two hundred survivors were officially listed.

Landed in pinnace at Lyme Regis (48)

Master At Arms ALBERT E. COOPER, Chief Electrical Artificer JOHN RIDLEY, Able Seaman BERTIE SIMMING, Petty Officer E.T. MARNPRIZE, Ordinary Seaman H. COX, Ordinary Seaman ROBERT I. MAY, Able Seaman A.E. SIMMONS, Telegraphist G.W. WILSON, Stoker H.H. STEVENS, Signalman E.H. MERTON, JOHN W. LAMBERT, DONALD McDONALD (RNR), Able Seaman JAMES AUCHTERLORNE, Armourer JOHN COWAN (RFR), Youth GEORGE MUNDAY, Boy CYRIL A. GREGG, Engine Room Artificer WILLIAM TAYLOR, Electrician ALFRED W. DAY, Boy J. BARRELL, Stoker REUBEN A. SMITH, W.E. NORWOOD, E.G. SIMS, Youth P.N. SEARLE, Leading Seaman THOMAS CARROLL, Leading Stoker W.D. PARR, ALBERT J. SNELL, Leading Seaman AARON MORRIS, Stoker JOSEPH FARRAR, Able Seaman G.A. WHITTINGTON, Able Seaman GEORGE DARVILL, Able Seaman CHARLES T. STOAKES, Stoker DAVID HOWARD, Boy A.E. GOOD, Boy THOMAS BEARDALL, Able Seaman A. ALDERTON, Stoker H. SNOWDEN,

Petty Officer Stoker ARTHUR PETTS, Stoker G.H. FOWLER, Leading Stoker G.H. TULLETT, Ship's Cook A.H. KNIGHT, Officer's Steward H.A.J. HART, Able Seaman W.F. RICHARDSON, Boy F. SHEE, Petty Officer HERBERT A. BING, Leading Stoker J. TAPLIN, Able Seaman GEORGE HAMMOND (RFR), Able Seaman ALFRED WALTER BOOTH and Stoker J.F. CONNOR.

Brought in by HMS *Topaze* (43)

221497 Yeoman of Sigs. FREDERICK HAROLD AMES, J/20414 Ordinary Seaman WILLIAM EDWARD AVERY, 239290 Able Seaman ERNEST BACKHOUSE, 181126 Leading Seaman JAMES FREDERICK BROWN, 238660 Leading Seaman VICTOR CHARLES BAVIN, J/2999 Able Seaman JAMES ARCHIBALD BURKE, J/11899 Able Seaman HENRY DANIEL BROWN, M/7483 Carpenter's Crew CHARLES BIRBECK DAVIS, V/1673 Stoker WILLIAM E. FRANCIS (RNR), J/14897 Able Seaman JACK FISHER, J/29902 Ordinary Seaman JOHN CHARLES FAULKNER, J/22110 Able Seaman JOHN HARLOW, 170221 Chief Stoker HENRY THOMAS HOPKINS, SS/4985 Ordinary Seaman GEORGE ANTHONY HALL, J/10644 Able Seaman JOHN NEWTON JONES, J/18663 Ordinary Seaman WILLIAM MAYNARD JEALOUS, 226693 Able Seaman CHARLES HENRY KERSLAKE, J/6089 Able Seaman SIDNEY EVANS LAW, S/1817 Stoker JAMES McNESTER (RNR), A/3090 Able Seaman JOHN McCLEOD (RNR), 179500 Able Seaman JOHN WILLIAM MARTIN (RFR), J/14326 Able Seaman FREDERICK WILLIAM MALLET, J/29899 Ordinary Seaman CHARLES SMILLIE MURIE, 193451 Able Seaman JOSEPH NODEN, M/3369 Sick Berth Attendant WILLIAM POWELL, 204950 Able Seaman ELVISE PERKS (RFR), J/24014 Ordinary Seaman SAMUEL RAINSBURY, 306784 Leading Stoker GEORGE RICHARDSON, 134780 Chief Petty Officer GEORGE RICHARD RICHARDSON, CH/14009 Private (RMLI) CHARLES EDWARD SHARP, 218172 Able Seaman HENRY GEORGE SAYER, 218835 Able Seaman FREDERICK SPEIGHT,

222326 Able Seaman HENRY ALBERT TURNER, 208119 Leading Seaman JAMES THORNTON, J/5657 Able Seaman EDWARD CHARLES THURGWOOD, J/5216 Able Seaman WESLEY HARRY WRIGHT, J/26434 Boy 1st Class JOHN ROBERT WHITE, 215138 Able Seaman HENRY WATSON, J/6217 Able Seaman SIDNEY CHARLES WHITNEY, 191158 Petty Officer 2nd Class PERCY HENRY WHALE (RFR), Private (RMLI) JOSEPH WOOLFORD (RFR), T/2675 Stoker WALTER WILSON (RNR) and 268280 Engine Room Artificer 1st Class JOHN WICKHAM.

Brought in by Brixham trawler *Provident* (71)

Gunner DANIEL HORRIGAN, Boatswain GEORGE TAYLOR, 214334 Able Seaman THOMAS GEORGE ARSCOTT, 306888 Stoker Petty Officer AMBROSE ASHBY, Ordinary Seaman WALTER DAVID ANDREWS, Youth ALFRED BELCHIN, J/12101 Boy HARRY BARRY, SS/4897 Boy ARTHUR JOHN BUKER, Boy EDWARD BARTHRUM, Able Seaman PERCY CECIL BARROW, 38463 Able Seaman MARK BELL, 217378 Leading Seaman ALBERT EDWARD BAKER, 183438 Able Seaman FRED CLIFT, 197560 A. CULLEN, 5070 A.C. CHURCH (RNR), 219040 A.E. CROUCH, J/22865 F.G. DAWE, J/16874 N.M. DUGGEN, H.L. DORTON, 136830 C.F. DAVIES, SS/114883 Stoker H.F. FIELD, 344937 G.W. FORD, 310838 Leading Stoker G.E. SELTON, 228840 PERCY GARWOOD, 193916 Petty Officer J. GARF, Stoker A.W. HUMPHREYS, 233211 E.F. HALWORTH, 183639 H.B. HAMBLING (RFR), SS/111881 A. HAWKER, 224858 Signalman R. HARRIS, CH/15224 Marine E.A. HUNT, 3214 Gunner WILLIAM HUGHES, J/8718 N. HARFORD, M/6331 E.J.R. HUGHES, K/10015 S. HART, Boy C.J. HULL, K/106 G.C. KING, CH/13122 Marine S. KNOCK, 235059 H. LICENCE, 155790 Leading Boatman H. LUMSEY, J/18437 WILLIAM JOHN LAVERTY, Youth A. LAWRENCE, 208886 FREDERICK MARTIN, D/2005 A. MARTIN, CH/17877 Marine R.P. MATCH, 16932 J.G. MITCHELL, J/11140 Able Seaman J. MATHER, Ordinary Seaman

F.T. MAWE, J/6228 WILLIAM F. OLDER, Engine Room Artificer R. PHILLIPS, 155068 G. PRESTON, J/16766 W.C. POUND, 213615 G. PAYNE, 350315 E.A. PERKS, 213587 R.L. PEEBLES, F. RACKSTRAW, 193859 W.G. ROBINSON, 186574 Petty Officer C.H. SINCLAIR, CH/16157 Marine F. J. STAFFORD, K/17828 Stoker S.W. STUD, 201669 R. SMITH, 181484 J. SITTERDALE, K/501 B.W. STILL, Boy G.T. STRANGE, SS/4922 J.D. SAUNDERS, 222409 Able Seaman F. STOW, 9140 C.R. SMITH (RFR), 9926 Stoker H. SMITHURST (RFR), 17001 Youth H. WANDBY, Youth E. WHEATLEY and M/1817 C. WRIGHT.

Brought in by HMS *Diamond* (37)

Engineer Commander C.J.M. WALLACE, Lieutenant H.D. SIMONDS, Lieutenant B.W. GREATHED, Lieutenant J.C.S. SOUTTER, Assistant Paymaster S.W. SAXTON, Assistant Paymaster F.H. WAKEFORD (RNR), Carpenter S.C. McCLOUNAN, Artificer Engineer JOHN STOBART, Midshipman T.C.T. WYNNE, Midshipman W.D. STEPHENS, Midshipman W.L. AGNEW, Midshipman N.F. HURD-WOOD, Midshipman E.J. GUINNESS, Midshipman D.E. PELLEY, 168159 Chief Petty Officer W.T. COOK, 238840 Leading Seaman E. FALCONER, 238474 Able Seaman A.E. HICKFORD, 221557 Able Seaman G. SAKER, J/26881 Ordinary Seaman T. WALKER, L/5021 Boy Domestic A.E. ASH, J/29923 Ordinary Seaman W.H. FLETCHER, 187497 Able Seaman F. MARTIN (RFR), J/27157 Boy 1st Class L.G. GRINT, 220910 Leading Signalman W.A. BOWN, J/3035 Signalman R.W. MILBURN, J/23234 Signal Boy W. WHITLEY, A/4176 Seaman THOMAS BRUCE STOLLERY (RNR), 153616 Chief Stoker (Pensioner) A.G. SIMMONDS, K/26667 Stoker G. GREEN, 232679 Stoker 1st Class E.J. GLOVER, K/16292 Stoker 1st Class A.E. PEARCE, Stoker W. HAWKINS (RNR), 116315 Officer's Steward 1st Class FREDERICK JACKSON, 365933 Officer's Steward 2nd Class H.E.G. MILLER, CH/12834 Corporal (RMLI) W. FOX, CH/17780 Private (RMLI) F.E. SIRKETT and CH/16973 Private (RMLI) H.W. BEAL.

Miscellaneous (1)

Ordinary Seaman R.C. ATKINS (received on board HMS *Implacable* from HMS *Diamond)*.

One Midshipman, officially listed on the Admiralty roll of the "missing presumed lost" was Ivor Gregor Macgregor. Fortunately the young sailor had been transferred from the *Formidable* on December 26, 1914, to HMS *Diamond*, just six days before the sinking and the Admiralty roll had not been updated. He was appointed Sub-Lieutenant on April 25, 1916 and served on the *Diamond* until January 18, 1917, and then on the "Q" ship HMS *Paxton* from February 1, 1917. This ship was sunk by a U-boat on May 20, 1917, but Ivor, although wounded, survived the ordeal and was awarded the DSC for his valour during the encounter. He remained in the Royal Navy Reserve and on April 25, 1934 was promoted to the rank of Commander RNR. Another survivor, Thomas Beardall, held the distinction of being the youngest survivor - at just fourteen years of age. After serving for a further nine years on HMS *Forward*, he joined the London Fire Service and was fire fighting during WW2. After the war, he worked for the Home Office as resident Fire Officer at 10 Downing Street, where he remained until retirement. Signalman E. H. Merton, who had landed at Lyme Regis, certainly had his share of good fortune, and would survive three sinkings in the first five months of the war. On the morning of August 6, 1914 he was aboard the light cruiser HMS *Amphion*, when it was mined, with the loss of 148 men, and would be the first British naval loss of the war. Transferred to HMS *Cressy* after he had recovered, this was sunk along with her sister ships by a lone German U-boat on September 22, 1914. His next ship he served on was the *Formidable*.

Unfortunately not all the survivors listed here survived the war. A few days after returning to their respective ports, the men of the old *Formidable* were assigned to new ships, either in the Royal or Merchant Navy. On August 18, 1915, Able Seaman William John Laverty, aged

20, was killed in an incident aboard HMS *Lilac*. He had been one of the 71 saved by the Brixham fishing smack *Provident*.

On May 31, 1916, the long awaited clash of the British Grand Fleet and the German High Seas Fleet finally took place in waters off Jutland in the North Sea. In this inconclusive battle, the Royal Navy would lose 6,000 men to the Germans 2,500. Among the British casualties was Able Seaman Frederick Martin, aged 31, who had been landed at Brixham by the *Provident* after the sinking of *Formidable*. He had been aboard HMS *Defence* when the cruiser was sunk in the battle with all 903 crew members lost.

On August 8, 1918, Petty Officer Thomas Bruce Stollery, aged 25 (rescued on January 1, 1915 by HMS *Diamond*), died while aboard SS *Celtic Prince*. Leading Stoker Walter Wilson, originally rescued by HMS *Topaze*, died just after wars end, on November 27, 1918, while at HMS *Pembroke II*.

There is little doubt that more of the survivors did not live to see the Armistice, but due to the lack of Christian names, service numbers and rank information in the official records, it has been very difficult to make positive identifications.

MEMOIRS OF A SURVIVOR

One survivor of the *Formidable* sinking, Able Seaman Alfred Walter Booth, who was landed in the pinnace at Lyme Regis, later wrote a story of his life in the Royal Navy from the turn of the century until he left the Navy. Here we include part of this story, up to and including the sinking.

'As the train puffed and chuffed its way through the tunnel beneath the Great Lines, some of the passengers in the tightly packed third class carriage began to ease themselves up and removed their bags from the netted rack above their heads. I sat in the corner seat facing the

engine wearing an overcoat and flat peaked cap. I nervously thrust my hand into my pocket and reassuringly clutched the envelope which reposed therein. My name is Alfred Booth and until recently had served as an apprentice butcher in Dover. The precious letter in my pocket contained instructions from the Admiralty for me to report to HMS Pembroke for training as a Seaman in His Majesty's Navy. The year was 1902. Autumn was well advanced and I had attained my 18th birthday just two months previously. When it emerged from the tunnel the train had slowed almost to a crawl. It approached the station and with a final flurry of steam, braked and came to a standstill on the 'up' platform. "Chatham! Chatham!" shouted one or two of the platform staff. "Hurry along there please." I waited a few moments to give the other passengers opportunity to alight. I stood up and with some difficulty removed my two suitcases from the luggage rack. With even more difficulty I clambered clumsily to the platform. For a few seconds I must have looked bewildered. Already, intending passengers for stations towards London were scrambling past me and forcing their way into the rapidly filling carriages. This was the first time I had travelled alone by train but I was determined not to show it and felt confident enough I could cope. With my ticket clutched tightly in my left hand I did my best to carry my suitcases and joined the crowd as they made their way towards the ticket barrier. They proceeded up the steps which were dimly lit by gas lamps and I eventually reached the barrier where I surrendered my ticket to the collector. I stood for a moment and looked about myself. Near the station entrance stood a porter little older than myself. I walked towards him and, deliberately adopting as nonchalant an attitude as I could, asked him "Tell me, my man, where can I catch a tram to take me to the dockyard?" The porter looked bemused. For a few seconds he stared blankly at me but finally replied. "I guess you'd better go to the one outside the station, son. They run every ten minutes or so." Guessing my purpose for asking he added humorously, "Be careful of the Chief Petty Officers. They eat young 'uns like you for breakfast." I grinned and followed the directions I had been given, and joined the few people already waiting at the stop. Sure enough after a few minutes the tram arrived and the passengers boarded the vehicle. The destination board displayed 'BROMPTON' and I confirmed with the conductor that I was on the correct tram. I placed my suitcases under the stairs and seated myself nearby where I could keep an eye on my luggage. The tram started with a jerk and moved slowly forward, gradually picking up a speed of about fifteen miles per hour. It turned into Railway Street in the direction of Military Road. The conductor collected my fare and clipped me a ticket from those held by a spring on his clip board. The vehicle moved across the High Street where the tram stopped to allow passengers to alight and others to board. Whilst the tram was still stationary I looked across to the recently constructed Town Hall buildings which had been opened two years earlier by the Earl of Rosebery. It was an impressive building reaching a height of just over 130 feet. The metal wheels clattered noisily over the points as the tram jerked to the left past the Gun Wharf and up the incline towards the Parish Church. The tram stopped once again, this time outside the Royal Marines Barracks where I gazed interestingly at the young recruits being drilled on the parade ground. I sat back and contemplated. For as long as I could remember I had set my heart on joining the Royal Navy. Now that day had dawned and for a fleeting moment I wondered whether I had made the right decision. I immediately dismissed such a thought from my head; I knew there could be no turning back.

I had been born near the sea at St. Margaret's Bay just outside Dover. As a youngster my favourite pastime had been to sit on the cliff near the South Foreland lighthouse and watch passing ships through an ancient telescope given to me by a retired sailor who claimed it once belonged to an officer who had served aboard HMS Victory at the Battle of Trafalgar. Nearby was the Cornhill Coastguard and Semaphore Station which was one of the many lookout stations dotted along the Kent and Sussex coastline but which had served it's purpose and would probably soon be demolished as progress demanded more sophisticated means of tracking shipping and the sometimes illegal activities such as smuggling liquor from France. I came too suddenly when the conductor called out "Next stop, Dockyard Main Gate" and stood up waiting for the tram to stop. I collected my suitcases and stepped on to the cobbled road. I was no longer feeling as confident as I tried to look. However, I pulled myself up to my full height of 5'6" and walked smartly up to the helmeted policeman at the gate and handed him my letter from the Admiralty. The entrance to the Dockyard was impressive. Two tower-like structures supported the centre piece which displayed the Royal Coat of Arms. The gate dated back to 1720 when it was completed to complement the new and higher boundary wall. The policeman, a member of the Metropolitan Police (Dockyard Division) looked carefully at the letter, apparently pondering over every word. He finally declared himself satisfied that it was genuine and not the ruse of a devious spy and directed me to no.2 Dock where reposed the three hulks comprising HMS Pembroke (formerly Duncan), Royal Adelaide and HMS Forte. I strolled on my way. I gazed in awe at the various ships I passed and took particular interest in the battleships Irresistible and Goliath berthed alongside within sight of my destination. I stood for a while as I took in the impressive looking hulk before striding purposefully up the covered gangway which led to the main deck where, in days of yore, had reposed the ships cannons housed ready for action. When I reached the head of the brow I paused for a moment and took in a deep breath. The invigorating aroma of tarred hemp pervaded the ship. Had I done the right thing? I pondered. Deep down I knew that I had. My cogitation was abruptly interrupted by the ship's corporal who demanded to see my credentials. I produced these from my pocket and waited apprehensively whilst these were again perused. The petty officer carefully eyed me up and down whilst behind his back a young sailor grinned broadly and made rude gestures towards the petty officer's back. He had failed to reckon, however, with the sixth sense developed by the Master-at-Arms' assistant during his long service with the Royal Navy. Whilst the petty officer continued to look towards me, he addressed the sailor behind him, "When you've finished skylarking, Hitchcock, take this new recruit to his messdeck and introduce him to his fellow nozzers." The now sober looking Ordinary Seaman indicated to me that he should follow him and led the way along passages and down ladders until I felt completely confused. I felt sure I would never again find my way through this maze unaided. We finally emerged into a large compartment where I saw several other lads of similar age sorting out their belongings and stowing them in wooden lockers. The sailor introduced me by saying "Ere's anuvver for the slaughter 'ouse" and left me to select a locker from those that were left. The other recruits paused from their labours and turned to gaze at me. "Welcome aboard Jack" said one of them, smiling, his arm outstretched. I acknowledged the greeting and grasped the proferred hand. The others followed suit and already I was beginning to feel that I belonged.

A short time later we were joined by an older sailor wearing an anchor and three stripes on his left arm who announced himself as Leading Seaman Bell. " I shall be your sea daddy for the next few weeks. Any problems – bring 'em to me. Don't ask anyone else because they either won't tell you – or if they do it will probably be wrong. Do I make myself understood." Almost immediately we replied that we did, whereby Leading Seaman Bell ordered us to follow him to collect our bedding. For the next hour or so he instructed us how to rig and sling our hammocks. First he laid flat on the deck the rectangular sheet of canvas which had small holes pierced at either end. The 'clews' consisted of a rope's end to which was attached several thinner pieces of twine which he referred to as 'nettles.' These were threaded through the holes at one end of the canvas and a similar operation repeated at the other end. "Now we're ready to test whether or not we've done the job properly. You there!" Bell indicated to one of the audience who answered to the name of Sims; a rather tubby, fresh faced lad who was looking rather bemused. "Take this end of the clews and pass it through that iron bolt secured in the bulkhead." Like most of the others I felt somewhat bewildered but could follow most of the instructions we were given. Bell continued, "Pass the end back through the ring to which the nettles are fastened and secure with a half hitch like this." With a few deft movements Bell secured the rope's end and gave it a tug to establish it was now safe to take a weight. "This is the only way to sling your 'ammick" he proclaimed. "Do it any other way and you'll meet with disaster. Any questions?" We looked blank. Most of us were confused but were too scared to admit it. Bell looked towards me. "'Ere you are son. Show me how to do it." I deftly threaded the nettles as I had been shown. I secured the clews to the ringbolt, but had overlooked the correct procedure for fastening. The hammock looked secure enough but Bell's eagle eye had spotted the mistake. "Jump in, lad, and test the hammock." I heaved myself up by grasping an overhead rail and lowered myself into the canvas. For a few moments it remained steady, but as my weight took charge the clews began to slip. Just in time Bell caught the hammock before it slipped towards the deck taking me with it. "Not so clever as we thought, are we?" snarled Bell. I looked shamefaced. The others laughed nervously, content in the knowledge that they had not been the victim. However, they were not to get away with it. "Come along. Now it's your turn." Bell looked at Sims but handed the hammock to another lad named Fowler. The remainder chuckled, but in a respectful way, mindful of the fact that they could well be next. For the next hour or so we all practised the art of slinging a hammock until we were sufficiently proficient to satisfy the Leading Hand. Beneath his granite looking exterior Bell was a kindly man who had spent nearly seventeen years in the Navy. He was a good man at his job but unlikely to progress any further up the promotion ladder. He enjoyed what he was doing but had no ambition to seek further responsibilities. By teatime the hammocks were all slung in Admiralty fashion and we enthusiastically repaired to our meal. We were ravenous. We soon got chatting to each other and exchanged information about ourselves. Eddie Sims came from Norfolk not far from the village of Burnham Thorpe where Admiral Lord Horatio Nelson was born in 1758. Eddie had worked as a farm labourer since leaving school but had become restless and thought he would try his luck with the Royal Navy. One of the others, Ted Fowler, had commenced an apprenticeship as a carpenter. At one time he had hoped to train as a Shipwright. His home was in London but having failed to obtain one of the preciously sought after places on a training course in Chatham Dockyard he too had decided to enter the Navy as a Seaman. No doubt his knowledge of woodwork would stand him in good stead at some stage of his career. Most of the lads had similar interesting accounts to relate as to why they had decided to join and were eagerly looking forward to completing their training and going to sea. By this time we were beginning to gel as a group. I realized how important this would become – not just during my training but for the remainder of my service.

I sat there entranced, reviewing the events of the day and endeavouring to arrange them in some semblance of order. This was an interesting era. Fresh life was beginning to take shape after the developments of the 19th century. The wooden walls were being phased out as more heavily armed ships were brought into service. Dreadnought was the first of these, known as an ironclad. It had been laid down in 1859 and was launched at the end of 1860. Now, even more powerful ships were being mooted which would be built entirely of steel and would be powered by steam. I felt it was an exciting time to join the Royal Navy.

"Wakey, wakey – rise and shine. You've had your time – now I'll have mine. Don't turn over – TURN OUT!" Dawn was barely breaking when the raised voice of a petty officer resounded throughout the messdeck. It was complemented by the occasional muttered epithet as he swiped blindly with his rope's end at the underside of the hammocks containing occupants who were slow to respond to his command. The petty officer answered rather aptly to the name of Barker! I blinked and rubbed my eyes. For a moment I could not recall where I was but as my eyes focused in the gloom I gradually became more orientated with my bearings. I looked at my watch and it was 5.30am. It must still be dark outside. I slid deftly out of my hammock and landed lightly on the deck. Around me in the dimness the other lads were doing likewise. The more athletic types made for the ablutions to avoid having to queue. On the deck above I could hear the sound of running feet and raised voices. This was soon followed by a swishing noise which seemed to move to and from above my head. I could just make out the shouted orders, "Scrub for'd, scrub aft" and "'vast

scrubbing." On this our first day the new recruits were excused falling in for 'both watches' but from tomorrow we would be required to take our allotted place among the others who were employed in cleaning ship. After breakfast we were issued with our kit which included 2 blue suits, 2 white canvas duck suits, a white sennet (or straw) hat to be worn with No.1 dress, 2 blue caps and 3 yellowish tinged flannel vests each with a square neck edged with blue tape. A black oilskin raincoat reached almost to my ankles. Two cap ribbons with the name HMS Pembroke depicted in gold wire completed the kit. We were also provided with a wooden ditty box in which to keep our more personal items such as letters from home. We were also given a "housewife" containing needles, thread and red silk cotton with instructions how to embroider our names in our kit to prevent items becoming lost or stolen.

During the next few weeks me and my chums were to learn a whole new language. From henceforth the floor would be known as the deck; the ceiling as the deckhead and the walls were called bulkheads. A gannet was not only a seabird – but described a person who enjoyed a surfeit of food. Numerous other expressions peculiar to the Navy would enable me to converse with others of like ilk whilst leaving the uninitiated land-lubbers completely in the dark. Training began the following day. We were gradually introduced to the art of seamanship. I seemed to have a natural bent towards anything which had a direct concern with the sea. I was particularly interested in boat handling and listened intently as instructions were given about how to pull a whaler and rig the sails. I recalled the time when I had watched sailing ships make their way majestically past Dover on their way to foreign climes. The instruction was given mainly by Chief Boatswain William Batt. He was dressed in a long dark blue frock coat and trousers and wore a pudding style cap with a badge surrounded by gold laurel leaves. His face was partially hidden by a thick, bushy beard and moustache. All in all Mr. Batt presented an awesome sight. He ruled the class with a rod of iron. Heaven help any lad he found skylarking or otherwise being inattentive when he should have been heeding what was being said. Mr. Batt's fearful appearance, however, concealed a heart of gold. When he found that I and some of the other recruits were exhibiting more than a usual interest in the subject he arranged to take us sailing at the weekends and would permit us to take the tiller and give orders as we tacked and turned about. On some occasions Mr. Batt and us lads would proceed along Gillingham Reach into the wider part of the River Medway, past Queenborough Spit towards the Thames Estuary as far as Sheerness. This to me was what I had always yearned for. I enjoyed every moment and longed for the day when I would be qualified to take away and cox'n a boat unsupervised.

For three weeks we were forbidden to go 'ashore' to enjoy the local amenities. We had first to complete our initial instruction as how to wear the naval uniform smartly and with pride. At last the long awaited day finally arrived. I could hardly contain myself. As soon as we had finished our dinner we began to change into our best suits. Complete with straw hats we looked every inch a sailor. We assisted each other to square our collars and straighten our lanyards whilst we stood eagerly awaiting the pipe for libertymen to fall in. The call duly arrived and I and several of the others made our way to the upper deck where we fell in for inspection. Standing stiffly to attention we waited nervously to see whether we passed muster. The ritual over we made our way down the gangway where we split into small groups each anxious to impose their presence upon the local civilian population. By this time me, Eddie and Ted had become inseparable chums and it seemed natural that we would team up to explore the delights of Chatham. We set off with a jaunty swagger. At first I felt somewhat self-conscious of my new status and felt that everyone I passed was staring at me. However, as the novelty began to wear thin so my confidence increased. As we passed through the main Dockyard gate I noticed it was the same policeman on duty who had passed me through the gate on my first day. This now seemed a lifetime ago. I glanced at the policeman searching for any sign of recognition but there was none. We continued on our way. Eager to reach the town as quickly as possible we increased our stride to a brisk pace, whilst at the same time endeavouring to maintain step with each other. Several other sailors were travelling in the same direction but at varying speeds depending on whether or not they had previously visited the area. It was easy to distinguish the recruits from the more seasoned seafarer. As our trio approached Military Road I glanced at my watch. The time was just after 1pm. To my right was the river Medway overlooked by the ancient castle and nearby cathedral. Barges of varying sizes and speeds looked resplendent with their large sails. Alongside the Gun Wharf lay barges busy loading and offloading ammunition destined for the local military and naval establishments. Ahead lay the main shopping area where there abounded public houses available to slake the thirst of local servicemen. By now we three mates had slowed almost to a crawl in order to take in the sights around us. Suddenly Ted spied the Old George Inn in Globe Lane. It was situated on the junction with Medway Street. The original six upstairs windows had been reduced to four; the two centre ones had been bricked up to reduce the effects of the window tax. There were two entrances each at either end of the building and Ted suggested we call in and have a drink. Outside a group of dockyard mateys were just departing in the direction from which we had approached. We smiled as we drew ourselves up to our full height in a gesture designed to impress the workmen. We were, however, completely ignored by the dockyard men who had probably seen more recruits still wet behind the ears than I had hot breakfasts. Inside the public house I felt in my pocket for the few pence necessary to purchase a round of drinks and approached the bar. I felt the perfect sailor as I did so and confidently ordered three pints to take back to my friends. I looked around. In one corner of the room was a pianola and the walls were decorated with ornate mirrors. We sat around a large rectangular table enjoying our drinks. The pub was not overcrowded but there were some other customers, all men, sitting at the tables. Next to me was a well built, jovial man who introduced himself as a member of the crew of one of the lighters. We stayed awhile exchanging pleasantries and about an hour later decided to depart. We continued on our way into Chatham High Street. On the left was the Theatre Royal which was advertising the Japanese musical play

'The Geisha.' It was the tale of a Tea House and did not strike us as being our 'cup of tea!' However, further along the road on the opposite side was Barnard's Palace of Varieties. It was still decorated with flags and bunting celebrating the coronation of King Edward VII which had taken place but a few weeks earlier. We looked at the list of performing artistes exhibited outside the entrance. It was a variety programme which included continental acrobats and tumblers known as the Haydes Troupe, an Australian comedian known as Billy Summers, three Flora Dora girls and other supporting acts. We looked at the prices which varied from 2d to one shilling and decided to compromise by purchasing 4d admission tickets for the matinee due to commence at 2.30pm. In the auditorium I gazed around. We had been directed towards the rear of the upper circle. Other seats were rapidly being filled by other sailors, soldiers and a few civilians. Some were accompanied by their wives, or more probably, by their girl friends. Above us were the 'Gods' where, resting against a shoulder high metal bar were those who had chosen to view in the cheapest possible way. A roll of drums from the pit just below the stage indicated that the show was about to begin. The babble of voices reduced to a murmur as the lights dimmed; the footlights were turned up and a board announcing the first act was placed at the front of the stage. We laughed and clapped with the audience throughout the various acts. It was the first time I had attended a variety show and I enjoyed every minute of it. All too soon the final act brought the entertainment to a close. The audience stood while the theatre pianist played 'God save the King.' It still seemed strange not to sing 'God save the Queen,' but they would soon get used to it. This act of respect completed we quietly shuffled from our seats out of the auditorium. It was cold and dark as we made our way slowly through the foyer and out into the main street. It was raining steadily but before we stepped out into the night, each in turn assisted the others by holding the corners of the blue sailor's collar as we donned our overcoats and squared our caps. The street was crowded with people emerging from the theatre and wending their way home. We decided to proceed to the Navy House Club where we could get

warm and enjoy a cheap meal before partaking of something stronger at a public house before returning to the barracks. We ambled along gazing into the windows of shops which were gradually being closed for the weekend. The lamplighter had completed his job and the ghostly, yellowish tinged lights flickered and cast weird moving shadows on the rainsoaked pavements and adjoining walls. We strolled with our heads down and gloved hands holding our coat collars in a vain attempt to protect our ears from the elements. We turned into Clover Street and walked the short distance to the Navy House. Inside, the club was crowded with other sailors and marines who, like ourselves had decided to seek shelter from the rain. A coal fire was blazing in the corner of the room. Soaked to the skin we squeezed our way as best we could towards the comforting flames. All in all it had been a very enjoyable excursion and, well satisfied with our achievements we made our way back to the ship– and so to our hammocks.

Training continued for the next few weeks but on a certain day in December an air of merriment could be detected as we fell in for inspection. It even extended to Petty Officer Barker who could be seen joking and exchanging light hearted banter with the men. The occasion was the Christmas Leave party who were waiting to proceed after the usual formalities had been completed. This over, we filed over the brow in an orderly fashion to the jetty where we again fell in ready to be marched off. Petty Officer Barker temporarily resumed his position of authority. "From the right, number," he ordered. A staccato response from right to left! "Form fours," he roared. Although normally a simple manoeuvre, some of the even numbers, ladened with baggage, were finding it difficult to take a pace to the rear with the left foot before taking an almost simultaneous pace to the right, bringing the left foot back in line with right. However, on this occasion there were no rebukes: only laughter, and nobody was taken to task as would have been the norm on other occasions. The various evolutions finally completed, the detachment was moved to the right and marched to the Dockyard Gate. At that point we were dispersed to board the several trams which had been contracted to transport us to the railway station. At the station the parties disembarked and made their way to the platforms where they displayed their travel warrants to the ticket collector as they passed on their way. Most of the sailors, including Ted and Eddie, were travelling in the direction of London and they shouted their farewells to those mates who were proceeding in the opposite direction. Meanwhile I made my way towards the down line to await the train to the east coastal towns. On the platform I spied an empty seat and sat down. I dumped my kitbag and case on the ground beside me and settled down to await the arrival of my train. Across the track the London bound sailors were rapidly filling the train which was already at the platform. I glanced up to see Eddie and Ted waving frantically from a crowded compartment in which they had been lucky enough to secure window seats. "Trust those two to do alright for themselves," I mused light-heartedly as I acknowledged their wave. Whistles could be heard, followed by the instruction to "Mind the doors." To the sound of cheers the train pulled slowly out of the station with the pair still waving in my direction. I again returned their wave and continued to do until, because of the oblique angle, it became impossible to distinguish one compartment from another. The station was now comparatively quiet. Two other sailors approached the seat and sat alongside me. I knew both of them by sight and we nodded acknowledgement to each other. For a few moments we sat bemusedly watching the antics of two sparrows who, totally oblivious of the presence of humans, were battling over a crust of bread. We laughed and began to converse. One was a young man who, because of his stature – his height being over six feet – was known as 'Tiny' Kimmins. Like me, he too hailed from Dover. The other was Zach Larder who came from nearby Deal. Both had joined the navy four weeks earlier than me and were due to complete their training early in the new year. All of a sudden a feeling of excitement rose among us as we heard an approaching train. In anticipation we stood up and moved our belongings nearer the edge of the platform. The sound of the engine grew louder until it appeared round the curve, preceded by a belch of smoke. Disappointment reflected clearly in our faces as a small shunter engine drove past and through the station without stopping. A few minutes later, however, our patience was rewarded when a much larger passenger train drew to a halt in front of us. The train was not very full and we were able to secure an empty compartment where we settled down to enjoy the journey. As the train picked up speed we started discussing how we were going to spend our leave. The general consensus was that we were all going to get drunk and would enjoy ourselves as much as we could before returning to Chatham in two weeks time.'

Chapter 2 – 'THE BIG 'OUSE'

Dawn broke to reveal a dull, overcast sky. The morning of Thursday 30th April 1903 started much the same as any other day but with an important difference. This was the day destined to oversee a change of accommodation arrangements which had been designed to improve the standard of life for hundreds of sailors currently based in the Chatham area and for those of future generations. We were roused from our slumbers as usual at an early hour by the raucous bellow of Petty Officer Barker's now familiar voice. I yawned and stretched. Me and Eddie Sims slid nimbly from our hammocks almost simultaneously. We were closely followed by the other recruits fearful lest they fall foul of the rough edge of Barker's tongue; or even worse, experience a taste of his rope's end. Ablutions completed and hammocks lashed and stowed, amid a babble of excited chatter, we settled down at the mess table for a hurried breakfast. "It seems strange" I commented "that the next time we do this we shall be on dry land." Ten minutes later the petty officer returned and instructed us to collect our kit and carry it over the brow ready for it to be conveyed to our new quarters. There was a great deal of milling about whilst we sorted ourselves out and finally fell in four deep ready to march off. Petty Officer Barker strode up and down until he appeared satisfied that all was as correct as it ever would be. He reported to the officer in charge and gave the order to turn right. This was not easy with all the kit we had to carry, but was finally carried out to his satisfaction. At a much slower pace than usual the column moved off in the direction of the new barracks. Me and my friends – or 'oppos' as they now preferred to be known – had previously visited the barracks and therefore had an idea of where we were going. There was a lot of banter which, despite Barker's protestations, continued until we entered by the main barrack's gate. "March at attention," roared the petty officer's stentorian voice. Silence gradually befell and the procession proceeded to the parade ground. Here we were turned into line and stood easy whilst another petty officer referred to a clip board and detailed us to our new quarters. The southern side of the parade ground was bordered by a red brick wall which rose to a height of thirty feet, forming a battlement like structure which divided the accommodation blocks and the terrace road which fronted them, from the drill area below. There were six blocks of which the one nearest the main entrance housed the Wardroom Mess; the next in line was occupied by Chief and Petty Officers. In the remaining four lived the sailors who were allocated according to which branch of the Service they belonged. Me and my two friends were directed to Duncan Block, together with many others of my seaman peer group. The petty officer dismissed the ratings with instructions to make our way to the Block by way of the centre steps leading from the parade ground to the road above. We struggled as best we could, laden as we were with kit. For most it entailed leaving some of it at the foot of the steps to await their return. The barrack rooms in each block occupied two floors. Each room contained twelve mess tables, each of which was designed to accommodate fourteen men. Along one side of each room were racks which provided for the stowage of kitbags and hammocks. We looked about taking stock of the situation. Suspended from the ceiling were iron girders spaced at regular intervals to enable hammocks to be slung at night. Quickly, I gathered about myself about a dozen of the sailors with whom I had made friends aboard the hulk and between us we established a territorial claim to one of the mess tables. As best we could we stowed our kitbags and hammocks before making our way back to the parade ground ready to return to the ship.

At no time did we give a thought to the security of our kit: woe betide any man caught thieving from his shipmates. It was now approaching 4pm. The time destined for us to depart the hulks. We were fallen in ready to again march the short distance to the barracks. Since 1877 one of the accommodation ships had always been known as HMS Pembroke and it had been felt appropriate that this name should be preserved by transferring it to the new base. As eight bells was sounded the detachments were ordered to march off, led by the Depot brass band. I took one long lasting look at the hulk with a mixture of hate and affection. In keeping with many of the others, it was difficult for me to assimilate that me and my shipmates were leaving her for the last time. The column left the dockyard by the Alexandra Gate – named as a tribute of the launching of HMS Alexandra by Princess Alexandra in 1875 – and proceeded along Dockyard Road. It was an imposing sight which was witnessed by a large number of people who had assembled not only along the route, but also in the barracks grounds. The procession entered the barracks by the main entrance and once again marched on to the now familiar parade ground. Rumours were rife amongst the sailors that either one of the Lords of the Admiralty or even a member of the Royal Family would be present to receive us prior to the formal opening. Together, I and my comrades looked in vain: there was no-one of importance there to greet us. Instead, as the procession arrived at its destination, the assembly received a short welcoming address by the Captain before we were dismissed with instructions to proceed to the rooms to which we had been allocated earlier in the day. "What a disappointment," I thought. Perhaps it was an indication of what those in high places thought of the navy in its peacetime role. After a satisfying tea, myself, Eddie and Ted decided to explore more fully our new 'home' and familiarise ourselves with the surroundings. We made our way through the main entrance of the block which led on to the Terrace Road. We crossed to the other side of the road where, from the ornamental balustrade we could see the parade ground below. The drill shed was situated on the far side of the parade ground and above its roof we could make out the masts of the ships in the dockyard rising above the trees which divided the barracks from the 'yard.' To our left, in the distance, was the main Pembroke Gate. We decided to walk in the opposite direction, past the front of the other accommodation blocks, and followed the road as it inclined gently downwards to the left. Past the eastern end of the drill shed where the road turned sharply left along the front of the building, and again in the direction of the Pembroke Gate. Several of the other sailors had been of like mind and were availing themselves of their new found freedom from the confined messdecks they had suffered in the past. We also passed a few officers whom we proudly saluted. As we turned left again, up the incline which led back towards the Blocks, we crossed to the other side of the road where we stepped on the adjacent path. Simultaneously there was an explosion as a stentorian voice bellowed, "Git orf that path, you free. Don't you know it's for orficers only?" We froze, hardly daring to turn round. At last we plucked up enough courage to do so only to find ourselves staring straight into the face of Petty Officer Barker, resplendent in his knee high, khaki blancoed gaiters. "Blimey!" I thought "Have we moved into the 'Big House' or the 'Mad House?'"

Chapter 3 – TO THE LIMITS AND BEYOND

"Shoulders back. Keep the arms straight – don't bend 'em at the elbows. Dig those 'eels in. 'Old yore 'ead up, Booth!" Four years had elapsed since me and my chums had completed our training. We had left Pembroke to join various ships. I had served three years on a cruiser on the China Station but had now returned to the barracks to train as a member of the depot's field gun crew. The squad was being marched to the Lower Gun Battery under the watchful eye of a Gunner's Mate. Together with 35 other ratings I had been selected to participate in the Field Gun competition at the Royal Naval and Military Tournament at Olympia. The squad was halted at the Battery; dismissed and ordered to re-form alongside the gun and limber. The gun was similar to the 12 pounders which had been landed from HMS Powerful and HMS Terrible

and used at Ladysmith in 1899 during the Boer War. Volunteers for the gun's crew had been sought throughout the Fleets from all ranks and branches. Those chosen had to undergo strenuous tests before final selection. Many aspirants had failed to meet the required standard and had been returned from whence they had come. The tournament had evolved from contests between various factions of the Army and had been brought together in June 1880 at the Agricultural Hall, Islington in London. The Navy had provided performances since 1896. At appearances during earlier years the 12 pounder guns had been brought into the arena where, after a short march, one round had been fired. Both wheels of the gun carriage had been changed after which the gun had been hauled round in front of the audience at the double and advanced in close order, reversed twice and then wheeled into the centre of the arena for the salute in the Royal Box. Since 1903 obstacles had been introduced which included two four foot walls and two bridges. The previous year the Tournament had been transferred to Olympia and this year, 1907, for the first time, teams of eighteen men from the Portsmouth, Devonport and Chatham Divisions were to compete against each other. The squad was divided into two teams. I was selected for 'A' team. The team was numbered and instructed to take up position alongside the drag ropes. We were marched back to the main road, followed by 'B' team who were fallen in behind. The order to march off was given and the procession made off proudly at a brisk pace towards the track behind the Gunnery School at the east end of the barracks. "Left, right, left, right. Watch your dressing!" The Gunner's Mate had positioned himself alongside the wheel of the gun carriage and was calling the pace. I looked sideways through the corner of my eye and was aware of the admiring glances from passers-by. Awaiting the two crews were the Gunnery Battery Officer, Lieutenant Wood, and the Parade Gunner, Mr. Frostick. Standing nearby was a Chief Petty Officer wearing under his jacket a white singlet bearing the insignia of a Physical Training Instructor. The Gunner's Mate halted the teams, saluted the Gunnery Officer and reported them correct. The Gunnery Officer stepped forward and stood the men at ease.

"Congratulations on being selected for training for this, the first inter-port Field Gun competition. However, this is just the beginning. During training some of you may fall by the wayside. Injuries or lack of physical ability are but two of the reasons for which you could be removed from training. From both of the crews the object is to produce one 'super' crew which will be capable of taking on and beating the other two Port Divisions. No doubt they are being given a similar pep talk and I am sure they will put up a good show. It will not be easy but I feel sure we can achieve success. It is going to require maximum effort and devotion to duty from everyone concerned. For myself, I shall give you 100 per cent encouragement and support to ensure that your every need is met. You will have your own quarters; will mess separately from the remainder of the barrack's personnel, and arrangements have been made to ensure you receive balanced, wholesome meals adequate to sustain the energy you will need. Each day you will rise at 5.30am, ready to undertake a five mile run before breakfast. That is just for starters before the day's training really begins. If anyone wishes to drop out, now is the time to do so." Nobody moved. *"Thank you gentlemen. Your number one trainer will be CPO PTI Perry and his assistant will be Petty Officer Gunner's Mate Dalton whom you have already met. I will now turn you over to their capable hands. Thank you very much and I wish you the best of luck in you training."* The chief PTI stepped forward, saluted the Gunnery Officer and turned to face the gun's crews. *"Fall out 'B' team,"* he snapped. *"'A' team take up the drag ropes. Ten times round the track – double march."* The training had begun. The next day both crews were roused from their slumbers at 5 o'clock. Enthusiastically we leapt from our bunks and within half an hour were washed, shaved and fallen in on a cold and dark February morning on the road outside the hut. In rigs akin to those of pirates we were dressed in sports shirts of various colours, blue bell-bottomed trousers, boots and gaiters. Sweat rags adorned most of our foreheads. The PTI was in charge and after a nominal head count turned us left and moved us off at the double. Morale was high and even a slight drizzle didn't dampen our spirits. Through the

main gate and left along Khyber Road (known locally as the Khyber Pass), past the Royal Engineers Barracks which was still in darkness where all except those on duty were probably still sleeping. The few people who were about watched in silence as the group went by. When we returned some three quarters of an hour later the depot was just beginning to come to life. Lights in the barracks' rooms were gradually being switched on as the sailors turned out and went about their ablutions. A brisk wash and change of clothing and it was time for breakfast. We tournament competitors were messed separately from the barracks' complement and were fed on bacon, two eggs, sausages and fried bread. "We must have been mad to have volunteered." Commented the man seated next to me. "but I'm glad I did." This seemed to sum up the attitude of the teams and high spirits prevailed. After a quick tidy up of the hut the teams were paraded before the gun carriage and limber standing on the dirt track. Various parts of the equipment were pointed out. The crews learned how to remove the lynch pins and wheels simultaneously. Changing wheels became a formality. One by one, as our names were called, the Gunner's Mate allocated us to various positions on the limber and drag rope. We took up our respective places, patiently awaiting the next instruction. I was positioned on the inside of the drag rope on the right hand side immediately in front of the limber. My immediate neighbour on the outside of the drag rope was a cheerful Stoker from London named White who later introduced himself to me as 'Chalky.' "Some people call me 'Knocker' but I prefer to be known as 'Chalky'" To his left, also on the inside of the drag rope was a young gunnery rating answering to the name of Ernest Chipchase. With everyone in position the Gunner's Mate called for attention. "At the order 'Take up the drag rope' you will bend the knees and grab the leather bound handgrip. At the order 'Rise' you will straighten up, resuming the position of attention. Is that clearly understood?" Everyone nodded assent so the Gunner's Mate continued. "Remember" warned the petty officer, "there are no brakes. You cannot afford to make a mistake. The men on the limber handle are primarily responsible for stopping the 'beast'. To assist them, the two men on the drag ropes in front of the handle will turn IMMEDIATELY to grab the handle and assist them to stop on each occasion that the order is given to halt. Any hesitation on their part will be met with a hefty great thump on the back of the neck. There is no allowance for a slow response. Do I make myself clear?" I shuddered. I realised only too well. I was one of those to whom the Gunner's Mate was referring. "Take up drag ropes. Rise. Quick, March. Double March. Halt." This evolution was repeated many times until halting the gun carriage within a distance which became shorter on each consecutive occasion became second nature. I and my companion, Ernest soon mastered the art of protecting our necks. The training was intensive and by the end of each day the crews were exhausted. Nevertheless, I and my companions enjoyed the challenge. Some injuries were inevitable but were generally of a minor nature and could be patched up by the local sick bay. Physical fitness formed a major part of the curriculum and an hour in the morning and a similar period during the afternoon was devoted to this subject. Two courses were erected. These were similar to those which would be experienced at Olympia. The two crews competed against each other at least twice every day. Regular inquests were held when each run was analysed to perfection and suggestions made as to how the performance could be improved. Friendly inter-branch rivalries were temporarily set aside as Seamen, Stokers and Torpedo men were gradually moulded into one unit. Misdemeanours, however minor, were dealt with severely. For dropping a lynch pin whilst attempting to secure a wheel to the field gun's axle, I was ordered to complete one circuit of the perimeter carrying a heavy sandbag on my back. My clumsiness had cost several seconds in time. However, all this was taken in good part. New friendships were formed. Friendly rivalry developed between the two teams. Each day we became fitter; the runs smoother and faster. The day of the tournament drew nearer. Rumours began to circulate about the prowess of the Portsmouth and Devonport crews. At last the great day dawned. The tournament was due to last from 16th May until 1st June 1907. The guns and limbers had been transported by lorries from their barracks a few days earlier whilst the sailors had travelled by train. For the first time the crews were able to observe their contemporaries from the other Port Divisions at first hand. Arrangements had been made for each Division to compete with the others on a twice daily basis. The rota had been so designed that by the end of the tournament each Division would have battled against the other two Divisions on an equal number of occasions. The atmosphere was electric. There were numerous troops from various Regiments, each milling around like ants, but who seemed to know what they were doing and where they were going. I was fascinated. It was my first experience of anything so spectacular. Everything was so alive. In the arena the ever popular Musical Drive by a Battery of the Royal Horse Artillery was drawing to a close. For the past quarter of an hour the six guns had circled and crossed the arena at a gallop. I could hear the crowd clapping as three guns from each end charged towards each other, missing each other by inches. The applause raised to a crescendo as the salute was taken and the teams left the arena. The display had been an unqualified success since it was first introduced by 'D' Battery in 1896. A short interlude then took place. The resident orchestra played martial music whilst a working party of blue-jackets prepared the stage for the next event which was the Field Gun competition. An announcement was made that Captain Van der Byl of the 16th Lancers had been adjudged the winner of the 'Sword versus Sword Mounted' contest. A hush fell over the audience as the announcer explained the background of the Royal Naval display and what it was designed to achieve. The military band struck up and to the resounding beat of 'Hearts of Oak' the two teams, one from Chatham; the other from Devonport, marched proudly into the arena. The layout was exactly as it had been during practice runs. The obstacle of planks fixed eighteen inches from the ground; the four foot wall which had to be crossed and the final run to the other end of the arena where a round was to be fired. I was on the drag rope immediately in front of the limber handle. As the gun was lifted I and my opposite number swiftly turned to assist the two men behind to stop the limber just as we had been taught. We all remained still whilst the Training Officer struck a thunder flash and dropped it by his side. The resulting explosion triggered off an instant response from both teams. The crowd went wild with excitement. Many were chanting "Oggy, oggy, oggy" to the Devonport team, but it seemed to me that the majority were shouting support to 'Chatty Chats'. Both teams roared up the planks, reached the wall almost abreast and began to dismantle the guns. Over the wall and reassembly took place. Chatham was just in the lead. The teams kneeled in their respective positions. The tampion was removed and the firer pulled sharply on the lanyard. The pin struck the percussion cap and Chatham had won that round by a couple of seconds. A short pause whilst another thunder flash was discharged and the teams raced back to the original start. After a short consultation between referees whilst penalties were assessed it was adjudged that Chatham had been a close winner to our worthy opponents.

Chapter 4 – SURVIVOR

Proudly displaying my newly acquired hook, or anchor on my left arm, and supported by my two more aged and tarnished good conduct stripes, I stepped aboard the trot boat which was to take me to my new ship, the battleship Formidable. From the shore on the quay at Sheerness I had already identified some of the ships lying off shore. They were the Agamemnon, Prince of Wales, and London together with six other capital ships. Two similar two funnelled craft were obviously Formidable and her sister ship Implacable – but which was which I wasn't sure. Both had been completed in 1901, shortly before Irresistible had completed the trio. I couldn't help glancing at my badge of rank and felt that my long wait to be advanced had been well worth it. Only a few weeks earlier, at the end of June, the heir to the Austro-Hungarian throne, the Archduke Franz Ferdinand, and his wife the Duchess of Hohenburg had been assassinated by a 19 year old Serbian student, Gavrilo Princip, during their visit to Sarajevo, capital of Bosnia. I didn't understand all the politics involved but because of various long standing treaties, war now seemed inevitable. All being well, I hoped I would not have to wait too long for the next step up the ladder to petty officer. The boat pushed off and after calling at the Queen, Venerable and London it finally arrived at the quarterdeck of Formidable where it disembarked two officers and thence made it's way to the for'd ladder where I and two Able Seamen climbed out and clambered up. The Petty Officer of the day was there to meet us and directed us to the ship's Police Office where we completed the necessary joining forms before being allocated to our respective messes. My mess was No.12 mess situated two decks down on the port side. There I found an empty locker into which I placed some of my belongings, leaving the rest in my kitbag. The time was fast approaching 11am. Suddenly the Bos'ns Mate could be heard, preceding with a shrill note on his 'call', the announcement "Up spirits. Senior hands of messes muster for rum." Like magic, members of No.12 and nearby messes appeared and introduced themselves to me. In addition to my normal duties, I discovered I was to be 'killick' of the mess. As such I was the senior mess member and responsible for the orderly running of the mess and to ensure a peaceable existence. A three badged Able Seaman known affectionately as 'Stripey' arrived with a 'fanny' containing rum mixed with two parts water – known as grog. This was after Admiral Vernon who invariably wore a cloak made of Grogram and was nicknamed 'Old Grog'. It was he who had arranged for such a mixture to be issued to all ratings below the rank of petty officer. As each man received his tot, having proffered 'sippers' to Stripey as his reward for collecting and issuing the rum, tongues became loosened. Naturally, members of the mess were interested to hear something about me. One or two faces were familiar, such as Ted Fowler, Eddie Sims and Bert Lambton, with whom I had served before. Others who introduced themselves were Percy Smithers, Chris Shaw and Derek Whiteside. Smithers was a one time pianist at a picture palace in London who, like so many others, had been mobilised because of the likelihood of war. Already Smithers had proved himself a popular shipmate who could be relied upon to liven up runs ashore by persuading local landlords to permit him to play their pianos to encourage community singing amongst the lads. The landlords were usually only too pleased because the better the entertainment the more money the sailors were likely to spend at their hostelry.

The collier berthed alongside just before first light and was secured by members of the morning watch. She was a dirty vessel, well grimed from the thousands of tons of coal transported over the years. Meanwhile the rest of the ship was beginning to come to life. Between decks the shrill sound of the bos'ns calls could be heard preceding the customary invitation to "Wakey, wakey, rise and shine!" Men began wiping the sleep from their eyes as they stirred and slid gently from their hammocks. Coaling ship was not the most popular of pastimes and it involved all members of the ship's company, including officers, and sparing only those privileged to be excused by reason of essential duties. All those participating dressed in their oldest and worn clothes. By the end of the day they would be ingrained with coal dust which would resist even the most vigorous efforts to remove it. This applied equally to the nooks and crannies throughout the ship, and as much of the deck and paintwork as was possible had been covered by protective canvas sheets to minimise the damage. Nevertheless, it would undoubtedly take several days – or even weeks – before the ravages of the coal dust was finally eradicated. On this occasion the ship's company enjoyed an early breakfast before mustering for both watches. I fell in on the foc'scle with the other Leading Rates, facing the hands as they were accounted for and detailed for their respective duties. My party, which included Fowler, Sims, Smithers, Whiteside and two other men whom I had not yet met were instructed to scramble down into the colliers hold where we were responsible for filling bags with coal. I looked around. Fowler and Sims were busy assisting each other to fill bags as quickly as they could. Smithers, Whiteside and the other two were doing likewise. I stumbled and slithered over the coal to assist them to hook the bags to a rope ready to be hoisted inboard. These were snatched eagerly by artisan ratings on the upper deck who unhooked the bags and placed them in barrows which were wheeled away by members of the Royal Marines detachment. Out of sight of me and my companions, the contents were tipped down hatches into the bunkers where the coal was finally stowed by stokers in the bowels of the ship. The whole evolution was performed under the watchful eyes of observant young officers of Lieutenant's rank and woe betide anyone caught, or thought to be, skulking. The ship was a hive of activity. As the bags were emptied and passed back up the hatches they were seized enthusiastically by Ordinary and Boy seamen who hurriedly returned them to the holds in the collier ready for re-filling. This went on until Stand-easy when we were permitted to relax for ten minutes before returning to our arduous duties. And so it went on – hour after hour – until late evening by which time 600 tons of coal had been transferred to the ship's engine room. My party and I were weary. We were covered from head to toe with coal dust. I sent Fowler and Smithers to fetch some buckets from the mess with the idea of washing as much of the grime from our bodies as was possible. This was more easily said than done. Many of the others had similar ideas and it was 2100 hours before we were proclaimed clean enough to return to the mess-deck where we tucked into some well earned grub. Now, under the overall command of Rear Admiral Sir Lewis Bayly, the Fifth Battle Squadron was ready to proceed to Portland to participate in gunnery exercises in what were considered to be safe waters.

The sound of sixteen bells ringing in my ears roused me from my slumbers. At first I feared it was the call to 'Action stations' but then I realised it was the Quartermaster's light hearted gesture of farewell to the Old year and a welcome to the New. For a while I lay collecting my thoughts. I was not due to start my watch until 4am. But I was fully dressed. My thoughts wandered over what had happened over the past year. Within a few weeks into the war the three armoured cruisers Hogue, Aboukir and Cressy had been sunk within hours of each other by the same German submarine. Later other British ships had been successfully attacked by U-boats. For some while, ships of the 5th Battle Squadron, of which Formidable was part, had been carrying out firing exercises in the Channel. On Thursday 30th December 1914 they had been ordered to proceed to Portland. Under the command of Vice Admiral Sir Lewis Bayly, Commander-in-Chief of the Channel fleet, in his flagship Lord Nelson, the squadron set sail as instructed. I felt weary. The crews had been exercising all day and I had only turned in two hours ago. Now it was New Years Day. Rumour had it that we would arrive at Portland on Saturday. With any luck we would be in time for the non-duty watch to be granted shore leave. I would welcome a run ashore. In my mind's eye I planned a trip to Weymouth where I could revisit old haunts where me and my mates could enjoy a drink before returning on board. I was dozing fitfully and reminiscing when at about 2.30am. there was a terrific explosion. The night was cloudy but visibility was clear up to two miles. The sea was choppy and the wind was getting up. The squadron had arrived between Portland and Start Point nearly 24 hours earlier but on the orders of the Commander-in-Chief had remained exercising in the area. The explosion came without warning. None of the British Squadron had been aware of the presence of a submarine and at first there was confusion as to whether or not it had been a mine. Formidable heeled over by at least 20 degrees. The throb of the engines stopped but was replaced by a roaring bellow of escaping steam as they rapidly lost pressure. A sudden hush prevailed as the bugler sounded the 'still' followed a few minutes later by 'carry on.' The sound of feet could be heard as men hurried to their stations. Suddenly there was a second explosion, bringing the ship to an even keel but down by the bow. It was becoming obvious that the stricken ship was doomed. Fortuitously I was fully clothed. I moved hurriedly towards the upper deck, battled fiercely to maintain my balance as the ship continued to list to port. I eventually arrived at my boat station where I waited patiently for further instructions. The first boat to be lowered was smashed against the ship's side and the occupants pitched into the ever roughening sea. Whilst the remainder waited their turn, any item which would float was hurriedly thrown into the sea. I suddenly realised I could hear the sound of a piano and men singing. Some of the younger crew members and indeed some of the not so young were feeling apprehensive. Nevertheless discipline prevailed and they joined lustily in the singing. I wondered what has inspired a fellow crew member to think of others whilst the ship around him was sinking fast. The Captain had given the order to abandon ship. I looked around and decided to conform. I peered over the side. Waves were crashing against the stricken ship. It took a lot of effort to pluck up enough courage and jump. Too late, I realised I had neglected to bring my lifejacket with me. There was no time to think about that now. I kicked off my sea boots and murmured a few words of prayer, took a deep breath, closed my eyes and leapt into the angry waters below. The icy water encompassed my body as I hit the surface and continued to sink beneath the waves. Everything was going black. My lungs felt as if they were going to burst. My senses became dull and blurred. Lights flashed before my eyes. Then all went black.

I regained consciousness to find myself being hauled unceremoniously into a sailing pinnace. "He's still alive," I heard someone shout. "Only just." replied another. I attempted to mutter my gratitude but no words emerged. I was too cold and frightened. I glanced around. The boat was crowded. It was being tossed in mountainous seas. The waves were reaching over thirty feet in height. One moment we were lost at the bottom of a trough, the next on the crest of an enormous wave. I estimated there were over sixty men in the boat which had been designed to carry far fewer. I spied a shipmate slumped near the side and managed a feeble wave. He acknowledged by a flicker of the eyes. There were six men on either side each pulling as best they could but already they appeared exhausted. By now we were about a mile from the stricken ship. Someone shouted "She's going!" Those who could, looked in the direction of Formidable as she slid slowly but gracefully beneath the surface. Tears were apparent amongst many of those who witnessed her demise. I felt sick. I just wanted to die. Suddenly one of the oarsmen stopped rowing. He flopped over his oar and fell heavily to the bottom of the boat. His body lay awash with water which had poured in. One of the crew leant forward and shook his head. The man was dead. As gently and as reverently as they could, other survivors lifted the body and floated it over the side. Those who had the strength removed their sea boots and endeavoured to bale. It was a soul destroying evolution. As quickly as they removed the water it was replaced by twice as much. One man took off his jacket and with the assistance of a mate, placed it beneath the bilge water and gave it a sudden jerk, heaving the water over the gunwhale. This seemed to be effective and after a few repetitions the water had noticeably reduced. Two more men expired and their bodies were committed to the angry sea. The oarsmen were replaced by less exhausted men. Someone shouted above the noise of the storm "While there's life there's hope. Pull boys, pull. One, two three – pull!" I recognised him as Leading Seaman Bing. Master-at-Arms Cooper – the senior rating aboard – was remarkable and did what he could to maintain morale. He and the coxswain started to sing a ditty and gradually others joined in. The boat continued to be buffeted by the waves. The heavy rain became a mixture of hail and sleet. We were soaked. Suddenly someone in the boat shouted excitedly, "There's a ship." I turned my head slowly. About a mile away I could sea the lights of what appeared to be a liner. As the boat crashed down, the lights vanished, but re-appeared shortly after the boat shot up towards the sky. Those who were able started to shout. They failed however, to rise above the crescendo of the storm. Gradually we realised they could not be heard, neither had we been seen. The ship continued on its way distancing itself further from the boat, oblivious to our plight. Despondently we sank back in the boat. More bodies were disposed of. Somebody had brought a blanket with him which, with the aid of a mop pole, was hoisted as a temporary sail. Daylight came. The storm continued unabated. Men continued to die. The coxswain and Master-at-Arms Cooper carried on singing. Croaked voices accompanied them. The oarsmen battled on. By this time I had recovered a little and volunteered to do a stint on the oars. The man I relieved looked exhausted. We pressed on making little headway.

Two more men died, others looked near to death. Night fell with no sign of land. I handed over my oar to another volunteer and sank back to 'enjoy' a fitful sleep.

Then suddenly I was awoken by a disturbance in the boat and before I could come to my senses, realised that we were in a raging surf, with several men trying to pull the boat ashore. Thank God, I thought, we had by some sort of miracle reached the coast. When my eyes become accustomed to the light, I noticed through the gloom, lights and the shoreline. Gradually, the efforts of the men trying to get us ashore paid off. One of the boat's occupants managed to throw a painter over the side which a police constable grabbed. Slowly they guided the boat towards the beach. The powerful waves did the rest, heaving it high on to the shingle. The wind and rain continued to pound it, but our brave rescuers hung on. The more able crew members, including myself, passed our injured and fatigued comrades over the side, but some were too weak to stand unaided and collapsed on to the beach. More policemen arrived on the scene as well as several locals, who had been alerted and arrived ready to do what they could. Messengers were sent to inform the local medics and in no time at all, two doctors were available to treat the hapless men. Some of those stretched out suffering from exposure, had been brought round by assiduous rubbing and the use of stimulants. Several others however were beyond any human aid. Being one of the more fortunate, I helped as best I could and carried several of my shipmates to one of the nearby hostelries, which turned out to be the Pilot Boat Inn. The landlord and his wife immediately proffered their hospitality to the unfortunate men. Wet clothing was removed and replaced with temporary clothing, often too big or too small, and warm blankets. The wood fire in the largest room was soon blazing merrily and hot drinks and food were served to us by many willing hands. Slowly but surely, the men started to feel a bit more comfortable although many were still suffering from the shock of the ordeal. My shipmate and myself sat together offering each other mutual comfort and support. Suddenly I tapped his arm and pointed towards the far corner of the room. Stretched out, apparently dead, was a sailor whom he knew, and we both look horrified to see the landlord's dog making his way towards the prone body, then start to lick the salt off the face of the sailor. My shipmate was just about to pull the dog away, when an excited voice shouted over for help, as he was positive that he had seen the sailor's face twitch. He looked again and sure enough, his initial thoughts that the sailor was indeed very much alive were proved right, when his eyes flickered open. Quickly one of the doctors was summoned and in no time at all the sailor was sitting up, back in the land of the living. We later learned that we had landed on the Dorset coast at Lyme Regis. Arrangements for the funeral of those who had succumbed, were made for the Monday following the sinking, but during the weekend, Master At Arms Cooper, who had assumed temporary command of the survivors, received a message from the Admiralty postponing burial until the following Wednesday, to enable those relatives who wished to make private arrangements to do so. Almost at the same time, we were relayed instructions from another Admiralty department, that all survivors who were fit to travel, should return to HMS Pembroke on the Monday. On hearing this we all felt downcast as we had hoped to attend the funerals of our late shipmates. However we had no need to worry, as Master At Arms Cooper made the decision that all men were unfit to travel and instead arranged with the Admiralty that we should leave Lyme Regis on the day following the funerals. On the day of the funerals, flags were flown at half mast from the parish church, town hall and many other public and private places. Throughout the morning an endless procession of wreaths and other floral tributes were delivered to the temporary mortuary at the Drill Hall. Here for the last time sorrowing relatives bade their farewells to their loved ones. By midday vast numbers of people had arrived in town, many of them had travelled from outlying districts, either by train, car or on foot. A muffled peal was rung on the bells of St, Michael's, signalling the start of the funeral procession and at 1.30pm, the coffins containing the bodies of six of our shipmates were carried from the Drill Hall. Petty Officer Feldon, who I knew quite well, was placed on a gun carriage drawn by twenty or so bluejackets. The other five coffins were carried by the local townsfolk. The funeral procession moved off, slowly passing the Pilot Boat Inn, before turning left up the hill towards the church. My thoughts returned back for a moment to the incident with the dog who had helped revive the 'dead' sailor. My shipmate was convinced that we would have been burying seven bodies today but for the intervention of the landlord's clever little dog. We followed behind the cortege, every one of us carrying a beautiful floral tribute. The streets were packed with people who bowed their heads as the cortege passed by. At the entrance to the church, a troop of boy scouts formed a bodyguard. We entered the church which was full to capacity. I felt close to tears when the choir and congregation sang "Let Saints on Earth in Concert Sing," although I am sure I was not alone in my grief. After a sermon by the bishop, and with the short service concluded, we left the church to the strains of Chopin's funeral march and proceeded up the steep incline to the local cemetery. In a quiet secluded corner, the coffins were placed side-by-side ready for burial in a communal grave. I felt somewhat comforted that they were being buried together. Benediction was pronounced and "Jesus Lives" was sung. The Last Post was sounded and the firing party fired a last salute. The echo from the rifles seemed to last forever. Myself and the rest of the survivors filed slowly past the grave and laid our wreaths. Slowly, those gathered around the grave slowly dispersed, leaving only the grieving relatives to make their peace and pay their farewells. Outside the cemetery gates, we resumed our places and marched sadly back to the town centre in readiness of our departure back to the barracks at Chatham. On the way back down the steep hill, some of the survivors swore revenge for the sinking. I was among them, vowing to pay back the enemy who had killed so many of my shipmates.'

After the *Formidable* sinking, Alfred joined HMS *Calliope* (with the majority of the crew made up of survivors from HMS *Formidable*, *Cressy*, *Hogue* and *Aboukir*) on May 4, 1915, and in this ship would be present at the Battle of Jutland. Among the many other British sailors in action that day was Alfred's father, who was aboard HMS *Sparrowhawk*. Alfred died on May 5, 1965, ironically just nine days before his son, Ray, who served during World War Two, gained his commission in the Royal Navy.

THE ADMIRALTY'S VERDICT

Someone had to be made accountable for the loss of HMS *Formidable* and 547 men - many of whom had not even fulfilled their teenage years. The Admiralty pointed the finger firmly in the direction of Vice-Admiral Bayly. They wrote a letter to him, dated January 11, 1915, pointing out several errors in the way the squadron had gone about its exercises. The first main point criticised him for keeping the squadron at sea for a period of 24 hours in an area, in their opinion, "infested" with enemy submarines. Their other main points of concern were with the slow speed of the squadron, its close formation on a straight course, and the positioning of the light cruisers astern. These errors, they concluded, afforded an easy target for a submarine attack. Summing up, the Admiralty stated that Vice-Admiral Bayly had not acted with the proper caution and was *'marked by a want of prudence and good seamanship in the avoidance of unnecessary risks inexplicable in an officer holding high and responsible command.'*

Vice-Admiral Bayly defended his actions in a reply two days later. On the first point, he stated that not a single submarine had been reported in the Channel since he had hoisted his flag in this command, so refuted the claim that the Channel was "infested" with submarines and thought the area was reasonably safe following the Sixth Battle Squadron's firing exercises, which had just been completed at Portland. On the other main criticisms, he noted that the squadron carried out exercises at an average speed of around 12.5 knots and the 16 point alteration of course executed after dark was carried out at a speed of 19 knots. As for his decision to steam in close order, he commented, that if the squadron had been steaming at four or five cables (800-1,000 yards) apart, then there would have been more time for an enemy submarine to get in a position and take aim, and he felt that if he had not carried out this formation, possibly two vessels could have been lost. As for steering a straight course, he stated that he had never done or experienced zig-zagging at night and was in fact only steering a straight course between 19.00 and 03.00. The accusation of positioning the cruisers astern, led him to conclude that if they had not been in this position, then the loss of life on the *Formidable* could have been far greater, as nobody would have been aware that the battleship was in distress, due to the failure of its wireless.

On February 4, 1915, the Admiralty received a letter from Vice-Admiral Bayly making an application for trial by Court Martial. This however was rejected and he was directed to haul down his flag. Vice-Admiral The Hon. Sir Alexander Bethell was appointed in his place. Vice-Admiral Bayly took over the Presidency of the Royal Naval College at Greenwich, but six months later, when the submarine menace became acute, was recalled to active command and appointed to the Coast of Ireland Station at Queenstown.

ADMIRAL SIR LEWIS BAYLY

Fairly or unfairly treated by the Admiralty over the *Formidable* incident, Sir Lewis Bayly was held in the highest esteem by many, in the British and American Navies for his service at Queenstown. Born on September 28, 1857, he was the son of Captain Neville Bayly of the R.H.A and a great nephew of Admiral Sir Richard Keats. He entered the Navy on July 15, 1870 and in June 1872 passed out of the training ship *Britannia* and with 42 other cadets (he was one of four navigating cadets) was ordered to join the frigate HMS *Ariadne* at Portsmouth. At the time, along with her sister ship, she was the largest frigate afloat and capable of 12 knots. In his first year the *Ariadne* cruised around Madeira, the Azores, Halifax Nova Scotia, Lisbon, Cadiz and Gibraltar. In August 1873 he was appointed as navigating midshipman on the 1,400 ton corvette HMS *Encounter*, which was commissioned for the West coast of Africa. Here he would take part in action against Congo natives after several British crew members of a trading schooner were killed.

After three years on the *Encounter*, he left the ship at Barbados to return home to pass the examination for navigating sub-lieutenant. After a brief spell aboard HMS *Euryalus* in the East Indies, he was appointed in 1879 to the Irish built man-of-war HMS *Lynx*, as an acting navigating lieutenant and then the Indian troopship HMS *Serapis*, steaming regularly between Portsmouth and Bombay. In the same year HMS *Iris* became his new home, notable for the fact that the ship could steam at 19 knots and cross the Atlantic and back at 8 knots without re-coaling. After a brief spell aboard the training brig *Nautilus*, he was finally promoted to lieutenant in August 1881. A year later, he underwent a short course of gunnery and torpedo instruction, which interested him so much, that he decided to leave the navigating side of the Royal Navy and concentrate all his efforts on becoming a torpedo lieutenant. To qualify for this, he had to remain at sea for a year as a watch-keeper. After qualifying he was appointed to HMS *Warrior* in the Reserve Fleet. The *Warrior* held the distinction of being the first sea-going iron clad warship ever constructed, having been launched in 1861. A posting to HMS *Agincourt* followed at Alexandria, where he saw action during the Eygptian War. In September 1883 he was sent to Greenwich College for a nine-month course and a further course at HMS *Vernon* saw him carry off the first prize of £80. From there he proceeded to the Torpedo School at Devonport on HMS *Defiance* and it came as no surprise to anyone when he gained his promotion to torpedo lieutenant in April 1886 and posted to HMS *Colussus*, which boasted electric light and was the first warship to boast breech-loading guns.

In May 1890 he was appointed to HMS *Vernon* and also commanding torpedo boats in exercises in home waters. His next appointment was as second-in-command on the cruiser HMS *Endymion*, which had the task of carrying ships companies to Australia and bringing back the relieved crews. In 1892 he married Yves Henrietta Voysey Stella and in the role as commander saw himself appointed to the new cruiser HMS *Talbot*, which had been commissioned in 1896 for North America and the West Indies and took part in the Spanish-American War. August 1899 saw him briefly as Acting-Captain of HMS *Indefatigable* in the West Indies, before returning to the *Talbot* as commander. On January 1, 1900 he was promoted to captain of HMS *Scotia* and from 1900-1902 he served as Naval Attaché in Washington, USA, where his knowledge of American history, politics and institutions, stood him in good stead when working with American officers who would later serve under him at Queenstown. He then returned to his old ship HMS *Talbot* and in January 1904, due to the high possibility of war between Japan and Russia, the *Talbot* was sent to Korea to relieve the *Cressy* and became embroiled in the opening shots of the war during exchanges between Japanese and Russian gunboats.

After returning to England in July 1904, Bayly was granted his wish by the Admiralty and given command of the battleship HMS *Queen*, a unit of the Mediterranean Fleet, stationed at Malta. In 1907 with the paying off of HMS *Queen*, he took command of the North Sea destroyers and given the rank of second-class commodore. After a two-year stint, he was appointed President of the War College and promoted to the rank of Rear-Admiral. During his time here, he prepared war plans for the operation of the fleet against different enemies for the First Sea Lord Sir John Fisher. In February 1911, he was given command of the Battle Cruiser Squadron, hoisting his flag on HMS *Indomitable*. In July 1912 he raised his flag on the newly-completed HMS *Lion*, but on March 1, 1913, Admiral David Beatty took over the ship, when Bayly was requested by the Admiralty to work out details of a proposed war with Germany. On July 1, 1913, he took command of the Third Battle Squadron, hoisting his flag on HMS *King Edward VII*, as a Rear-Admiral until December 12, 1913, and then as an Acting Vice-Admiral from December 13 until June 21, 1914. From June he hoisted his flag on HMS *Malborough* and took command of the First Battle Squadron from Admiral Colville, with Admiral Bradford taking command of the Third Battle Squadron.

After taking part in the great Spithead Review of July 1914 and just after the declaration of war in August 1914, he was promoted to the rank of Vice-Admiral on September 14, 1914. In December following the German raids on the Yorkshire coast, he received orders to leave the Grand Fleet and hoist his flag in HMS *Lord Nelson*, commanding the Channel Fleet, exchanging commands with Sir Cecil Burney. The Channel Fleet had been strengthened to prevent further raids on the east coast and also to pose a possible threat by taking offensive action against the German submarine bases on the Belgian coast and also assisting Allied land operations by attacking the German flank. However his new role was short-lived when the *Formidable* was sunk and he was ordered to haul down his flag, but remain on full pay. After this unfortunate incident he was appointed President of the Greenwich College, but with the German submarine threat intensifying around the waters of the British Isles, he was summoned by the Admiralty in July 1915 and given command of the Western Approaches, while based at Queenstown, Ireland. This area stretched from the Sound of Mull to Ushant, and therefore covered the coast of Ireland, Irish Sea, St. George's Channel, Bristol Channel and the entrance to the English Channel. At his disposal he was given the light cruiser HMS *Adventure* as well as a fleet of sloops and around thirty "Q" or "Mystery" ships. These ships sailed disguised as unarmed merchantmen but carried concealed naval armaments. As they were generally too small to merit attack with torpedo, they seemed easy prey for the guns of a surfaced U-boat. This is where the "Q" ships took advantage by revealing their guns and several submarines were sunk employing these tactics.

At the beginning of 1916, Bayly was made up to Commander-in-Chief and was part responsible for quelling the Easter Irish Rebellion by preventing German arms landing to aid the rebellion. Further ships were sent to Queenstown to aid the battle with the U-boat and this total improved when the United States entered the war in 1917 and a number of US destroyers (arriving on May 4, 1917) were put under Bayly's direct orders. Throughout the remainder of the war he would command 92 US ships and teach his American counterparts the art of submarine warfare. On November 3, 1917, he finally received notification from the Admiralty of his promotion to Admiral. At the war's end, Bayly left Queenstown and retired after nearly fifty years service, when hauling down his flag on April 1, 1919. Among the honours bestowed upon him were the C.V.O. in 1907, K.C.B. in 1914 and was created K.C.M.G. in 1918. The King of Denmark conferred on him personally the Grand Cross of the Dannebrog, he held the United States Distinguished Service Order, was a commander of the Legion of Honour and also held the Order of the Crown of Italy.

On March 20, 1919, some five months after the war's end, the Admiralty received a letter from Admiral Bayly stating his hopes that the case involving the loss of HMS *Formidable* could be re-opened with a view *'to justice being publicly done; and in order that the official history of the war should contain a true history of the facts.'* His letter also contained letters and telegrams to substantiate the case. The reply, dated April 25, 1919, rejected the application due to the lapse of time and the questioning of the decision of a former Board of the Admiralty.

Despite his fall-out with the Admiralty over the *Formidable* affair, he received a letter of thanks from the Admiralty on April 5, 1919 thanking him for his efforts at Queenstown.

'Sir, On the termination of your appointment as Commander-in-Chief, Coast of Ireland, I am commanded by My Lords Commissioners of the Admiralty to convey to you their appreciation of the manner in which you have carried out the important duties of that command and their satisfaction with the very high standard of efficiency maintained by H.M. Ships and Naval Establishments under your orders.'

'My Lords are aware of the difficulties with which you had to contend, and they thank you for your many valuable suggestions which you put forward in connection with the anti-submarine campaign, trade routes, and protection of convoys, and other war measures, and desire to record their recognition of your able administration of the vessels placed under your orders, including many of the United States Naval Forces. The judgement shown by you was evidenced by the smooth and efficient working of the joint Services.'

'In the protection of sea communications in the vital waters of the area within your command by offensive and defensive measures, and by the safeguarding so far as possible through these waters of vessels carrying reinforcements and warlike and essential commodities, your services have been of great value towards the successful prosecution of the War.'

In America however, Admiral Bayly was so admired by the US officers who had served under him, they formed a Queenstown Association, so when Admiral Bayly and his niece visited the United States in December 1920, they were treated better than royalty. In May 1934 he returned to the States and was again welcomed with open arms. During the visit, he dined at the White House with President Roosevelt and on returning to England was received by King George V, who was keen to hear of his words with the President. He died on May 16, 1938, aged 80.

THE FIFTH BATTLE SQUADRON'S WAR RECORD

As for the remaining units of the Fifth Battle Squadron, all the battleships would serve during the Dardanelles campaign as the strength of the Channel Fleet was dramatically reduced. Between them, they would take part in the bombing of the forts in the Narrows and in the Anzac, Cape Helles and Suvla landings. All units survived the war's conclusion apart from HMS *Irresistible*. The *Lord Nelson* went to the Dardanelles in February 1915 and became flagship of Vice Admiral

Wester Wemyss until December 22, 1915 and then Sir John de Robeck until June 1916. She then became flagship in the East Mediterranean and the Aegean. After the Armistice, she passed through the Dardanelles and into the Black Sea, where she remained as flagship until April 1919. HMS *Agamemnon* went to the Dardanelles with her sister ship and took part in all the bombardments and was also struck by gunfire at least fifty times. She then earned distinction on May 5, 1916 when shooting down a Zeppelin (LZ 85) over Salonika (using a 6 pdr.). With her sister ship, she remained at Mudros or Salonika in case of a breakout by the German battlecruiser *Goeben*. The Turkish Armistice was signed aboard her and she returned to Chatham in February 1919, where she was converted to a radio-controlled target ship. HMS *Venerable* bombarded the Belgian coast in March 1915, before being ordered to the Dardanelles in May 1915 to relieve HMS *Queen Elizabeth*. She took part in the Suvla landings (August 14-21), but was then transferred to the Adriatic, to help the Italian Navy in their fight with Austria. She returned to home waters early 1918 and was reduced to harbour service. HMS *Prince of Wales* went to the Dardanelles in March 1915 and took part in the Anzac landings on April 25. She also was ordered to the Adriatic on May 12, 1915, remaining there until 1918 and was also reduced to harbour service on her return. HMS *Queen* was ordered to the Dardanelles in March 1915, covering the Anzac landings and was then ordered to the Adriatic. She remained at Taranto as a base ship until 1918, but before her return, her main armament were removed and transferred to the Italian Navy. As for HMS *London,* she was transferred to the Dardanelles early 1915 to replace losses, then transferred to the Adriatic in May 1915, before returning home in 1917 for conversion to a minelayer. She then became a unit of the 1st Minelaying Squadron in January 1918. HMS *Implacable*, the only surviving Formidable class battleship, was ordered to the Dardanelles in March 1915, and covered the landings at Helles ('X' beach) on April 25. She too was also transferred to the Adriatic in May 1915 and remained there until November. After this, she supported the blockade of the Greece and Bulgarian coast, and supported the Suez Canal Patrol.

After a refit at Plymouth in April 1916, she remained in the Mediterranean, during the abdication of King Constantine, but in July 1917, returned home and was paid off at Portsmouth, to provide crews for anti-submarine vessels. In March 1918, was selected as a depot ship in the Northern Patrol, and at the war's end was placed on the disposal list.

THE LOSS OF HMS IRRESISTIBLE

HMS *Irresistible*, along with HMS *Majestic*, sailed to the Dardanelles on February 1, 1915. She served there as a unit of the 2nd Division, along with HMS *Vengeance, Albion, Cornwallis* and *Triumph*, and took part in the opening bombardment of the entrance forts on February 18-19. On March 18, while in action attempting to silence the defences of the Narrows, HMS *Irresistible* struck a floating mine at 4.15pm while in Erenkui Bay, which flooded the engine room so quickly, that only three of the occupants escaped alive. The explosion caused an almost immediate seven degree starboard list, and she was also down by the stern. Seeing her in distress only intensified the fire from the forts as HMS *Ocean* stood by to tow her clear of the bombardment. *Irresistible's* condition worsened, and her commander, Captain Dent, decided to abandon ship. This was carried out with shells crashing down on the deck, as 28 officers and 582 men were transferred over to the destroyer HMS *Wear*, with 10 men left aboard to try and get out a wire to the *Ocean*. However the list became so pronounced, that the remaining men were removed and taken aboard HMS *Ocean*, who herself began to withdraw under a barrage of shells. At 5.50pm, *Irresistible* was left to drift, with the intention of attempting to save her with destroyers and minesweepers after dark. Then at 6.05pm, further tragedy struck, when HMS *Ocean* struck a mine. Realising the situation was hopeless, Captain Hayes-Sadler, abandoned ship, with the crew quickly taken aboard the destroyers *Colne, Jed* and *Chelmer*. Despite a desperate search which lasted until midnight, neither ship was found. According to Turkish reports, HMS *Irresistible* had drifted after being caught in cross-currents and carried within range of the Narrows forts, where she was pounded until she sank at 7.30pm. As for the *Ocean*, she too drifted, this time into Morto Bay, and sank around 10.30pm.

In 1920, HMS *Prince of Wales, London, Venerable, Queen* and *Lord Nelson* were sold for breaking up. A year later, HMS *Implacable* suffered the same fate along with the light cruisers HMS *Topaze* and *Diamond*. HMS *Agamemnon,* the final surviving unit of the old Fifth Battle Squadron, was finally sold for breaking up in 1927.

RUDOLPH SCHNEIDER AND U-24

As for *U-24*, she continued to be a menace following the sinking of HMS *Formidable* and on August 15, 1915 left Borkum for a patrol in the Irish Sea, via the north of Scotland. At 5.00am on August 16, off the Cumberland coast, she opened fire on the small works at Lowca, situated between the towns of Whitehaven and Workington. The works had been targeted because of the production of coke, naphtha and benzol. A total of 55 shells were fired on the works during a twenty-five minute period, causing some damage but no casualties. Continuing down the Irish Sea, *U-24* was set-upon by a patrol trawler off Tuskar. By August 19, she had reached a position south of the Old Head of Kinsale where *U-27* and *U-38* were also operating. When in St. George's Channel, *U-24* attacked the liner *City of Exeter*, but Schneider was compelled to break off the attack and dive, when the liner opened fire on her. Later that day, some 48 miles from the Old Head of Kinsale, *U-24* spotted the stricken SS *Dunsley* and was in the throes of finishing her off with gunfire when Schneider spotted a much bigger prey – the 15,801 ton White Star liner *Arabic*. Learning from his previous encounter with the *City of Exeter*, *U-24* decided to attack submerged, and at close quarters fired a torpedo into her side. The *Arabic* en-route for New York, took just 10 minutes to sink. Of the 429 passengers and crew, 44 were lost, but the fact that three of the victims were American, rekindled anger in the United States, just four months after the sinking of the *Lusitania*, which had claimed 124 American lives.

On the same day as the *Arabic* sinking, the sailing vessel *St. Olaf* and the SS *New York City* were sunk in the same area by gunfire from a U-boat and on August 23, the steamers *Trafalgar* and *Silvia* were also sunk. It is highly likely that either *U-24* or *U-38* were responsible for these sinkings.

As the *Arabic* sinking put Germany on a collision course with America, and fearing their entry into the war, the unrestricted U-boat campaign in British waters was temporarily halted, to safeguard continuation of American neutrality. On August 30, 1915, the Kaiser ordered his U-boat commanders not to sink passenger steamers without prior warning or without seeing that the passengers were safe. America was informed of the order and on September 24, 1915, the U-boat campaign in British waters ceased and was not resumed again until March 1916. In May 1916, *U-24* operated alongside the High Seas Fleet during the Battle of Jutland, although was not engaged in any action. She would continue on war patrols until 1917, but was withdrawn from active service and used as a training school boat. *U-24* was surrendered on November 22, 1918 and would be eventually broken up at Swansea in 1922.

Its first commander and conqueror of the *Formidable* however would not survive the war's conclusion. Rudolph Schneider, born in Zittau an der Saale on February 13, 1882, joined the Kaiser's Navy on April 10, 1901. Between 1901-1902 he served his Sea Cadet Training on the *Stein* before moving on to the Naval School at Kiel. On April 22, 1902 he became a Midshipman where he served on the training ships *Mars* and *Blucher*. In Autumn 1904, he served on the gunboat *Luchs* and from 1906-07 the battleship *Schwaber*. On April 6, 1907 was promoted to the rank of Oberleutnant and in 1908-09 served on the battleship *Pommern*. In Autumn 1909, he became an instructor for ship's gunnery in Sondenburg and between 1909-11, a Company Officer with the 2nd Dockyard Division in Wilhemshaven. After serving on the cruiser *Von Der Tann*, he was promoted to Kapitan Leutnant on April 25, 1912. On August 1, 1914 he took command of *U-24*, which had been commissioned on December 6, 1913. On February 26, 1917, he took command of *U-87*, but on October 13, 1917, was washed overboard in the North Sea and dragged unconscious from the water. All attempts to revive him failed and he was buried at sea at the very spot he was washed overboard. He would figure in the top twenty German U-boat commanders of the war in terms of tonnage sunk.

THE NEW FORMIDABLE

In 1937, a fourth Royal Navy vessel was given the name HMS *Formidable*. The *Illustrious* class fleet aircraft carrier was ordered on March 19, 1937 and work began on her at Harland & Wolff on June 17, 1937. She was launched on August 17, 1939 and commissioned on November 24, 1940. In 1935 the Admiralty had deemed that the next generation of carriers to be constructed, would be afforded the same protection as the big-gun units. Previous aircraft carriers had been partly armoured, but the *Illustrious* class carriers were to have hangar protection against 5,000lb bombs and 6" shells, which meant armouring the flight deck and extending the vertical armour upwards to meet it. HMS *Formidable's* displacement was 30,530 tons standard and 35,500 tons fully loaded. She could reach 30 knots, and at 14 knots could travel 11,000nmiles. She was 781 feet long and carried a crew, including officers, ratings and air crew, of 2,200 and over 60 aircraft. During her service in World War Two, she operated mainly in the Mediterranean. Her initial role was to accompany a convoy to Capetown from December 1940, until January 1941, but was transferred to the Mediterranean to replace HMS *Illustrious* in February 1941. She then took part in the Battle of Matapan (March 27-29, 1941) against units of the Italian Navy, and in the following months was involved in convoy escort. However on May 27, while supporting operations in Crete, she suffered serious damage from an air attack when she was hit by 1,000kg bombs, which put her out of action for six months. Between June and December 1941, she underwent repairs in the United States, after which she sailed for the Indian Ocean, remaining there between March and

August 1942. In October 1942, she returned to the Mediterranean and remained there until October 1943, where she took part in the North African landings in November 1942, the Sicily landings in July 1943 and the Salerno landings in September 1943. On completion of her Mediterranean tour of duties, she took part in an Artic convoy in October 1943. Between January and June 1944, HMS *Formidable* underwent a re-fit, before her aircraft took part in Operation Mascot, which was the attack on the German battleship *Tirpitz* in Norway on July 17, 1944 and then further attacks on her on August 22, 24 and 29 as part of Operation Goodwood. On September 16, 1944, she sailed for the Far East and was stationed at Gibraltar until January 1945 after a machinery breakdown. She finally joined the British Pacific Fleet in place of HMS *Illustrious* on April 16, 1945 and took part in air attacks against Sakishima Gunto between April - May, 1945. Between May 4 - 9, she was hit by Kamikazes, yet was able to operate her aircraft a few hours after the attack. Between July - August 1945, her aircraft would attack Japanese home islands, before she arrived in Sydney, Australia on August 23, to undertake troop voyages to Britain from September 1945 until November 1946. HMS *Formidable* was reduced to reserve in March 1947 at Rosyth, stricken in 1950 and sold in 1953. She was scrapped at Inverkeithing from November 1956.

Port and starboard shots of the 1898 *Formidable*.

(Top) *U-24* on war patrol c1915 and (left)
Kapitanleutnant Rudolph Schneider.

Admiral Sir Lewis Bayly at Queenstown on the US destroyer *Cushing*.

(Top left) Able Seaman Alfred Booth who's memoirs appear on page 104. (Top right) Ivor Gregor McGregor who was transferred from *Formidable* to HMS *Diamond* just days before the sinking.

(Left) A seaman's boot found at the bottom of the pinnace landed at Lyme Regis, which was used for bailing purposes. It is now on display in the Philpot Museum, Lyme Regis. (Right) A lifebelt washed ashore, a few days after the sinking.

(Top) Survivor Percy Garwood, pictured with his wife Lillie, some years after the sinking. Percy was saved by the Brixham trawler *Provident*. (Below) Ex-Petty Officer Roy Emmett (right) who served on the aircraft carrier HMS *Formidable* during WW2. In 1976 he set out to track down the 48 survivors landed at Lyme Regis. His search found two men, one of which was ex-Stoker Reuben Smith who survived the sinking when he was blown from the deck, landing on the heads of the occupants of the pinnace. Roy Emmett is pictured presenting a photograph of the old HMS *Formidable* to Reuben and his wife.

Ex-units of the Fifth Battle Squadron, Channel Fleet. (Top) HMS *Irresistible* sinking during the disastrous Dardanelles campaign. (Below) HMS *Implacable* protecting the "X" beach landings at Gallipoli on April 25, 1915.

THE ROLL
OF HONOUR
TO THE
FALLEN

The Chatham Naval War Memorial. Many of the
***Formidable* casualties are listed on the panels.**

THE ROLL OF HONOUR TO THE FALLEN

This Roll of Honour is made up from the Admiralty list (ADM), stored at the Public Record Office and the Commonwealth War Graves Commission (CWGC) printout, plus additional details gleaned from books, period newspapers and information supplied by relatives or friends of the men listed. Any conflicting information will be marked with an asterisk with the alternative also recorded. As both documents are known to contain the odd error, any listing known to be incorrect will be rectified in future reprints of this book.

SS/4918 Ordinary Seaman **JAMES WILLIAM ABON** - Commemorated on the Chatham Naval Memorial, Kent, England (10).

Assistant Clerk **GEORGE WILLIAM HENRY ADAMS** - Commemorated on the Chatham Naval Memorial, Kent, England (9).

212907 Leading Seaman **HENRY "HARRY" ADAMS** - Aged 33. Son of Henry James and Mary Ann Adams of West Croydon. Served in the Boer War. Commemorated on the Chatham Naval Memorial, Kent, England (9).

J/29939 Boy 1st Class **ROBERT SMITH AIRD** - Born Govan, Glasgow. Son of Robert and Mary Aird of 57, West Campbell Street, Glasgow. Commemorated on the Plymouth Naval Memorial, Devon, England (6).

K/89 Petty Officer Stoker **JOHN FRANCIS ALLAN** - Aged 27. Son of Lennard and Mary Allan of Richmond, Yorkshire. Husband of Anna M. Nicholson (formerly Allan) of 89, St. Peter's Road, Byker, Newcastle-upon-Tyne. Commemorated on the Chatham Naval Memorial, Kent, England (11).

195952 (RFR/CH/B/437*) Able Seaman **DAVID WILLIAM ALLEN** - Born Liverpool. Son of David William and Mary Jane Allen and husband of Mary Jane Allen of 52, Gordon Street, Liverpool. Commemorated on the Chatham Naval Memorial, Kent, England (9). *3437 on CWGC.

CH/16544 Private (RMLI) **HENRY ALLEN** - Aged 28. Son of W. H. Allen of 17, Woodland Hill, Upper Norwood, London. Commemorated on the Chatham Naval Memorial, Kent, England (13).

K/20652 Stoker 1st Class **ALFRED JOHN ANDERSON** - Commemorated on the Chatham Naval Memorial, Kent, England (11).

Canteen Manager **ALFRED PHILIP ANDREWS** - Aged 24. Husband of E. J. Adamson (formerly Andrews) of 14, High Street, Stonehouse, Plymouth. Employee of R. Dickeson and Co. Ltd., Canteen Tenants aboard HMS *Formidable*. Commemorated on the Plymouth Naval Memorial, Devon, England (10).

237780 Leading Seaman **GEORGE STANLEY ANDREWS** - Commemorated on the Chatham Naval Memorial, Kent, England (9).

J/24877 Boy 1st Class **HAROLD JOHN ANDREWS** - Aged 17. Son of Walter John and Kate Andrews of 31, Westfield Road, Hornsey, London. Commemorated on the Chatham Naval Memorial, Kent, England (10).

CH/17910 Private (RMLI) **LEWIS THOMAS ARNOLD** - Aged 20. Son of E. J. W. Arnold of "North Dene," 93, Campbell Road, Lower Walmer, Deal, Kent. Previously employed at the Walmer Brewery, along with William Bennett, another of *Formidable's* crew, who also perished. They also lived in the same street. An original member of the crew and rejoined the *Formidable* one day after the declaration of war. Commemorated on the Chatham Naval Memorial, Kent, England (13).

J/29895 Ordinary Seaman **CHARLES FREDERICK ARTHY** - Aged 18. Son of Mr and Mrs F. C. Arthy of Earls Colne, Essex. Commemorated on the Chatham Naval Memorial, Kent, England (10).

J/14309 Able Seaman **GEORGE WALTER ASHBEE** - Aged 20. Son of William and Rose Ashbee of 15, Raglan Road, Bromley, Kent. Buried Janval Cemetery, Dieppe, Seine-Maritime, France (U.1).

SS/4976 Ordinary Seaman **JOHN ASHBY** - Commemorated on the Chatham Naval Memorial, Kent, England (10).

J/19260 Ordinary Seaman **SIDNEY ASHBY** - Aged 18. Son of George Edward and Lydia Agnes Ashby of 23, Far Fold, Armley, Leeds. Commemorated on the Chatham Naval Memorial, Kent, England (10).

J/11188 Able Seaman **GEORGE ERNEST ASHWOOD** - Aged 22. Son of the late Mr and Mrs George Ashwood. Commemorated on the Chatham Naval Memorial, Kent, England (9).

J/2055 Leading Seaman **ERNEST ALEXANDER LANE BABER** - Buried Portland Royal Naval Cemetery, Dorset, England (545).

SS/4919 Ordinary Seaman **FRANCIS NIXON BAKER** - Buried Portland Royal Naval Cemetery, Dorset, England (547).

J/27855 Boy 1st Class **HERBERT FRANCIS BAKER** - Commemorated on the Plymouth Naval Memorial, Devon, England (6).

K/3655 Stoker 1st Class **SIDNEY HERBERT BAKER** - Aged 26. Son of Ernest and Telia Baker of 57, Coopersale Road, Homerton, London. Commemorated on the Chatham Naval Memorial, Kent, England (11).

SS/4978 Ordinary Seaman **THOMAS WILLIAM BALL** - Aged 18. Native of Sheffield. Son of Thomas Platts and Louisa Ball of 35, Chesley Gardens, East Ham, London. Commemorated on the Chatham Naval Memorial, Kent, England (10).

Commander **CHARLES FREDERICK BALLARD** - Aged 35. Born Rock, Washington, Sussex, March 23, 1879. Son of the late Lieut. Col. John Fane Ballard (Duke of Cornwall's Light Infantry) and Mary Ballard. Joined the *Britannia* in 1892, passing out in eighth. Appointed Midshipman January 1895, Sub-Lieut. July 1898, and Lieut. in November 1900. He was made Commander in June 1913. Married Violet Hazel, daughter of Admiral Sir Cecil Burney at St. Mary Abbotts, Kensington on July 15, 1913. Appointed to HMS *Formidable* in August 1913. On January 1, 1915, Commander Ballard was last seen on the bridge of the *Formidable* with Captain Loxley. He had previously superintended getting the boats out and had ordered as much wood as possible to be thrown overboard for the men to cling to. Commemorated on the Chatham Naval Memorial, Kent, England (8).

CH/17969 Private (RMLI) **THOMAS GEORGE BANTON** - Aged 20. Son of Joshua and Elizabeth Banton of 58, Mynors Street, Stafford. Commemorated on the Chatham Naval Memorial, Kent, England (13).

SS/4737 Ordinary Seaman **HENRY RICHARD GEORGE BARNES** - Commemorated on the Chatham Naval Memorial, Kent, England (10).

285954 Mechanician **ALFRED JOSEPH BARTER** - Commemorated on the Chatham Naval Memorial, Kent, England (11).

SS/4982 Ordinary Seaman **ERNEST WILLIAM BARTLETT** - Commemorated on the Chatham Naval Memorial, Kent, England (10).

J/28285 Boy 1st Class **HORACE BATCHELOR** - Aged 17. Son of Alfred and Esther Batchelor of 20, New Houses, Powder Mills, Tonbridge, Kent. Commemorated on the Chatham Naval Memorial, Kent, England (10).

215592 Able Seaman **JAMES BAXTER** - Aged 30. Son of Edwin and Isabel Baxter of 5, Fernside Street, Bradford, Yorkshire. Commemorated on the Chatham Naval Memorial, Kent, England (9).

190777 Petty Officer **JOSEPH SECRET BEALES** - Commemorated on the Chatham Naval Memorial, Kent, England (9).

CH/14035 Private (RMLI) **FREDERICK JAMES BEAMS** - Commemorated on the Chatham Naval Memorial, Kent, England (13).

190480 Able Seaman **WILLIAM BEAZLEY** - Commemorated on the Chatham Naval Memorial, Kent, England (9).

343459 Armourer's Mate **WILLIAM JAMES BEECH** - Aged 31. Born Vale of Clwyd, Denbighshire. Son of Richard and Mary Beech of 13, Harriet Street, Higher Broughton, Manchester. Commemorated on the Chatham Naval Memorial, Kent, England (12).

CH/17875 Private (RMLI) **WILLIAM BENNETT** - Aged 17. Son of William and Elizabeth Bennett of 95, Canada Road, Walmer. His father and grandfather both served in the Royal Marines. Employed for a time at the Walmer Brewery, where another *Formidable* casualty had also worked (Lewis Thomas Arnold). Joined the Navy and served on HMS *Lord Nelson*. Was among the Marine force sent to Ostend during the early days of the war. On his return from action joined the *Formidable*. Buried Deal Cemetery, Kent, England (4. 1660).

CH/17273 Private (RMLI) **FRANK WILLIAM BENTLEY** - Aged 21. Born Chelsea. Son of Thomas Harry and Annie Bentley of 14, Wood Street, Chelsea, London. Commemorated on the Chatham Naval Memorial, Kent, England (13).

117236 Ship's Corporal 1st Class (Pensioner) **HARRY BERESFORD** - Aged 47. Husband of Clara Beresford of 104, Ramsden Road, Hexthorpe, Doncaster. Awarded Long Service and Good Conduct Medal. Commemorated on the Portsmouth Naval Memorial, Hampshire, England (9).

311695 Stoker 1st Class **JAMES BERESFORD** - Aged 27. Son of Samuel and Annie Beresford of 91, North Frederick Street, Glasgow. Commemorated on the Chatham Naval Memorial, Kent, England (11).

SS/112713 Stoker 1st Class **HORACE FRANK BERNTHALL** - Aged 21. Son of Henry Adolphus Bernthall of Slotters Cottage, Folly Lane, Walthamstow, Essex. Buried Lyme Regis Cemetery, Dorset (D. 14/17).

M/1295 Engine Room Artificer 3rd Class **SIDNEY GEORGE BETENSON** - Aged 29. Son of George (RN) and Emma Betenson of Portsmouth and husband of Alice Betenson of 4, St. Mark's Road, Portsmouth. Commemorated on the Chatham Naval Memorial, Kent, England (11).

M/4761 Cook's Mate **HARRY GEORGE BIDDLECOMBE** - Aged 24. Son of Joseph and Mary Ann Biddlecombe of 5, Spring Meadow, Forest Row, Sussex. Commemorated on the Chatham Naval Memorial, Kent, England (12).

CH/17624 Private (RMLI) **PERCY BIGG** - Aged 19. Born Lambeth, London. Son of Alfred Bigg of 12, Thornparch Road, Wandsworth, London. Commemorated on the Chatham Naval Memorial, Kent, England (13).

J/12563 Able Seaman **FRANCIS HERBERT BLACKMORE** - Son of John and Emma Blackmore of 60, Mayfield Road, Dalston, London. Commemorated on the Chatham Naval Memorial, Kent, England (9).

170876 Shipwright 1st Class **ALBERT GEORGE BLATCHFORD** - Aged 48. Husband of F. M. Blatchford of 117, Trafalgar Road, Gillingham, Kent. Commemorated on the Chatham Naval Memorial, Kent, England (12).

SS/113116 Stoker 1st Class **GEORGE FREDERICK BLAXLAND** - Aged 22. Son of Mrs K. Deeks of 21, Bridge Road, Rainham, Essex. Commemorated on the Chatham Naval Memorial, Kent, England (11).

J/29557 Ordinary Seaman **FREDERICK WILLIAM BOHANNAN*** - Commemorated on the Portsmouth Naval Memorial, Hampshire, England (8). *BOHANNON on CWGC.

CH/17916 Private (RMLI) **GEORGE JOSEPH BONFIELD** - Aged 24. Son of Albert and Charlotte Bonfield of 6, Long Lane, East Finchley, London. Commemorated on the Chatham Naval Memorial, Kent, England (13).

CH/16099 Private (RMLI) **ERNEST BOOTH** - Aged 24. Son of Emma of 11, Sutherland Street, Sheffield. Resided at Two Brewers, Rochester. Commemorated on the Chatham Naval Memorial, Kent, England (13).

177715 (RFR/CH/B/13553*) Able Seaman **GEORGE BORMAN** - Aged 36. Native of Goole. Son of the late George and Sarah Ann Borman and husband of E. Borman of 20, Fowler Place, Pitsmoor, Sheffield. Commemorated on the Chatham Naval Memorial, Kent, England (9). *3553 on ADM.

J/29552 Ordinary Seaman **JOSEPH NORMAN BOSWELL** - Commemorated on the Plymouth Naval Memorial, Devon, England (6).

J/10692 Able Seaman **ALBERT WICKSTEAD BOTLEY** - Aged 19. Son of Mr and Mrs Botley of 45, Henry Street, Luton, Chatham (previously at 148, Castle Street, Chatham). Commemorated on the Chatham Naval Memorial, Kent, England (9).

J/11392 Able Seaman **EDGAR BOVIS** - Aged 20. Native of Chatham. Son of Ernest and Clara Bovis of 21, Rhode Street, Chatham. Commemorated on the Chatham Naval Memorial, Kent, England (9).

J/26112 Boy 1st Class **FREDERICK JAMES BRADLEY** - Aged 16. Born London. Son of Frederick and the late Lilian Elizabeth Bradley of 93, Tredway Street, Bethnal Green, London. Commemorated on the Chatham Naval Memorial, Kent, England (10).

J/26399 Boy 1st Class **THOMAS BREED** - Aged 17. Son of Charles and Emily Breed of 22, Harrow Road, Leytonstone, London. Commemorated on the Chatham Naval Memorial, Kent, England (10).

J/3649 Leading Seaman **HERBERT WILLIAM BRENCHLEY** - Aged 23. Son of Austin and Eleanor Brenchley of Meopham Court Lodge, Gravesend, Kent. Commemorated on the Chatham Naval Memorial, Kent, England (9).

CH/17913 Private (RMLI) **JESSE BRIERLEY** - Commemorated on the Chatham Naval Memorial, Kent, England (13).

K/16918 Stoker 1st Class **ARTHUR HUGH BRITTER** - Commemorated on the Chatham Naval Memorial, Kent, England (11).

210679 Able Seaman **HERBERT WILLIAM BROAD** - Aged 29. Born London. Son of Mr and Mrs H. Broad of 54, Hampden Road, Hornsey, London. Commemorated on the Chatham Naval Memorial, Kent, England (9).

351213 Sick Berth Steward 2nd Class **JAMES BROAD** - Aged 28. Son of James and Lucy Broad of Wantage, Berkshire and husband of Priscilla F. Broad of 28, Stranmillis Gardens, Belfast. Commemorated on the Chatham Naval Memorial, Kent, England (12).

159503 Cook **THOMAS WILLIAM BROOM** - Aged 41. Son of Henry and Emma Broom of 27, Lords Street, Landport, Portsmouth. Commemorated on the Portsmouth Naval Memorial, Hampshire, England (9).

K/17384 Stoker 1st Class **ALFRED BROWN** - Aged 21. Son of Henry and Marion Brown of 11, Winchelsea Street, Dover. Commemorated on the Chatham Naval Memorial, Kent, England (11).

J/2685 Able Seaman **JOHN BROWN** - Commemorated on the Chatham Naval Memorial, Kent, England (9).

143956 (RFR/CH/A/1402) Chief Stoker **JOHN WESTON BROWN** - Commemorated on the Chatham Naval Memorial, Kent, England (11).

M/688 Electrical Artificer 3rd Class **RICHARD BROWN** - Commemorated on the Chatham Naval Memorial, Kent, England (12).

211313 Petty Officer **WALTER BRUMMAGE** - Commemorated on the Chatham Naval Memorial, Kent, England (9).

342453 Ship's Chief Cook **CHARLES BRYANT** - Aged 40. Son of Jonathan and Ann Bryant of Sedlescombe, Battle, Sussex and husband of Rosalie Bryant of "Fairview" Lenham, Maidstone, Kent. Commemorated on the Chatham Naval Memorial, Kent, England (12).

K/20120 Stoker 1st Class **WILLIAM EDWARD BRYANT** - Aged 19. Native of Deptford. Son of Frank Edward and Harriet Bryant of 16, Snead Street, New Cross, London. Commemorated on the Chatham Naval Memorial, Kent, England (11).

CH/17386 Private (RMLI) **SIDNEY JAMES BUCKLAND** - Commemorated on the Chatham Naval Memorial, Kent, England (13).

Gunner **GEORGE BUNYARD*** - Commemorated on the Chatham Naval Memorial, Kent, England (9) *BUNGARD on CWGC.

CH/16043 Private **DAVID BURBAGE** - Aged 23. Son of the late William Burbage. Commemorated on the Chatham Naval Memorial, Kent, England (13).

238256 Able Seaman **HORACE HUGH BURLEY** - Commemorated on the Chatham Naval Memorial, Kent, England (9).

CH/10463 Private (RMLI) **WILLIAM ARTHUR BURLEY** - Commemorated on the Chatham Naval Memorial, Kent, England (13).

M/10987 Senior Reserve Attendant **JAMES BURNELL** - Aged 33. Son of William and Sarah Ann Burnell of Newport Pagnell, Buckinghamshire and husband of Martha Burnell of 149, Alkington Road, Whitchurch, Shropshire (formerly 11, Myrtle Street, Crewe). Member of the Royal Naval Aux. Sick Berth Reserve and formerly worked in Crewe Works. Commemorated on the Chatham Naval Memorial, Kent, England (15).

SS/114859 Stoker 1st Class **ALFRED GEORGE BYATT** - Aged 21. Born Wandsworth, London. Son of Joseph and Louisa Byatt of 54, Foss Road, Lower Tooting, London. Commemorated on the Chatham Naval Memorial, Kent, England (11).

308718 Mechanician **JOHN BYGRAVE** - Aged 28. Son of George and Mary Jane Bygrave of Waterford, Hertford, Herts. Commemorated on the Chatham Naval Memorial, Kent, England (11).

Midshipman **ERNEST GEOFFREY CADLE** - Aged 16. Born Durham. Son of Charles Ernest and Elizabeth Rebecca Cadle of 26, North Bailey, Durham. Commemorated on the Chatham Naval Memorial, Kent, England (8).

J/11807 Able Seaman **DANIEL EDWARD THOMAS CANNON** - Aged 21. Son of Mr and Mrs Cannon of 93, Hillside Terrace, Buckland, Dover. Commemorated on the Chatham Naval Memorial, Kent, England (9).

195257 Able Seaman **WILLIAM JOSEPH PATRICK CARR** - Aged 33. Son of Mrs H. M. Carr of Buckland, Faringdon, Berkshire. Commemorated on the Chatham Naval Memorial, Kent, England (9).

J/29535 Ordinary Seaman **GEORGE EDWARD CASSELL** - Commemorated on the Portsmouth Naval Memorial, Hampshire, England (8).

297968 (RFR/CH/B/9853) Leading Stoker **THOMAS HENRY CHALLIS** - Son of Thomas and Louisa Challis and husband of H. Challis of 31, Lloyd Road, Walthamstow, London. Commemorated on the Chatham Naval Memorial, Kent, England (11).

343163 Shipwright 2nd Class **HERBERT CHAMBERLAIN** - Commemorated on the Chatham Naval Memorial, Kent, England (12).

302284 Petty Officer Stoker **ROBERT BETHEL CHANDLER** - Commemorated on the Chatham Naval Memorial, Kent, England (11).

2588/S (RNR) Stoker **ALEXANDER CHANTRELL** - Aged 18. Son of Joseph and Mary Chantrell of 31, Moses Street, Bowerfield Lane, Stockton-on-Tees. Buried Stockton-on-Tees (Durham Road) Cemetery, Durham (A1. D. 33).

307880 Leading Stoker **ALFRED STEPHEN CHAPMAN** - Aged 29. Son of Mr and Mrs Alfred Chapman of Chilham, Kent and husband of Jane Rose Chapman of 1, Garden Place, Tanner Street, Faversham, Kent. Commemorated on the Chatham Naval Memorial, Kent, England (11).

CH/17928 Bugler (RMLI) **HUBERT THOMAS MAY CHAPMAN** - Aged 16. Born Wouldham, Kent. Son of Henry and Louisa Chapman of 42, Fox Street, Gillingham, Kent. Commemorated on the Chatham Naval Memorial, Kent, England (13).

268200 Engine Room Artificer 1st Class **JOHN CHARLESWORTH** - Resided at 127, Rochester Avenue, Rochester. Commemorated on the Chatham Naval Memorial, Kent, England (11).

CH/17917 Private (RMLI) **FRANK CHEEK** - Aged 22. Son of Harry and Mary Cheek of Yew Tree Cottage, Little Saling, Braintree, Essex. Commemorated on the Chatham Naval Memorial, Kent, England (13).

J/4265 Able Seaman **WILLIAM CHENEY** - Aged 23. Son of William Alfred Cheney of 31, Farnham Street, Humberstone Road, Leicester. Commemorated on the Chatham Naval Memorial, Kent, England (9).

CH/16112 Private (RMLI) **ERNEST JOSEPH CHILDS** - Aged 23. Son of Thomas William and Kerenhappuch Childs of 7, St. George's Road, Peckham, London. Commemorated on the Chatham Naval Memorial, Kent, England (13).

309598 Leading Stoker **JOHN CHING** - Aged 26. Son of Mr T. and Mrs H. Ching of Christopher Street, Finsbury, London and husband of M. F .S. Ching of 14, Gloucester Road, Philip Lane, Tottenham, London. Commemorated on the Chatham Naval Memorial, Kent, England (11).

345978 Shipwright **GEORGE ERNEST CHURCH** - Commemorated on the Chatham Naval Memorial, Kent, England (12).

288089 Stoker 1st Class **JOSEPH CHURCHILL** - Aged 38. Son of Clifford and Jane Churchill of Broadbridge Heath, Horsham, Sussex and husband of Ellen Lucy Churchill of 3, Prin Cottages, Broadbridge Heath, Horsham, Sussex. Commemorated on the Chatham Naval Memorial, Kent, England (11).

CH/16398 (RMLI) Private **ALFRED CLAPHAM** - Buried Burton Bradstock (St. Mary) Church Cemetery, Devon, England.

122977 (RFR/CH/A/885) Petty Officer 1st Class **ARTHUR RICHARD CLARK** - Aged 56. Son of Thomas and Phoebe Clark. Commemorated on the Chatham Naval Memorial, Kent, England (9).

K/40 Stoker 1st Class **GEORGE CLARK** - Commemorated on the Chatham Naval Memorial, Kent, England (11).

301882 Petty Officer Stoker **GEORGE SAMUEL ROLAND CLARK** - Aged 29. Son of John Clark of Salisbury Street, North Unley, South Australia. Commemorated on the Chatham Naval Memorial, Kent, England (11).

J/14342 Able Seaman **HAROLD JAMES CLARK** - Commemorated on the Chatham Naval Memorial, Kent, England (9).

J/27307 Boy 1st Class **THOMAS STEPHEN CLARK** - Commemorated on the Chatham Naval Memorial, Kent, England (10).

SS/114908 Stoker 1st Class **WILFRED HARRY CLARKE** - Aged 18. Son of Harry and Mrs E. Clarke of 17, Chinnor Road, Thame, Oxon. Commemorated on the Chatham Naval Memorial, Kent, England (11).

192356 (RFR/CH/B/6564) Petty Officer 2nd Class **HORACE CLARKSON** - Aged 38. Son of Annie Elizabeth and the late Joseph Clarkson of 16, Gladstone Street, Loftus-in-Cleveland, Yorkshire. Commemorated on the Chatham Naval Memorial, Kent, England (9).

Artificer Engineer **HENRY CLAYTON** - Resided with his parents at Mills Hill Road, Middleton, Manchester opposite the Laurel Cotton Mill, where his father was employed. Commemorated on the Portsmouth Naval Memorial, Hampshire, England (7) and on the family gravestone by the north wall of St. Gabriel's Parish Church.

J/29544 Ordinary Seaman **GEORGE HENRY CLIFFORD** - Commemorated on the Chatham Naval Memorial, Kent, England (10).

204142 (RFR/CH/B/6795) Able Seaman **WILLIAM HEBRON CLIMO*** - Commemorated on the Chatham Naval Memorial, Kent, England (9). *CLIME on ADM.

J/29530 Ordinary Seaman **JAMES HALCOMB CLINTON** - Aged 18. Son of Phoebe and the late Samuel Clinton of 15, Lockington Road, Battersea, London. Commemorated on the Chatham Naval Memorial, Kent, England (10).

161867 Leading Seaman* **FREDERICK JAMES COE** - Commemorated on the Chatham Naval Memorial, Kent, England (addenda) *Able Seaman on CWGC.

Midshipman **JOHN SMILEY COEY** - Aged 16. Son of Edward and Mary Coey of Merville, Whitehouse, Co. Antrim Commemorated on the Chatham Naval Memorial, Kent, England (8).

239711 leading Seaman **LEONARD COLLETTE** - Aged 23. Son of the late Mr and Mrs Collette of Wimbledon, London and husband of Elsie Louisa Collette of 42, Cornwall Road, Handsworth, Birmingham. Awarded Messina medal. Commemorated on the Chatham Naval Memorial, Kent, England (9).

223049 Leading Seaman **ALFRED WALTER FRANK COLLINS** - Aged 27. Son of the late Walter and Matilda Collins. Commemorated on the Chatham Naval Memorial, Kent, England (9).

CH/13674 Private (RMLI) **GEORGE WILLIAM COLLINS** - Aged 36. Son of the late Mr and Mrs E. Collins of 44, Portland Street, St. Albans, Hertfordshire. Commemorated on the Chatham Naval Memorial, Kent, England (13).

179013 Petty Officer **HENRY ROBERT COLLINS** - Aged 37. Husband of M. A. Collins of 7, Wornington Road, North Kensington, London. Commemorated on the Chatham Naval Memorial, Kent, England (9).

169942 Petty Officer 1st Class **SAMUEL COLVILLE** - Aged 30 (39?). Husband of Mrs M. Colville (nee Dowling). Resided at 4, Gundulph Road, Chatham. Until war broke out, worked in the Coastguard Service at South Shields and later at Leigh-on-Sea. Commemorated on the Chatham Naval Memorial, Kent, England (9).

316V (RNR) Stoker **THOMAS CONDON** - Aged 45. Son of the late David Condon of Cork and husband of the late Margaret Condon. Commemorated on the Chatham Naval Memorial, Kent, England (14).

K/5791 Stoker 1st Class **THOMAS CONNOR** - Aged 23. Son of William Connor of 11, Newton's Rents, Twine Court, Cable Street, Shadwell, London c. Chatham Naval Memorial, Kent, England (11).

J/13460 Able Seaman **WILLIAM ALFRED COOK** - Aged 18. Stepson of E. C. Dean of 126, Frith Road, Leytonstone, London. Commemorated on the Chatham Naval Memorial, Kent, England (9).

K/20988 Stoker 1st Class **CHARLES ALFRED COOPER** - Aged 20. Son of Mrs E. Cooper of 14, Riley Street, King's Road, Chelsea, London. Commemorated on the Chatham Naval Memorial, Kent, England (11).

K/20638 Stoker 1st Class **CHARLES ARTHUR COOPER** - Aged 18. Son of James and Mary Ann Cooper of 6, Vale Road, Sutton, Surrey. Commemorated on the Chatham Naval Memorial, Kent, England (11).

J/29898 Ordinary Seaman **ERNEST FREDERICK COOPER** - Aged 18. Son of John Henry and Jane Cooper of 38, Westville Road, Shepherds Bush, London. Commemorated on the Portsmouth Naval Memorial, Hampshire, England (8).

K/23071 Stoker 1st Class **GEORGE CHARLES COOTE** - Aged 27. Son of William and Caroline Coote of Barrington, Cambridgeshire and husband of Laura Coote (nee Adams). Commemorated on the Chatham Naval Memorial, Kent, England (11).

Gunner **JOSEPH URIAH COPLAND** - Aged 36. Husband of Priscilla Copland of Gillingham, Kent. Commemorated on the Chatham Naval Memorial, Kent, England (9).

233814 Stoker 1st Class **WILLIAM COPPING** - Aged 26. Son of James and Sarah Copping of Sunny Side, Hacheston, Wickham Market, Suffolk. Commemorated on the Chatham Naval Memorial, Kent, England (11).

Canteen Assistant **ALFRED CHARLES CORBY*** - Aged 21. Son of George Ernest and Rebecca Maria Corby* of Erwarton, Ipswich. Employee of R. Dickeson and Co. Ltd., Canteen Tenants aboard HMS *Formidable*. Commemorated on the Chatham Naval Memorial, Kent, England (15). *ALBERT CORDY on ADM.

216350 Able Seaman **ARTHUR COWIE** - Aged 29. Son of William and Sarah Cowie of Nacton, Ipswich. Commemorated on the Chatham Naval Memorial, Kent, England (9).

Lieutenant **HUGH CLIFFORD HOLLED COXE** - Aged 23. Son of Mr and Mrs H. R. H. Coxe of Ozendyke, Watlington, Oxfordshire. Commemorated on the Chatham Naval Memorial, Kent, England (8).

J/29435 Ordinary Seaman **BERT CRAWFORD** - Aged 18. Foster son of Charles and Emily Lavinia Crawford of 2, Down Cottage, Bursledon Road, Sholing, Southampton. Commemorated on the Portsmouth Naval Memorial, Hampshire, England (8).

J/7655 Able Seaman **SOMERVILLE DANZEY CRESSWELL*** - Aged 21. Son of Sackville Cresswell* of the Square, Wingham, Canterbury. Commemorated on the Chatham Naval Memorial, Kent, England (G). *CRESWELL on ADM.

221515 Able Seaman **ROBERT CRIGHTON** - Son of John and the late Elizabeth McLauchlan Crighton of The Crescent, Luncarty, Perth. Commemorated on the Chatham Naval Memorial, Kent, England (9).

157774 Ship's Corporal 1st Class **JACK CRIPPS** - Aged 39. Husband of Frances Cripps of 10, Chaucer Road, Gillingham, Kent. Commemorated on the Chatham Naval Memorial, Kent, England (12).

SS/116014 Stoker 1st Class **THOMAS RANSON CROSBY** - Commemorated on the Chatham Naval Memorial, Kent, England (11).

269824 Chief Engine Room Artificer **JOHN SAMUEL CROSS** - Commemorated on the Chatham Naval Memorial, Kent, England (10).

182769 Petty Officer Stoker **HERBERT HORACE CROUCHER** - Commemorated on the Chatham Naval Memorial, Kent, England (11).

K/15901 Stoker 1st Class **EDWARD JOHN CROWHURST** - Aged 20. Son of Mr and Mrs G. E. H. Crowhurst of 18, North Cray Road, Bexley, Kent. Commemorated on the Chatham Naval Memorial, Kent, England (11).

CH/11454 Private (RMLI) **JOHN HAROLD CROXFORD** - Commemorated on the Chatham Naval Memorial, Kent, England (13).

350161 Ship's Corporal 1st Class (Pensioner) **HENRY THOMAS CROXSON** - Aged 45. Born Ipswich, December 31, 1869. Son of Jonathan and Jane Croxson of Ipswich and husband of the late Mary Ann Croxson (married at St. Matthew's Church, Ipswich on October 26, 1896). Entered the Navy on July 31, 1888. Awarded Long Service and Good Conduct Medal on November 27, 1903. Commemorated on the Chatham Naval Memorial, Kent, England (12).

K/4150 Leading Stoker **WALTER HENRY CULLEN** - Commemorated on the Chatham Naval Memorial, Kent, England (11).

M/7745 3rd Class Writer* **HERBERT GEORGE CUNNINGTON** - Aged 21. Native of London. Son of the late Henry Opten Jeffs and Elizabeth Cunnington c. Chatham Naval Memorial, Kent, England (12) *3rd Class Waiter on CWGC.

J/29890 Boy 1st Class **EDWARD JOHN CURRIE** - Aged 17. Son of George Edward and Rose Currie of Goss Street, Northam, Devon. Commemorated on the Plymouth Naval Memorial, Devon, England (6).

L/3909 Officer's Steward 2nd Class **HENRY GEORGE DAKERS** - Commemorated on the Chatham Naval Memorial, Kent, England (12).

J/20906 Boy 1st Class **THOMAS ERNEST DALTON** - Aged 17. Native of Dalston, London. Son of Ernest and S. A. Dalton of 21, Lakes Road, Keston, Kent. Commemorated on the Chatham Naval Memorial, Kent, England (10).

6405A (RNR) Seaman **ARTHUR CHARLES DAVIDSON** - Aged 18. Son of William and Minnie Davidson of 38, Holmby Street, Albany Road, Camberwell, London. Commemorated on the Chatham Naval Memorial, Kent, England (14).

214594 Yeoman of Signals **EDMUND THOMAS DAVIES** - Commemorated on the Chatham Naval Memorial, Kent, England (10).

233246 Able Seaman **WILLIAM ROBERT DAVIS** - Son of William Davis of Shoreditch, London and husband of A. B. Pugh (formerly Davis) of 60, Bridport Place, Hoxton, London. Commemorated on the Chatham Naval Memorial, Kent, England (9).

K/8310 Stoker 1st Class **ALEXANDER DAY** - Aged 24. Native of West Hoathly, Sussex. Son of Spencer and Isabella Day of Holly Cottage, Ardingly, Sussex. Commemorated on the Chatham Naval Memorial, Kent, England (11).

J/23037 Ordinary Seaman **OLIVER WILLIAM JAMES DAY** - Aged 18. Son of Mr and Mrs W.M. Day of 12, King's Road, Belmont, Surrey. Commemorated on the Chatham Naval Memorial, Kent, England (10).

Captain (RMLI) **JOHN CYRIL DEED** - Aged 38. Born St. Albans, Hertfordshire May 22, 1876. Son of Reverend Canon John George (Vicar of Nuneaton, Canon of Coventry and Rural Dean of Atherstone) and Elizabeth Deed of Nuneaton Vicarage, Nuneaton, Warwickshire. Educated at St. Albans Grammar School and Greenwich College. Gazetted Second Lieut. in the Royal Marines on February 1, 1894, promoted to Lieutenant January 1, 1895 and to Captain October 10, 1900. When he retired he joined the Reserve of Officers. Went to British Columbia and on the outbreak of war, he was asked to raise and command the 1st East Kootenay (Fernie) Contingent. He trained and commanded this unit until September 1914, when he was ordered to return to England. He rejoined his old Corps at Deal on October 10, 1914 and was posted to HMS *Formidable* on November 16. Commemorated on the Chatham Naval Memorial, Kent, England (13).

SS/4902 Ordinary Seaman **JOHN DELANEY** - Commemorated on the Chatham Naval Memorial, Kent, England (10).

226589 Petty Officer **WILLIAM DENHAM** - Aged 28. Born Stockton-on-Tees, October 10, 1886. Son of William and Jane (nee Lambert) Denham of 2, Paradise Place, Stockton-on-Tees. Joined the Navy in 1903 and served in both the Home and Mediterranean Fleets. Awarded the Messina Medal from the King of Italy, for services rendered there during the earthquake. Passed qualifying exam for Warrant Officer on November 30, 1914. Commemorated on the Chatham Naval Memorial, Kent, England (9).

360990 Ship's Cook **GEORGE HENRY DEWBERRY** - Commemorated on the Chatham Naval Memorial, Kent, England (12).

CH/16667 Corporal (RMLI) **WILLIAM JOSEPH DINGWALL** - Aged 22. Born Woolwich, London. Son of Mr R. and Mrs K. Dingwall of 18, Gildersome Street, Woolwich Common, London. Commemorated on the Chatham Naval Memorial, Kent, England (13).

306742 Stoker 1st Class **HARRY DITCHER** - Aged 29. Son of Eleanor Cheeseman of Two Brewers Inn, Yalding, Kent. Commemorated on the Chatham Naval Memorial, Kent, England (11).

J/27819 Ordinary Seaman **HAROLD DIXON** - Commemorated on the Plymouth Naval Memorial, Devon, England (6).

223154 Petty Officer **ALBERT EDWARD REDFERN DONOVAN** - Commemorated on the Chatham Naval Memorial, Kent, England (9).

CH/17570 Private (RMLI) **EDWARD DOSWELL** - Commemorated on the Chatham Naval Memorial, Kent, England (13).

CH/8462 Private (RMLI) **ALBERT FRANCIS DOUCE** - Aged 35. Son of Joseph John and Harriet (nee Matthews) Douce of 108, Chesterton Road, Kensington, London (at the time of Albert's death). Born on June 26, 1879 and enlisted in the RMLI in 1895, giving his birth date as 1877, as he was actually two years below the minimum age for engagement. Awarded Queen's South Africa War Medal while earned while serving on HMS *Barracouta* and posthumously awarded Naval General Service Medal with bar (Persian Gulf 1909 - 1914) earned while onboard HMS *Perseus*. Commemorated on the Chatham Naval Memorial, Kent, England (13).

J/29910 Ordinary Seaman **CHARLES ROBERT DOVE** - Aged 18. Son of Charles and Mary Ann Dove of 20, Clarendon Street, Paddington, London. Commemorated on the Plymouth Naval Memorial, Devon, England (6).

M/9463 Senior Reserve Attendant **MICHAEL DOYLE** - Member of the Royal Naval Aux. Sick Berth Reserve. Commemorated on the Chatham Naval Memorial, Kent, England (15).

K/8177 Stoker 1st Class **ALFRED GEORGE DRAPER** -Aged 23. Son of George and Annie Draper of 43, Milestone Road, Stone, Dartford, Kent. Commemorated on the Chatham Naval Memorial, Kent, England (11).

K/4064 Stoker 1st Class **HARRY DRINKWATER** - Aged 23. Son of James Taylor and Susannah Drinkwater of 47, Makin Street, County Road, Walton, Liverpool. Commemorated on the Chatham Naval Memorial, Kent, England (11).

J/29940 Ordinary Seaman **WILLIAM DUROW** - Aged 18. Son of Joseph and Mary Ann Durow of 132, Station Road, Stanley Village, Derbyshire. Commemorated on the Plymouth Naval Memorial, Devon, England (6).

CH/8738 Colour Sergeant (RMLI) **THOMAS DYKE** - Aged 38. Husband of Fanny Sarah Dyke of 105, Maida Road, Chatham. Commemorated on the Chatham Naval Memorial, Kent, England (13).

K/6644 Leading Stoker **JAMES EARLY** - Aged 29. Son of John James and Charlotte Early of Marylebone, London and husband of Esther Janie Early of 13, Ridley Road, Rochester, Kent. Commemorated on the Chatham Naval Memorial, Kent, England (11).

SS/106878* (RFR/B/9507) Stoker 1st Class **WILLIAM CHARLES ELEY** - Aged 24. Born Liverpool. Son of William and Ellen Eley. Buried Lyme Regis Cemetery, Dorset, England (D. 14/17). *SS/10687B on CWGC.

K/4464 Leading Stoker **ALBERT GEORGE ELLENDER** - Aged 29. Husband of Mabel Charlotte Ellender of 43, Liverpool Street, Dover. Commemorated on the Chatham Naval Memorial, Kent, England (11).

229338 Stoker 1st Class **CHARLES JOSEPH ELLIOTT** - Commemorated on the Chatham Naval Memorial, Kent, England (11).

J/29354 Ordinary Seaman **CHARLES WILLIAM ELLIOTT** - Aged 19. Son of Frederick and Martha Elliott, of Tooting, London. Commemorated on the Portsmouth Naval Memorial, Hampshire, England (8).

288851 Stoker 1st Class **GEORGE ELLIOTT** - Commemorated on the Chatham Naval Memorial, Kent, England (11).

K/11506 Stoker 1st Class **JAMES ALFRED ELLIS** - Commemorated on the Chatham Naval Memorial, Kent, England (11).

SS/109232 Stoker 1st Class **JOHN GEORGE FREDERICK ELLIS** - Aged 24. Husband of M. E. Dwyer (formerly Ellis) of 24, Elm Street, Strand Road, Bootle, Liverpool. Commemorated on the Chatham Naval Memorial, Kent, England (11).

J/22992 Ordinary Seaman **LEONARD JAMES ELLIS** - Commemorated on the Chatham Naval Memorial, Kent, England (10).

194837 Petty Officer 1st Class **ALBERT EDGAR ELMES** - Commemorated on the Chatham Naval Memorial, Kent, England (9).

J/29503 Ordinary Seaman **HAROLD ERIC CLIFTON ELTON** - Aged 20. Native of Clifton, Derby. Son of Thomas and Annie Elizabeth Elton of 2, Crescent Road, Cheetham Hill, Manchester. Commemorated on the Plymouth Naval Memorial, Devon, England (6).

290480 Stoker 1st Class **THOMAS ERWIN** - Commemorated on the Chatham Naval Memorial, Kent, England (11).

340857 Blacksmith **SYDNEY FRANK GEORGE EYRES** - Aged 41. Son of John Bray and Sarah Eyres of Lostwithiel, Cornwall and husband of E. M. F. Eyres of 28, Park Road, Gillingham, Kent. Commemorated on the Chatham Naval Memorial, Kent, England (12).

3159C (RNR) Seaman **MARTIN FAHERTY** - Commemorated on the Portsmouth Naval Memorial, Hampshire, England (10).

K/10036 Stoker 1st Class **FREDERICK GEORGE FARRINGTON** - Aged 22. Son of Joseph and Emma Farrington of Henham, Wangford, Suffolk. Commemorated on the Chatham Naval Memorial, Kent, England (11).

CH/17168 Private (RMLI) **GEORGE THOMAS PERCIVAL FAULKNER** - Resided in Belmont Road, Gillingham. Commemorated on the Chatham Naval Memorial, Kent, England (13).

303073 Stoker 1st Class **WILLIAM FAWKES** - Aged 32. Son of William and Ann Fawkes of 161, St. Vincent Street, Westoe, South Shields. Buried in Lyme Regis Cemetery, Dorset, England (D. 14/17).

178093 Petty Officer **WILLIAM FELDON** - Buried in Lyme Regis Cemetery, Dorset, England (D. 14/17).

K/19314 Stoker 1st Class **GEORGE HENRY JOHN FILLIES** - Commemorated on the Chatham Naval Memorial, Kent, England (11).

J/27159 Boy 1st Class **JOHN HYAMS FISHER** - Commemorated on the Chatham Naval Memorial, Kent, England (10).

CH/15332 Private (RMLI) **ARTHUR FITCH** - Commemorated on the Chatham Naval Memorial, Kent, England (13).

CH/14098 Private (RMLI) **WALTER EDWIN FLINT** - Aged 30. Son of Henry and Fanny Flint of Barn Street, Stoke Newington, London and husband of Emma Ann Flint of 13, Corfield Street, Bethnal Green, London. Commemorated on the Chatham Naval Memorial, Kent, England (13).

283150 Chief Stoker **WILLIAM JOHN FOAD** - Aged 38. Son of William and Susannah Foad of Hillborough, Herne Bay and husband of Mary Ann Foad of White Cottages, Marshside, Chislet, Canterbury. Commemorated on the Chatham Naval Memorial, Kent, England (11).

231797 Able Seaman **ALBERT GEORGE FORD** - Aged 27. Son of Frederick and Charlotte Ford of 36, Golfe Road, Ilford, Essex. Commemorated on the Chatham Naval Memorial, Kent, England (9).

K/17082 Stoker 1st Class **JOHN FORWARD** - Aged 21. Born Wadhurst, Sussex, December 30, 1893. Son of William Forward of 26, Winton Street, Alfriston, Sussex. Died two days after his 21st birthday. Commemorated on the Chatham Naval Memorial, Kent, England (11).

304150 Stoker 1st Class **JOHN ROBERT FOSTER** - Commemorated on the Chatham Naval Memorial, Kent, England (11).

J/29548 Ordinary Seaman **JOHN EDWARD FRANKLIN** - Aged 18. Born Camden Town, London. Son of Sidney and Annie Franklin of 33, Delverton Road, Walworth, London. Commemorated on the Chatham Naval Memorial, Kent, England (10).

190890 Able Seaman **WILLIAM FRASER** - Aged 33. Native of Inverness. Son of Margaret Black (formerly Fraser) of 12, Cornwall Street, Edinburgh. Commemorated on the Chatham Naval Memorial, Kent, England (9).

SS/4916 Ordinary Seaman **HERBERT CHARLES FREEMAN** - Aged 19. Son of Elizabeth Freeman of 5, Abbey Place, Faversham, Kent. Buried in St. Gerrans Churchyard, Cornwall, England.

299542 (RFR/CH/B/10295) Leading Stoker **JOHN FRENCH** - Aged 39. Son of the late George French of Hadleigh, Essex. Commemorated on the Chatham Naval Memorial, Kent, England (11).

K/18988 Stoker 1st Class **THOMAS EDWARD FRICKER** - Commemorated on the Chatham Naval Memorial, Kent, England (11).

J/6739 Signalman **EDGAR NORMAN FRIGHT** - Commemorated on the Chatham Naval Memorial, Kent, England (10).

CH/14856 Corporal (RMLI) **GEORGE FREDERICK FUGGLES** - Aged 24. Son of William (late Colour Sergeant in RMLI) and Mary Fuggles of Christ's Hospital, Horsham, Sussex. Enlisted in the Royal Marines as a bugler at the age of 16 and served aboard HMS *Cadmus* at Hankow, during the Chinese Revolution. Had served on *Formidable* for around nine months. Commemorated on the Chatham Naval Memorial, Kent, England (13).

127754 Chief Armourer (Pensioner) **WILLIAM GEORGE FUGLER** - Aged 51. Son of James and Jane Fugler of Tregoney, Cornwall and husband of Emma Jane Kent Fugler of 12, Copythorn Road, North End, Portsmouth. Commemorated on the Portsmouth Naval Memorial, Hampshire, England (8).

L/4907 Officer's Steward 2nd Class **SIDNEY ALFRED FUTCHER** - Commemorated on the Chatham Naval Memorial, Kent, England (12).

SS/114909 Stoker 1st Class **JAMES GAFFNEY** - Aged 21. Son of Patrick and Mary Gaffney of 3, Vincent Terrace, Glasnevin, Dublin. Commemorated on the Chatham Naval Memorial, Kent, England (11).

K/16971 Stoker 1st Class **CHARLES GARDNER** - Aged 20. Native of Tooting, London. Son of Mr and Mrs Gardner of 70, High Street, Colliers Wood, Merton, London. Commemorated on the Chatham Naval Memorial, Kent, England (11).

M/2962 Cook's Mate **FREDERICK ROY GAUNT** - Aged 23. Native of Chislehurst, Kent. Son of Charles and Rachel Gaunt of "Wellfield," Vicarage Road, Lingfield, Surrey. Commemorated on the Chatham Naval Memorial, Kent, England (12).

239503 Able Seaman **WILLIE VICTOR GAUNT** - Commemorated on the Chatham Naval Memorial, Kent, England (9).

4626B (RNR) Seaman **CHARLES BRUCE GEAR** - Aged 31. Son of Charlotte Gear of Brough, South Nesting, Shetland. Commemorated on the Portsmouth Naval Memorial, Hampshire, England (10).

2038S (RNR) Stoker **GEORGE WILLIAM GELDARD** - Commemorated on the Chatham Naval Memorial, Kent, England (14).

L/959 Officer's Steward 3rd Class **FRED GIBBON** - Aged 23. Son of the late William and Mary Gibbon of Normanby, Yorkshire. Commemorated on the Chatham Naval Memorial, Kent, England (12).

J/29536 Boy 1st Class **ROBERT GIBSON** - Aged 18. Native of Bethnal Green, London. Son of Frances E. Pomeroy (formerly Gibson) of 13, Wellington Street, Peterborough and the late Thomas Gibson. Commemorated on the Plymouth Naval Memorial, Devon (6).

J/26317 Ordinary Seaman **ERNEST WILLIAM GINELACK** - Aged 18. Adopted son of Thomas Frederick Hensen of 32, Ayenby Road, Peckham, London. Commemorated on the Chatham Naval Memorial, Kent, England (10).

K/14520 Stoker 1st Class **THOMAS HENRY GIRLING** - Commemorated on the Chatham Naval Memorial, Kent, England (11).

229847 Signalman **ALBERT STANLEY GODTSCHALK** - Aged 28. Native of Dulwich, London. Son of Charles and Matilda Godtschalk of 9, Stoneley Road, Tottenham, London. Commemorated on the Chatham Naval Memorial, Kent, England (10).

174897 Petty Officer 1st Class **HARRY GOLDS** - Aged 38. Native of Washington, Sussex. Son of John and Harriet Golds. Commemorated on the Chatham Naval Memorial, Kent, England (9).

CH/15290 Private (RMLI) **FRANK GEORGE HOWARD GOOCH** - Aged 28. Son of Ernest and Matilda Gooch of "Deynes House," Cowlinge, Newmarket, Suffolk. Commemorated on the Chatham Naval Memorial, Kent, England (13).

Boatswain (Bosun) **WILLIAM CHARLES GOSNEY** - Aged 34. Husband of Margaret Gosney of 291, Sydney Terrace, New Road, Copnor, Portsmouth. Commemorated on the Chatham Naval Memorial, Kent, England (9).

311416 Stoker 1st Class **FRANK DAVID GOWENS** - Aged 28. Husband of Sarah Ann Gowens of 9, Hermit Road, Canning Town, London. Commemorated on the Chatham Naval Memorial, Kent, England (11).

J/13375 Able Seaman **ROBERT GEORGE GRAND** - Aged 20. Son of George and Alice Mary Grand of 125, Armes Street, North Heigham, Norwich. Commemorated on the Chatham Naval Memorial, Kent, England (9).

K/1009 Leading Stoker **SIDNEY ARTHUR GRANT** - Aged 26. Son of Frederick William and Frances Elizabeth Grant of Hartland Road, West Ham, London. Commemorated on the Chatham Naval Memorial, Kent, England (11).

224900 Able Seaman **JOHN GRANTHAM** - Aged 29. Son of Mr and Mrs J. Grantham of 66, Albert Road, Croydon and husband of Henrietta Grantham of 7, Waddon New Road, West Croydon. Commemorated on the Chatham Naval Memorial, Kent, England (9).

CH/16300 Corporal (RMLI) **ARTHUR CHARLES GRAVES** - Aged 28. Son of Arthur and Minnie Graves of Debden Village, Saffron Walden, Essex and husband of Sarah Jane Matilda Graves of 16, Gravel Walk, Rochester, Kent. Commemorated on the Chatham Naval Memorial, Kent, England (13).

J/29418 Ordinary Seaman **HORACE SYDNEY GRAY** - Commemorated on the Portsmouth Naval Memorial, Hampshire, England (8).

J/16375 Able Seaman **WILLIAM GREALEY** - Aged 20. Son of John and Mary Grealey of Wolverhampton. Commemorated on the Chatham Naval Memorial, Kent, England (9).

236720 Able Seaman **CHARLES THOMAS GREEN** - Commemorated on the Chatham Naval Memorial, Kent, England (9).

J/29539 Ordinary Seaman **CHARLES WILLIAM GREEN** - Commemorated on the Chatham Naval Memorial, Kent, England (10).

CH/17915 Private (RMLI) **BENJAMIN NEWMAN GRIMSHAW** - Aged 19. Son of Mr and Mrs W. Grimshaw of 19, Ross Street, Ebury Bridge Road, Pimlico, London. Commemorated on the Chatham Naval Memorial, Kent, England (13).

J/26892 Ordinary Seaman **GEORGE GROOM** - Aged 18. Son of John and Lizzie Groom of Little Wymondley, Stevenage, Hertfordshire. Commemorated on the Portsmouth Naval Memorial, Hampshire, England (8).

K/497 Stoker 1st Class **ROBERT GUY** - Aged 25. Son of Margaret Guy of 48, Blandford Street, Hartlepool, County Durham. Commemorated on the Chatham Naval Memorial, Kent, England (11).

CH/17587 Private (RMLI) **WILLIAM HENRY CHARLES GUYMER** - Commemorated on the Chatham Naval Memorial, Kent, England (13).

J/387 Able Seaman **NORMAN ALEXANDER HAISMAN** - Aged 22. Son of William and Caroline Haisman of Maidstone, Kent. Commemorated on the Chatham Naval Memorial, Kent, England (9).

K/20996 Stoker 1st Class **ROBERT RAYMOND HALL** - Aged 19. Son of Ann Hall and the late George Hall of 57, Eleanor Street, Cullercoats, Northumberland. Commemorated on the Chatham Naval Memorial, Kent, England (11).

Gunner **PERCIVAL HENRY HALLETT** - Resided at 8, Holmeside, Gillingham. Commemorated on the Chatham Naval Memorial, Kent, England (9).

238519 Able Seaman **ALFRED COLIN HARDS** - Aged 23. Born Tolworth, Long Ditton. Son of Alfred and Ann Jane Hards of 4, Blackshaw Road, Tooting, London. Commemorated on the Chatham Naval Memorial, Kent, England (9).

290198 Leading Stoker **HERBERT JOHN HARE** - Aged 36. Husband of Alice Amy Hare of 2, Officer's Terrace, Ospringe, Faversham, Kent. Awarded Long Service and Good Conduct Medal. Commemorated on the Chatham Naval Memorial, Kent, England (11).

J/29537 Boy 1st Class **BERNARD HARRIS** - Aged 18. Son of William Harris of 105, Carver Street, Birmingham. Commemorated on the Portsmouth Naval Memorial, Hampshire, England (8).

J/4714 Able Seaman **CHARLES HARRIS** - Commemorated on the Chatham Naval Memorial, Kent, England (9).

SS/116016 Stoker 2nd Class **WILLIAM ALBERT HARRIS** - Aged 19. Son of Mr and Mrs G. Harris of 3, Charlotte Street, Plumstead, London. Commemorated on the Chatham Naval Memorial, Kent, England (12).

PLY/16501 Private (RMLI) **WILLIAM HARRIS** - Aged 26. Son of Mr J. Harris of 8, Sutherland Road, Tottenham, London. Commemorated on the Plymouth Naval Memorial, Devon, England (7).

M/476 Electrical Artificer 3rd Class **WALTER HENRY HARRISON** - Commemorated on the Chatham Naval Memorial, Kent, England (12).

Lieutenant Commander **WILLIAM CRAWFORD HARRISON** - Commemorated on the Chatham Naval Memorial, Kent, England (8).

K/22628 Stoker 1st Class* **WILLIAM VICTOR HARRUP** - Aged 17. Son of William and Sarah Harrup of Main Street, Caldecote, Cambridge. Commemorated on the Chatham Naval Memorial, Kent, England (12) *Stoker 2nd Class on CWGC.

J/29918 Boy 1st Class **GEORGE HENRY HARWOOD** - Commemorated on the Chatham Naval Memorial, Kent, England (10).

309773 Leading Stoker **FREDERICK HECTOR HASTINGS** - Aged 29. Son of Charles and Martha Hastings of Bishopsgate, Englefield Green, Surrey. Commemorated on the Chatham Naval Memorial, Kent, England (11).

215783* Able Seaman **FREDERICK THOMAS HASWELL** - Commemorated on the Chatham Naval Memorial, Kent, England (9). *215183 on CWGC.

K/13569 Stoker 1st Class **GEORGE JOSEPH HATCH** - Aged 22. Native of Shoreditch, London. Son of George John Hatch of 301, Globe Road, Bethnal Green, London. Commemorated on the Chatham Naval Memorial, Kent, England (11).

2163U (RNR) Stoker **DAVID HATHAWAY** - Aged 35. Commemorated on the Chatham Naval Memorial, Kent, England (14).

Lieutenant **GEORGE HUGH VANS HATHORN** - Born Tezpur, Assam, June 30, 1887. Son of Chales Hugh Vans and Emily Rose Hathorn (nee Bensley) of 6, Park Place, Cheltenham, Gloucestershire (formerly Seconce Tea Estate, Assam). George was the grandson of the late Admiral George Hathorn. Eduacted at Pretoria House, Folkestone and Dover College. Joined the R.M.L.I. on September 1, 1906 and promoted to Lieutenant on July 1, 1907. Served in the West Indies, Gibraltar and in Home Waters and was appointed to HMS *Formidable* on January 25, 1914. His youger brother Second Lieutenant Noel Hathorn lost his life in Iraq on July 14, 1915 aged 24. Had Lieutenant George Hathorn survived, the Admiralty would have expressed their appreciation of the good service rendered by him on the occasion of the sinking of the vessel. In a report by Lieut. V. C. V. Soutter, senior surviving executive officer of the *Formidable* he states; *'Lieut. Hathorn collected volunteers and searched the Marines' mess deck for any gear that would float. At a time when things became critical, this officer penetrated as far aft as the ward room, using the after hatch in the port battery and aided solely by the light of a small electric torch. His passage was greatly impeded by strung hammocks. His conduct was extremely plucky, for he continued to work there, collecting chairs etc., though it was apparent to all that the ship might capsize at any moment without warning. To add to this, the water was at a dangerous level on the starboard side of the same deck.'* Commemorated on the Chatham Naval Memorial, Kent, England (13).

J/29527 Ordinary Seaman **CHARLES WILLIAM HAWKES** - Aged 19. Brother of Mrs L. H. Furley of 10, Union Road, Stratford, London. Commemorated on the Chatham Naval Memorial, Kent, England (10).

SS/4984 Ordinary Seaman **BERT HAWKINGS** - Commemorated on the Chatham Naval Memorial, Kent, England (10).

151812 Leading Seaman **FREDERICK WALTER HAWKINS** - Aged 39. Son of Henry and Sarah Ann Hawkins of Poplar, London. Commemorated on the Chatham Naval Memorial, Kent, England (9).

1511U* (RNR) Stoker **EDWARD HAYES** - Commemorated on the Plymouth Naval Memorial, Devon, England (8). *1511V on CWGC.

M/1077 Engine Room Artificer 4th Class **WILLIAM CHARLES HAYES** - Aged 21. Son of Mary Ann Hayes of 9, King's Road, Luton, Chatham. Commemorated on the Chatham Naval Memorial, Kent, England (11).

166328 Petty Officer 1st Class **WILLIAM HAYTER** - Commemorated on the Chatham Naval Memorial, Kent, England (9).

CH/18005 Private (RMLI) **CHARLES WILLIAM HEBBARDS** - Commemorated on the Chatham Naval Memorial, Kent, England (13).

171083 (RFR/CH/JA/1806) Petty Officer Stoker **ARTHUR JAMES HEDDERSON** - Aged 44. Son of Joseph and Mary Ann Hedderson and husband of Annie Eliza Rogers (formerly Hedderson) of 11, Charter Street, Gillingham, Kent. Awarded Long Service and Good Conduct Medal. Commemorated on the Chatham Naval Memorial, Kent, England (11).

SS/101624 (RFR/CH/IC/386) Stoker 1st Class **ALFRED HEMMINGS** - Aged 28. Native of Canning Town, London. Commemorated on the Chatham Naval Memorial, Kent, England (11).

343786 Ship's Steward **HARRY HENDERSON** - Aged 37. Husband of the late Lilian Jane Henderson of Sittingbourne. Commemorated on the Chatham Naval Memorial, Kent, England (12).

288374 Petty Officer Stoker **JOHN HENDERSON** - Commemorated on the Chatham Naval Memorial, Kent, England (11).

Surgeon (RNVR) **SEPTIMUS HIBBERT** - Born Brasted, near Sevenoaks July 31, 1886. Son of Charles George and Clara Hibbert (nee Heseltine) of Talbot Avenue, Bournemouth. Educated at Tonbridge School, University College, Oxford and St. George's Hospital, London, where he was House Surgeon and Physician. Joined the Navy on the outbreak of war and was appointed Surgeon of the *Formidable*. Commemorated on the Chatham Naval Memorial, Kent, England (14).

272092 Engine Room Artificer 3rd Class **ARTHUR HILL** - Aged 24. Son of Thomas Peregrine and Emma Hill of 6, Owler Lane, Pitsmoor, Sheffield. Commemorated on the Chatham Naval Memorial, Kent, England (11).

Lieutenant **EDMUND ARNOTT HILL** - Aged 25. Son of George William and Esther Hill of 21, West Hill, Highgate, London. Awarded Naval General Service Medal with bar (Persian Gulf). Commemorated on the Chatham Naval Memorial, Kent, England (8).

K/20990 Stoker 1st Class **WILLIAM JOHN HILL** - Commemorated on the Chatham Naval Memorial, Kent, England (11).

2531T (RNR) Stoker **JOHN HILLEN** - Aged 33. Husband of Kate Hillen of 3, Oxford Street, Darlington, County Durham. Commemorated on the Chatham Naval Memorial, Kent, England (14).

K/20633 Stoker 1st Class **RICHARD HENRY HOBBS** - Aged 21. Son of James Lloyd and Alice Mary Hobbs of 13, Blakenham Road, Upper Tooting, London. Commemorated on the Chatham Naval Memorial, Kent, England (11).

311196 Leading Stoker **JAMES EDWARD HOOD** - Aged 26. Son of Edward John and Rhoda Hood of Addington Green, West Malling, Kent. Commemorated on the Chatham Naval Memorial, Kent, England (11).

CH/16593 Private (RMLI) **JOHN GEORGE HOPE** - Aged 29. Husband of Mrs Hope of 44, Sturla Road, Chatham. Previously fought during the Boer War. Commemorated on the Chatham Naval Memorial, Kent, England (13).

CH/15895 Private (RMLI) **GEORGE HAROLD HOPKINS** - Aged 25. Son of Mrs M. A. Hopkins and the late James Hopkins of 19, Grosvenor Road, South Norwood, London. Commemorated on the Chatham Naval Memorial, Kent, England (13).

162720 Petty Officer **HENRY WILLIAM HOPKINS** - Commemorated on the Chatham Naval Memorial, Kent, England (9).

157792 Chief Petty Officer **WALTER HORTON** - Aged 41. Son of Mr and Mrs Horton of West Street, Deal and husband of H. E. Horton of 18, Britton Street, Gillingham, Kent. Joined the Navy aged 16 and in November 1914 completed twenty-four years service. Awarded the Good Conduct Medal and also awarded the medal for operations against the Mad Mullah. Commemorated on the Chatham Naval Memorial, Kent, England (9).

CH/10615 Corporal (RMLI) **ERNEST WILLIAM HORWOOD** - Aged 34. Husband of May Emily Gertrude Horwood of 80,Charter Street, Chatham. Commemorated on the Chatham Naval Memorial, Kent, England (13).

161990 Stoker 1st Class **GEORGE ALEXANDER HOUGHAM** - Aged 41. Son of Charles Henry and Frances Louisa Hougham of London. Commemorated on the Chatham Naval Memorial, Kent, England (11).

1338U (RNR) Leading Stoker **WILLIAM EDWARD PHILIP HOWLAND** - Son of the late Sergeant Howland of the R.M.L.I. of Upper Deal. Had been expected home on leave on January 9. Commemorated on the Chatham Naval Memorial, Kent, England (14).

CH/17518 Private (RMLI) **WILLIAM GEORGE HUDDLE** - Aged 20. Native of Willesden, London. Son of Edward and Kate Huddle of 57, Bendall Street, Lisson Grove, Marylebone, London. Commemorated on the Chatham Naval Memorial, Kent, England (13).

179832 (RFR/CH/B/5444) Able Seaman **CORNELIUS HUGHES** - Aged 38. Son of John and E. Hughes of 2, Leonard's Cottages, Ashford Common, Middlesex. Commemorated on the Chatham Naval Memorial, Kent, England (9).

J/29541 Ordinary Seaman **HENRY EDWARD HULL** - Commemorated on the Chatham Naval Memorial, Kent, England (10).

181519 Able Seaman **JOHN HUME** - Aged 37. Son of James and Isabella Hume of 178, Canongate, Edinburgh. Commemorated on the Chatham Naval Memorial, Kent, England (9).

Lieutenant (RNR) **EDMUND WILLIAM ALFRED HUMPHREY*** - Commemorated on the Chatham Naval Memorial, Kent, England (13). *EDWARD (not EDMUND) on ADM.

J/29909 Boy 1st Class **ANDREW PERCY HURST** - Commemorated on the Chatham Naval Memorial, Kent, England (10).

154553 (RFR/CH/A/1742) Chief Stoker **WILLIAM ROBERT HUTTON** - Aged 43. Son of Thomas and Harriet Hutton of Croft, Lincolnshire and husband of Agnes Annie Hutton of 99, Alexandra Road, Grimsby. Commemorated on the Chatham Naval Memorial, Kent, England (11).

CH/19290 (RMR/B/398) Private (RMLI) **FRANCIS HUXTABLE** - Commemorated on the Chatham Naval Memorial, Kent, England (13).

J/7806 Able Seaman **WALTER FRANK HYDE** - Son of Frank and Ellen Hyde of 17, Cromwell Road, Grays, Essex. Commemorated on the Chatham Naval Memorial, Kent, England (9).

CH/17919 Private (RMLI) **GEORGE RICHARD JAMES INGS** - Aged 20. Son of George and Emma Ings of 66, Canning Road, Wealdstone, Harrow, Middlesex. Commemorated on the Chatham Naval Memorial, Kent, England (13).

J/29529 Boy 1st Class **ERNEST LEON JACKSON** - Commemorated on the Chatham Naval Memorial, Kent, England (10).

CH/17298 Private (RMLI) **HAROLD MUSCROFT JACKSON** - Aged 21. Son of John Bernard and Clara Jackson of 61, Bankfield Terrace, Burley, Leeds. Commemorated on the Chatham Naval Memorial, Kent, England (13).

203908 Petty Officer **HENRY PURCELL JAQUES** - Aged 31. Son of George and Mary Jaques of 39, Sandside, Scarborough. Commemorated on the Chatham Naval Memorial, Kent, England (9).

SS/101359 (RFR/CH/B/6820) **JOB JENKINS** - Commemorated on the Chatham Naval Memorial, Kent, England (11).

J/29555 Boy 1st Class **EDWARD WILLIAM CAPPS JENNER** - Aged 17. Son of Robert Capps and Elsie Capps Jenner of 12, Spurgeon Score, Lowestoft. Commemorated on the Chatham Naval Memorial, Kent, England (10).

287411 Petty Officer Stoker **EDWARD JOBLING** - Aged 37. Son of the late Gilbert and Elizabeth Jobling of Newbiggin-by-the-Sea, Northumberland. Commemorated on the Chatham Naval Memorial, Kent, England (11).

SS/115863 Stoker 2nd Class **ROBERT WILLIAM JOHNSON** - Aged 20. Son of William and Barbara Ellen Johnson of 19, Dene Terrace, Murton Colliery, County Durham. Commemorated on the Chatham Naval Memorial, Kent, England (12).

CH/17866 Private (RMLI) **CHARLES JOHN WILLIAM JONES** - Aged 19. Born London. Son of John Thomas and Kate Jones of 2,Whitegate Road, Southend-on-Sea, Essex. Commemorated on the Chatham Naval Memorial, Kent, England (13).

SS/4899 Ordinary Seaman **SAMUEL HENRY JONES** - Commemorated on the Chatham Naval Memorial, Kent, England (10).

J/29958 Boy 1st Class **WALTER ALFRED JONES** - Aged 17. Son of George Jones of 86, Hatherley Gardens, East Ham, London. Commemorated on the Chatham Naval Memorial, Kent, England (10).

L/4071 Officer's Steward 2nd Class **GEORGE CHRISTOPHER KEECH** - Aged 19. Born Deal, Kent. Son of Joseph (ex-R.M.L.I.) and Mary Ann Keech of 96, Whitworth Road, Alverstoke, Gosport, Hampshire. Commemorated on the Chatham Naval Memorial, Kent, England (12).

1966T (RNR) Stoker **JOHN KELLY** - Aged 34. Son of Patrick and Catherine Misset Kelly of Hartlepool. Commemorated on the Chatham Naval Memorial, Kent, England (14).

CH/12234 Private (RMLI) **ROBERT WALTER KEMP** - Aged 27. Husband of Clara Elizabeth Kemp of 232, Castle Road, Luton, Chatham. Commemorated on the Chatham Naval Memorial, Kent, England (13).

344024 Shipwright 2nd Class **THOMAS KENNEDY** - Commemorated on the Chatham Naval Memorial, Kent, England (12).

J/31055 Ordinary Seaman **THOMAS ABNER KENT** - Aged 18. Son of Alice Lee (formerly Kent) of 55, Bailgate Lincoln and the late J.P. Kent. Commemorated on the Plymouth Naval Memorial, Devon, England (6).

J/28855 Boy 1st Class **WILLIAM HENRY KENT** - Commemorated on the Chatham Naval Memorial, Kent, England (10).

M/1182 Cook's Mate **JOHN WILLIAM PETTIFER KERSWELL** - Resided in Lower Rainham. Commemorated on the Chatham Naval Memorial, Kent, England (12).

298725 Petty Officer Stoker **BERTIE KIFF** - Commemorated on the Chatham Naval Memorial, Kent, England (11).

SS/109432 Stoker 1st Class **GEORGE KING** - Commemorated on the Chatham Naval Memorial, Kent, England (11).

CH/14743 Private (RMLI) **GEORGE FREDERICK KING** - Aged 28. Son of George and Emma King of 82, Paradise Street, Rotherhithe, London. Commemorated on the Chatham Naval Memorial, Kent, England (13).

K/13571* Stoker 1st Class **SAMUEL KINGSTON** - Aged 22. Son of Mr and Mrs Kingston of 8, West Street, Grove Road, Walthamstow, London. Commemorated on the Chatham Naval Memorial, Kent, England (11). *K/113571 on CWGC.

M/10986 Senior Reserve Attendant **ALBERT EDWARD KINLAY** - Aged 23. Adopted son of Mrs Kinlay of 144, Henry Street, Crewe, Cheshire. Member of the R.N. Aux. Sick Berth Reserve. Previously employed in Crewe Works. Died on his birthday. Commemorated on the Chatham Naval Memorial, Kent, England (15).

J/26165 Ordinary Seaman **WILLIAM EDWARD KINSMAN** - Commemorated on the Chatham Naval Memorial, Kent, England (10).

J/28455 Ordinary Seaman **WILLIAM KIRBY** - Commemorated on the Chatham Naval Memorial, Kent, England (10).

347431 Ship's Steward 2nd Class **ARCHIBALD SAMUEL HENRY THOMAS KISSICK** - Aged 24. Son of Louisa Kissick and the late Archibald Kissick (former Master At Arms, Royal Navy) of Eddington Farm, St. Helens, Isle of Wight. Commemorated on the Chatham Naval Memorial, Kent, England (12).

232351 Able Seaman **WILLIAM ANDREW KNOWLES** - Aged 27. Son of Mr and Mrs Knowles of 92, Monier Road, Bow, London. Commemorated on the Chatham Naval Memorial, Kent, England (9).

M/2391 Sick Berth Attendant **THOMAS LAMING** - Aged 23. Son of Thomas and Mary Elizabeth Laming of 48, Laburnum Road, Wimbledon, London. Commemorated on the Chatham Naval Memorial, Kent, England (12).

CH/14623 Private (RMLI) **FREDERICK LANE** - Aged 30. Husband of Mary Ann Lane of 24, Askew Crescent, Shepherd's Bush, London. Commemorated on the Chatham Naval Memorial, Kent, England (13).

238393 Able Seaman **HENRY ALFRED CHARLES LANE** - Aged 24. Son of William Henry and Emma Louise Lane of 27, Talfourd Road, Peckham, London. Commemorated on the Chatham Naval Memorial, Kent, England (9).

CH/18064 Private (RMLI) **ROBERT ALLEN LAWRENCE** - Commemorated on the Chatham Naval Memorial, Kent, England (13).

K/20989 Stoker 1st Class **WILLIAM LAWRENCE** - Aged 19. Nephew of John Lawrence of 1, Tamplin Mews, Warlock Road, Paddington, London. Commemorated on the Chatham Naval Memorial, Kent, England (11).

M/6882 Ship's Steward Assistant **REGINALD ALFRED LAWS** - Aged 21. Son of Harry David and Alice Louisa Madge Laws of 18, Copnor Road, Portsmouth. Commemorated on the Chatham Naval Memorial, Kent, England (12).

310947 Stoker 1st Class **WILLIAM CHARLES LEACH** - Aged 28. Son of Fredrick and Helen Leach of Southwick and husband of Hannah Rose Leach of Honeysuckle Cottage, Priest Lane, Shenfield. Commemorated on the Chatham Naval Memorial, Kent, England (11).

310039 Stoker 1st Class **JAMES LEARY** - Aged 28. Son of James and the late Elizabeth Leary of Wexford. Commemorated on the Chatham Naval Memorial, Kent, England (11).

CH/16931 Private (RMLI) **FREDERICK ARTHUR LEE** - Aged 21. Son of James Lee of 25, Nelson Street. Deal, Kent. Previously served aboard HMS *Cyclops*, a repair ship in the Mediterranean. Had served in the Royal Marines about four years. Three brothers and three brothers-in-law also served during the war. Commemorated on the Chatham Naval Memorial, Kent, England (13).

187766 (RFR/CH/B/4471) Petty Officer 1st Class **RICHARDSON DUNBAR LESLIE** - Commemorated on the Chatham Naval Memorial, Kent, England (9).

CH/17291 Private (RMLI) **FRANK THOMAS LEWIS*** - Aged 20. Native of Ramsgate. Son of George and Elizabeth Lewis of 4, Dawes Street, Gillingham, Kent. Commemorated on the Chatham Naval Memorial, Kent, England (13). *FRED (not FRANK) on CWGC.

K/20169 Stoker 1st Class **THOMAS EDWARD LIDDIARD** - Aged 20. Son of George and Elizabeth Liddiard of 46, Armitage Road, East Greenwich, London. Commemorated on the Chatham Naval Memorial, Kent, England (11).

Fleet Paymaster **PERCY JOHN LING** - Commemorated on the Chatham Naval Memorial, Kent, England (9).

CH/17286 Private (RMLI) **ROBERT ARTHUR LITTLE** - Commemorated on the Chatham Naval Memorial, Kent, England (13).

CH/17279 Private (RMLI) **JOHN WILLIAM LIVSEY** - Aged 20. Son of John Thomas and Ann Livsey of 10, Palm Street, Boothtown, Halifax, Yorkshire. Commemorated on the Chatham Naval Memorial, Kent, England (13).

184048 (RFR/CH/B/5991) Petty Officer 2nd Class **EDWARD LLOYD** - Aged 33. Son of Robert and Ann Lloyd and husband of Catherine Lloyd of 23, Prince William Street, Dingle, Liverpool. Commemorated on the Chatham Naval Memorial, Kent, England (9).

347103 Sailmaker **FREDERICK JAMES LOCK** - Aged 30. Native of Halling, Kent. Husband of Minnie Lock of 87, New Street, Ashford, Kent. Commemorated on the Chatham Naval Memorial, Kent, England (10).

181617 Petty Officer 1st Class **ALEXANDER THOMAS VIVIAN LOOKER** - Aged 36. Son of Elias Looker of Twickenham and husband of Ada Elizabeth Looker of 163, Nelson Road, Whitton, Twickenham. Commemorated on the Chatham Naval Memorial, Kent, England (9).

181350 Leading Seaman **DAVID LORD** - Aged 36. Son of David and Lavinia Lord of Bolton, Lancashire. Commemorated on the Chatham Naval Memorial, Kent, England (9).

Captain **ARTHUR NOEL LOXLEY** - Aged 40. Son of Alice and the late Reverend Arthur Loxley of "The Little Cloisters" Gloucester and husband of Gladys Maud Loxley of Norcott Court, Northchurch, Hertfordshire. Two other brothers also lost their lives during World War One. Commemorated on the Chatham Naval Memorial, Kent, England (9).

J/29528 Boy 1st Class **CLIFFORD CHARLES LUCAS** - Son of William George and Elizabeth Lucas of 19, New Street, Weston-Super-Mare. Commemorated on the Plymouth Naval Memorial, Devon, England (6).

220867 Able Seaman **WILLIAM JOHN CASSIMER THOMAS MACDONALD** - Commemorated on the Chatham Naval Memorial, Kent, England (9).

J/29553 Boy 1st Class **HENRY WILLIAM JOHN MACKLEY** - Aged 17. Son of Mr H. R. and Alice Mackley of 9, St. John's Retreat, North Street, Barking, Essex. Commemorated on the Chatham Naval Memorial, Kent, England (10).

311779 Leading Stoker **WILLIAM DENNIS MALCHER** - Aged 26. Husband of Grace Dorothy Bishop (formerly Malcher) of 13, Gladeswood Road, Belvedere, Kent. Awarded Messina Medal. Commemorated on the Chatham Naval Memorial, Kent, England (11).

J/6412 Able Seaman **CHARLES ALFRED HORACE MANKIN** - Aged 24. Native of Walthamstow, London. Commemorated on the Chatham Naval Memorial, Kent, England (9).

SS/4921 Ordinary Seaman **HARRY MARCHAM** - Aged 20. Born Penge, London. Son of William Oliver and F. Marcham of 69, Hawthorne Grove, Penge, London. Commemorated on the Chatham Naval Memorial, Kent, England (10).

K/821 Leading Stoker **ERNEST MARSH** - Aged 24. Son of George and Annie Marsh of Boghurst Cottage, Cobham, Gravesend, Kent. Commemorated on the Chatham Naval Memorial, Kent, England (11).

J/5441 Able Seaman **THOMAS JAMES MARSH** - Aged 21. Son of Thomas and Jane Marsh of 10, Darlington Street, Folkestone. Commemorated on the Chatham Naval Memorial, Kent, England (9).

J/29949 Boy 1st Class **EDWARD VICTOR MARSHALL** - Commemorated on the Portsmouth Naval Memorial, Hampshire, England (8).

CH/17543 Private (RMLI) **FREDERICK JOSEPH MARTIN** - Aged 21. Son of Mr E. and Mrs J. H. Martin of Hampton, Middlesex. Commemorated on the Chatham Naval Memorial, Kent, England (13).

SS/102144 (RFR/CH/IC/418) Stoker 1st Class **GEORGE HENRY MARTIN** - Aged 36. Son of Jasper and Katherine Martin of London and husband of Katherine Jane Martin of 1, Berrymead Gardens, Acton, London. Commemorated on the Chatham Naval Memorial, Kent, England (11).

227705 Able Seaman **WILLIAM HENRY MARTIN** - Aged 26. Husband of Ada Blanche Martin of 63, North Lane, Canterbury. Commemorated on the Chatham Naval Memorial, Kent, England (9).

Midshipman **TREVOR MUNRO HOARE MASTERS** - Aged 16. Son of Lieutenant C. M. Masters (Royal Navy) and S. E. Masters of "Whiteknights," The Leazes, Newcastle-upon-Tyne. Commemorated on the Chatham Naval Memorial, Kent, England (8).

2122T (RNR) Stoker **HENRY MATES** - Aged 33. Son of Richard and Ellen Mates of 20, Beecham Street, South Bank, Yorkshire. Commemorated on the Chatham Naval Memorial, Kent, England (14).

J/29954 Boy 1st Class **GEORGE CLAUDE MATTHEWS** - Aged 17. Son of Mr and Mrs W. H. Matthews of Goff's Corner, Sturminster Newton, Dorset. Commemorated on the Portsmouth Naval Memorial, Hampshire, England (8).

SS/106850 (RFR/CH/B/9452) Stoker 1st Class **GEORGE WILLIAM MATTHEWS** - Aged 26. Son of John Albert and Ellen Matthews of Stourport, Worcestershire. Commemorated on the Chatham Naval Memorial, Kent, England (11).

347388 Carpenter's Crew **EDWARD WALLACE MAXWELL*** - Commemorated on the Chatham Naval Memorial, Kent, England (12). *Served as WILLIAM LEIGH.

CH/17143 Private (RMLI) **HENRY GEORGE MAY** - Aged 23. Son of Ellen Jane May of 15, Dolphin Street, Deal, Kent. Had completed three years in the Royal Marines in August 1914. In a letter received by his mother written on Boxing Day, he had written *'he would be glad to have a go at the Germans.'* Commemorated on the Chatham Naval Memorial, Kent, England (13).

K/13570 Stoker 1st Class **FREDERICK GEORGE MAYES** - Commemorated on the Chatham Naval Memorial, Kent, England (11).

215399 Able Seaman **GEORGE McCLURG*** - Aged 30. Born Belfast. Son of the late James and Anna Maria Fleeten McClurg.* Commemorated on the Chatham Naval Memorial, Kent, England (9). *McLURG on CWGC.

K/16979 Stoker 1st Class **CHARLES JAMES McCLURKIN** - Commemorated on the Chatham Naval Memorial, Kent, England (11).

M/5240 Painter 2nd Class **WALTER VALENTINE McDONALD** - Aged 25. Son of Walter and Adelina McDonald of 34, Telham Road, East Ham, London. Commemorated on the Chatham Naval Memorial, Kent, England (12).

K/706 Petty Officer Stoker **JAMES McLAREN** - Aged 25. Husband of E. G. McLaren of 73, Spa Road, Bermondsey, London. Commemorated on the Chatham Naval Memorial, Kent, England (11).

2850C (RNR) Seaman **MALCOLM McLEAN** - Aged 44. Son of Donald and Annie McLean of Breasclete, Stornoway, Ross-shire. Commemorated on the Chatham Naval Memorial, Kent, England (14).

298357 Stoker 1st Class **FREDERICK MEAD** - Buried Burton Bradstock (St. Mary) Church Cemetery, Dorset.

Surgeon **WILLIAM MEARNS** - Born Gateshead December 7, 1884. Son of Eldest son of William and Mary Mearns (nee Mellis) of 22, Bewick Road, Gateshead. Educated at Aldenham School and later at Aberdeen University, graduating M. B., Ch. B., in 1908. Entered the Navy in the same year and served aboard HMS *Action* 1909-1910; HMS *Redbreast* in the Persian Gulf, 1910-1911; HMS *Teal*, in the Upper Yangtse River 1911-1914. His father was a former Lt. Gen.of the Royal Army Medical Corps and at the time of the *Formidable's* sinking, was attached to the Royal Engineers. Commemorated on the Chatham Naval Memorial, Kent, England (9).

J/4085 Able Seaman **GEORGE EDWARD MEEKUMS** - Son of Margaret Meekums of 46, Earl Street, Plumstead, London. Commemorated on the Chatham Naval Memorial, Kent, England (9).

J/16840 Able Seaman **JOHN MEGGESON** - Commemorated on the Chatham Naval Memorial, Kent, England (9).

J/15440 Ordinary Seaman* **WALTER ERNEST MELHUISH***- Aged 18. Son of Ernest and Mary Melhuish* of 5x, Peabody Avenue, Ebury Bridge, London. Commemorated on the Chatham Naval Memorial, Kent, England (10). *Ordinary Signalman and MELLUISH on CWGC.

J/29533 Boy 1st Class **FREDERICK MILLER** - Aged 18. Son of Fred and E. Miller of 361, High Road, Streatham, London. Commemorated on the Portsmouth Naval Memorial, Hampshire, England (8).

SS/106674 (RFR/CH/B/9434) Stoker 1st Class **JOHN MITCHELL** - Husband of Eleanor Mitchell of 3, Wyndham Road, Camberwell, London. Commemorated on the Chatham Naval Memorial, Kent, England (11).

J/25866 Boy 1st Class **WILLIAM MOAT** - Aged 16. Son of William and Emily Moat of College Street, Sutton, Hull. Commemorated on the Chatham Naval Memorial, Kent, England (10).

213625 Able Seaman **PHILIP MOORE** - Son of Mr and Mrs Moore of High Street, Great Wakering, Essex and husband of Mrs F. E. Smith (formerly Moore) of 6, Lovelane Cottages, Shoeburyness, Essex. Commemorated on the Chatham Naval Memorial, Kent, England (9).

196630 Petty Officer Telegraphist **WALTER WILLIAM MOORE** - Aged 32. Son of Walter William (Chief Petty Officer, Royal Navy) and Clara Moore and husband of Marguerite Beatrice Moore of Heathfield, Oakleigh Road, Whetstone, London. Commemorated on the Chatham Naval Memorial, Kent, England (10).

J/28437 Ordinary Seaman **FREDERICK BARTER MORGAN** - Aged 18. Son of Thomas and Mary Jane Morgan of 16, Severn Street, Newtown, Mont. Commemorated on the Plymouth Naval Memorial, Devon, England (6).

Midshipman **JOHN WALTER MORRICE** - Commemorated on the Chatham Naval Memorial, Kent, England (8).

166709 Petty Officer 1st Class **ALFRED ERNEST MORRISON*** - Aged 38. Husband of Margaret Morrison of 98, Old Bidston Road, Birkenhead, Cheshire. Commemorated on the Chatham Naval Memorial, Kent, England (9). *ALBERT (not ALFRED) on CWGC.

J/29892 Boy 1st Class **JOHN THOMAS MORRISON** - Commemorated on the Plymouth Naval Memorial, Devon, England (6).

J/9918 Telegraphist **WILLIAM FREDERICK MORRISON** - Aged 20. Son of William Henry and Harriet Morrison of 244, Burrage Road, Plumstead, London. Commemorated on the Chatham Naval Memorial, Kent, England (10).

J/26479 Boy 1st Class **WALTER MUDDLE** - Aged 17. Son of Mr and Mrs Muddle of 8, Wade Street, Poplar, London. Commemorated on the Chatham Naval Memorial, Kent, England (10).

SS/109831 Stoker 1st Class **DESMOND MURPHY** - Aged 24. Son of the late Mr and Mrs Patrick Murphy of 21, Sixth Avenue, Fazakerley, Liverpool. Commemorated on the Chatham Naval Memorial, Kent, England (12).

1243U (RNR) Stoker **GEORGE MURPHY** - Commemorated on the Chatham Naval Memorial, Kent, England (14).

CH/17000 Private (RMLI) **SAMUEL THOMAS NAYLOR** - Son of Samuel and Phoebe Naylor of 42, Bridge Road, Toll End, Tipton, Staffordshire. Commemorated on the Chatham Naval Memorial, Kent, England (13).

CH/17878 Private (RMLI) **WILLIAM JOHN NEWELL** - Commemorated on the Chatham Naval Memorial, Kent, England (13).

J/22769 Ordinary Signalman **PERCY DAVID NEWING** - Aged 18. Native of Walmer, Kent. Son of George and Elizabeth Newing of 44, Stafford Street, Gillingham, Kent. Commemorated on the Chatham Naval Memorial, Kent, England (10).

223925 Able Seaman **PATRICK NEWMAN** - Commemorated on the Chatham Naval Memorial, Kent, England (9).

215509 Able Seaman **WILLIAM JOHN NEWSON** - Aged 30. Son of Charles Munro and Louisa Newson of 16, Bond Street, Ipswich. Commemorated on the Chatham Naval Memorial, Kent, England (9).

Warrant Engineer (RNR) **GEORGE NEWTON** - Commemorated on the Chatham Naval Memorial, Kent, England (13).

307479 Blacksmith's Mate **ALBERT HENRY GEORGE NICHOLLS** - Aged 27. Husband of Florence Noble (formerly Nicholls) of 7, Warner Street, Chatham. Commemorated on the Chatham Naval Memorial, Kent, England (12).

CH/14768 Private (RMLI) **HERBERT EDWARD NICHOLLS** - Commemorated on the Chatham Naval Memorial, Kent, England (13).

353324 Officer's Steward 1st Class **RICHARD CHARLES NOAKES** - Commemorated on the Chatham Naval Memorial, Kent, England (12).

CH/16945 Private (RMLI) **ERNEST EDWARD NOBES** - Aged 21. Son of Ernest Nobes of 128, Elgar Road, Reading, Berkshire. Commemorated on the Chatham Naval Memorial, Kent, England (13).

J/22908 Signal Boy **FREDERICK NORMAN** - Born November 28, 1897. Son of Mr and Mrs W. Norman of 88, Elm Road, Wisbech, Cambridgeshire. Former pupil of March Grammar School (January 12, 1911 - August 29, 1912). His body was washed ashore at Portland on February 6, 1915, over a month after the sinking. Buried March Cemetery, Cambridgeshire (A. 361).

SS/103011 (RFR/CH/B/7665) Stoker 1st Class **HERBERT NORRIS** - Aged 28. Son of James John and Catherine Norris of 74, Cambridge Street, Camberwell, London. Commemorated on the Chatham Naval Memorial, Kent, England (12).

312071 Stoker 1st Class **FREDERICK NORTH** - Aged 27. Son of James and Annie North of Church Street, Thame, Oxfordshire and husband of Frances Jane North of Church End, Tempsford, Sandy, Bedfordshire. Commemorated on the Chatham Naval Memorial, Kent, England (12).

SS/110581 Stoker 1st Class **RICHARD MARTIN ODELL*** - Aged 25. Son of Bessie and the late Stephen Odell* of 25, Hitchin Hill, Hitchin, Hertfordshire. Commemorated on the Chatham Naval Memorial, Kent, England (12). *O'DELL on CWGC.

J/26419 Boy Telegraphist* **GEORGE PERCIVAL OLDAKER** - Commemorated on the Chatham Naval Memorial, Kent, England (10). *Boy 2nd Class on ADM.

CH/17306 Private (RMLI) **HARRY WRIGHT OSTICK** - Aged 22. Son of John Henry and Mary Ostick of 25, Water Lane, Moorgate, Retford, Nottinghamshire. Commemorated on the Chatham Naval Memorial, Kent, England (13).

CH/16582 Private (RMLI) **JOSEPH JOSHUA JOHN OWENS** - Aged 21. Native of Belvedere, Kent. Son of Joseph George and Annie Owens of 24, Maximfeldt Road, Erith, Kent. Commemorated on the Chatham Naval Memorial, Kent, England (13).

J/31624 Able Seaman **SAMUEL JAMES OWENS** - Aged 21. Son of the late Thomas and Letitia Owens of Belfast. Commemorated on the Chatham Naval Memorial, Kent, England (9).

J/14888 Able Seaman **ALBERT EDWARD OXFORD** - Aged 18. Son of William and Ada Oxford of 147, High Road, Leyton, Essex. Commemorated on the Chatham Naval Memorial, Kent, England (9).

J/29550 Boy 1st Class **REUBEN EDWARD PARISH** - Aged 17. Son of Edward Parish of 2, Ivy Cottages, Hardaway Head, Barnstaple, Devon. Commemorated on the Plymouth Naval Memorial, Devon, England (6).

J/950 Able Seaman **EDWIN MORTIMORE PARKER** - Commemorated on the Chatham Naval Memorial, Kent, England (9).

SS/106583 (RFR/CH/B/9349) Stoker 1st Class **HARRY WALTER PARKER** - Aged 27. Son of Walter and Emma Parker of Grays, Essex. Commemorated on the Chatham Naval Memorial, Kent, England (12).

174534 Able Seaman **JAMES WELDON PARKER** - Aged 37. Son of James Weldon and Elizabeth Weldon Parker of Gateshead, County Durham. Commemorated on the Chatham Naval Memorial, Kent, England (9).

CH/17831 Private (RMLI) **ROBERT RICHARD PARRY** - Aged 18. Son of James and Mary Elizabeth Parry of 75, Whitland Road, Fairfield, Liverpool. Commemorated on the Chatham Naval Memorial, Kent, England (13).

5856A (RNR) Seaman **CHARLES FREDERICK PARSK** - Aged 21. Son of Walter Parsk of 4, Epsom Terrace, Kirkley Run South, Lowestoft. Commemorated on the Chatham Naval Memorial, Kent, England (14).

CH/17276 Private (RMLI) **HENRY PASCALL** - Aged 22. Son of Henry and Elizabeth Pascall of Barking, Essex. Commemorated on the Chatham Naval Memorial, Kent, England (13).

SS/4915 Ordinary Seaman **EDWARD REGINALD ERNEST PAY** - Aged 19. Son of Edward and Annie Pay of Staple Street, Hernhill, Faversham, Kent. Commemorated on the Chatham Naval Memorial, Kent, England (10).

M/216 Leading Cooks Mate **FREDERICK PAYNE** - Son of Frederick and Annie Payne of Chatham and husband of Edith Maud Payne of 7, Alfred Street, Chatham. Commemorated on the Chatham Naval Memorial, Kent, England (12).

K/9231 Leading Stoker **HERBERT JAMES PAYNE** - Commemorated on the Chatham Naval Memorial, Kent, England (11).

K/516 Leading Stoker **JOHN WILLIAM PELLS** - Buried King's Lynn Cemetery, Norfolk, England (Y. 268).

J/26891 Ordinary Seaman **JOSEPH ROGERSON PERCIVAL** - Aged 18. Son of Abraham and Elizabeth Percival of Ivy Cottage, Rockcliffe, Carlisle. Commemorated on the Plymouth Naval Memorial, Devon, England (6).

J/4183 Leading Seaman **OSCAR REGINALD PERKINS** - Aged 21. Son of Philip Perkins of 34, Commerell Street, Greenwich, London. Commemorated on the Chatham Naval Memorial, Kent, England (9).

K/1348* Leading Stoker **CHARLES PETTITT** - Aged 25. Son of John and Jane Pettitt of The Lodge, Bromswell, Woodbridge, Suffolk. Commemorated on the Chatham Naval Memorial, Kent, England (11) *R/1348 on CWGC.

298089 Petty Officer Stoker **JOHN PETTYFER** - Aged 31. Son of Mr and Mrs Pettyfer of Chapel Street, Woolwich, London and husband of Rebecca Emily Pettyfer of 45, Quinn's Buildings, Popham Street, Islington, London. Commemorated on the Chatham Naval Memorial, Kent, England (11).

CH/12415 Private (RMLI) **HERBERT STANLEY PHILLIPS** - Aged 32. Son of Walter Phillips and husband of Edith Mary Phillips of 166, Castle Road, Luton, Chatham. Commemorated on the Chatham Naval Memorial, Kent, England (13).

295127 Mechanician **HARRY PHIPPS** - Aged 41. Son of Enoch and Annie Phipps of Yew Cottage, Victoria Avenue, Borrowash, Derbyshire. Resided in Church Road, Gillingham. Commemorated on the Chatham Naval Memorial, Kent, England (11).

L/4340 Officer's Cook 3rd Class* **PERCY JAMES PIKE** - Aged 21. Son of the late Edmund Pike of 34, Church Street, Gillingham, Kent. Commemorated on the Chatham Naval Memorial, Kent, England (12). *Officer's Steward 3rd Class on CWGC.

208727 Petty Officer **ALBERT EDWARD PIPE** - Aged 30. Son of William and Rose Pipe of Nacton, Suffolk and husband of Edith Florence Pipe of 100, Dover Road, Ipswich, Suffolk. Commemorated on the Chatham Naval Memorial, Kent, England (9).

236288 Able Seaman **JOSEPH PLUCK** - Aged 24. Son of Jane Catherine Pluck of 53, Blackthorne Street, Devons Road, Bow, London c. Chatham Naval Memorial, Kent, England (10).

J/24838 Signal Boy **STANLEY POOLE** - Native of Battersea, London. Son of Mr and Mrs Poole of 33, Cathall Road, Leytonstone, London. Commemorated on the Chatham Naval Memorial, Kent, England (10).

191310 Leading Seaman **WILLIAM JAMES PORT** - Aged 36. Son of Mr J. D. and Mrs L. Port of 2, Manchester Villas, Crescent Road, Birchington, Kent. Awarded the Long Service and Good Conduct Medal. Commemorated on the Chatham Naval Memorial, Kent, England (9).

211556 (RFR/PO/B/10910) Leading Signalman **ALBERT EDWARD PORTER** - Commemorated on the Portsmouth Naval Memorial, Hampshire, England (8).

K/20691 Stoker 1st Class **WILLIAM JOHN PORTER** - Aged 26. Born Woolwich. Son of William John Porter of 27, Sirdar Road, Bramford Road, Ipswich. Commemorated on the Chatham Naval Memorial, Kent, England (12).

239121 Able Seaman **WILLIAM POSTLETHWAITE** - Aged 24. Son of Robert Wilson Postlethwaite of 9, Joshua Street, Everton, Liverpool and husband of Ellen Postlethwaite. Commemorated on the Chatham Naval Memorial, Kent, England (10).

J/15117 Able Seaman **HARRY CLIFFORD POTTER** - Aged 19. Son of Harry and Alice Potter of 3, Long's Cottages, Weston Green, Thames Ditton, Surrey. Commemorated on the Chatham Naval Memorial, Kent, England (10).

342186 Painter 1st Class **CHARLES VICTOR POTTS** - Aged 38. Son of Charles Pool and Mary Rebecca Potts of Poplar, London. Commemorated on the Chatham Naval Memorial, Kent, England (12).

J/10540 Ordinary Seaman **CECIL FRANK POWELL** - Commemorated on the Chatham Naval Memorial, Kent, England (10).

K/6341 Stoker 1st Class **JAMES GEORGE PRETIOUS** - Commemorated on the Chatham Naval Memorial, Kent, England (12).

173317 Chief Writer **THOMAS HENRY PURDY** - Aged 40. Son of John Dryden and Isabella Purdy of Sheerness and husband of Alice Maud Purdy of 13, Wells Road, Upper Sydenham,

London. Awarded Royal Humane Society's Medal. Commemorated on the Chatham Naval Memorial, Kent, England (12).

239959 Able Seaman **WALTER QUICK** - Aged 24. Son of Joseph and Catherine Quick of 13, Melville Street, Princes Park, Liverpool. Commemorated on the Chatham Naval Memorial, Kent, England (10).

K/17055 Stoker 1st Class **GEORGE DAGONET RAINBIRD** - Commemorated on the Chatham Naval Memorial, Kent, England (12).

SS/109202 Stoker 1st Class **JOHN WILLIAM RAMSDEN** - Commemorated on the Chatham Naval Memorial, Kent, England (12).

J/9472 Signalman **WILLIAM GEORGE RAVENHILL** - Aged 21. Born Hampstead, London. Son of Jeremiah and Emily Ada Ravenhill of 48, Carlton Street, Kentish Town, London. Commemorated on the Chatham Naval Memorial, Kent, England (10).

CH/11358 Sergeant (RMLI) **JOHN LANCELOT REED** - Aged 29. Born Lowestoft. Son of John Lancelot and Mary Reed and husband of Ellen Reed of 75, Mount Road, Chatham. Resided at 16, Ernest Road, Chatham. Commemorated on the Chatham Naval Memorial, Kent, England (13).

312284 Leading Stoker **SAMUEL JOHN REED** - Commemorated on the Chatham Naval Memorial, Kent, England (11).

CH/17153 Bugler (RMLI) **STANLEY CHRISTOPHER REED** - Aged 16. Son of William and Margaret Reed of 45, Skinner Street, Chatham. Awarded Royal Humane (Life Saving) Society's Certificate. Commemorated on the Chatham Naval Memorial, Kent, England (13).

343606 Carpenter's Mate **GEORGE RICHARDSON** - Aged 29. Son of Mr G. and Mrs M. F. Richardson of 126, Berridge Road, Sheerness. Commemorated on the Chatham Naval Memorial, Kent, England (12).

M/7475 Armourer's Crew **LEONARD CHARLES RICHARDSON** - Aged 20. Son of Frederick and Elizabeth Richardson of 1, Ridler Place, Holland Street, Blackfriars, London. Commemorated on the Chatham Naval Memorial, Kent, England (12).

191918 Petty Officer **THOMAS RICHARDSON** - Aged 33. Son of James Richardson of Silloth, Cumberland and husband of Louisa Richardson of 6, Tot Hill Terrace, Minster, Ramsgate. Commemorated on the Chatham Naval Memorial, Kent, England (9).

284906 Stoker 1st Class **CHARLES RILEY** - Brother of Alfred Riley of 95, Military Avenue, Shorncliffe. Commemorated on the Chatham Naval Memorial, Kent, England (12).

M/4157 Engine Room Artificer 4th Class **JOHN RITCHIE** - Aged 24. Son of Joseph and Sarah Ritchie of 257, Maria Street, Elswick, Newcastle-upon-Tyne. Commemorated on the Chatham Naval Memorial, Kent, England (11).

185730 Able Seaman **JOHN ROBERTSON*** - Aged 39. Native of Forfar. Son of Alexander and Jane Robertson of 11, Herons Lane, Lochee, Dundee. Commemorated on the Chatham Naval Memorial, Kent, England (10). *ALEXANDER (not JOHN) on CWGC.

THE SINKING OF HMS FORMIDABLE

Chaplain the Reverend **GEORGE BROOKE ROBINSON** - Former curate of Burton Bradstock. Resided in West Bay. Commemorated on the Chatham Naval Memorial, Kent, England (9).

J/10080 Able Seaman **WESLEY ROBINSON** - Son of Ruth Robinson of 32, Clifford Street, Byker, Newcastle-upon-Tyne. Commemorated on the Chatham Naval Memorial, Kent, England (10).

218604 Able Seaman **CHARLES FREDERICK ROGERS** - Aged 30. Husband of Alice Rogers of 6, Burlington Parade, Cricklewood, London. Commemorated on the Chatham Naval Memorial, Kent, England (10).

CH/17544 Private (RMLI) **JAMES ROLLINGS** - Commemorated on the Chatham Naval Memorial, Kent, England (13).

CH/17899 Private (RMLI) **FRANK LOUIS ROYES** - Aged 18. Second son of Mr and Mrs E. G. Royes of 1, Camden Cottages, Mill Road, Deal, Kent. His brother Private Thomas Percy Royes, also of the Royal Light Marine Infantry, died on September 22, 1914 when HMS *Aboukir* was sunk off the Hook of Holland. The last letter recieved by Frank's parents was dated the day before the *Formidable* was lost, describing the Christmas festivities on board. Commemorated on the Chatham Naval Memorial, Kent, England (13).

CH/17912 Private (RMLI) **JAMES HENRY RUSSELL** - Aged 19. Son of Mary Russell of 16, Porlock Street, North Kensington, London (previously 15, Treverton Street, North Kensington). Commemorated on the Chatham Naval Memorial, Kent, England (13).

CH/16024 Private (RMLI) **CECIL ARTHUR SAMPSON** - Aged 21. Born Walmer, Kent. Son of Colour Sergeant George Gale Sampson of 37, Waverley Avenue, Wembley Hill, Middlesex. Commemorated on the Chatham Naval Memorial, Kent, England (13).

SS/4933 Ordinary Seaman **ROBERT SAMUEL SAUL** - Aged 21. Son of William and Sarah Saul of Stepshot, Borough Castle, Great Yarmouth. Commemorated on the Chatham Naval Memorial, Kent, England (10).

J/29587 Boy 1st Class **WILLIAM SAUNDERS** - Son of James Saunders of Flexford Farm, Wanborough, Guildford, Surrey. Commemorated on the Portsmouth Naval Memorial, Hampshire, England (8).

232097 Leading Seaman **ERNEST JAMES SAVILL** - Son of Amelia Savill of 33, Fitzroy Avenue, Cliftonville, Margate. Commemorated on the Chatham Naval Memorial, Kent, England (9).

SS/114882 Stoker 1st Class **HARRY SAYER** - Aged 21. Son of Mr and Ellen Sayer of 4, Watlington Cottages, Watlington Grove, Lower Sydenham, London. Commemorated on the Chatham Naval Memorial, Kent, England (12).

J/26335 Boy 1st Class **CHARLES RICHARD SCHLINGLER*** - Son of Richard Schlingler* of 30, Benbow Road, Hammersmith. Commemorated on the Chatham Naval Memorial, Kent, England (10). *SCHINGLER on CWGC.

J/18908* Ordinary Seaman **REGINALD JAMES SCRIVEN** - Aged 18. Adopted son of Mrs Jane Scriven (aunt) of 256, Luton Road, Chatham (previously 8, Edward Street, Chatham). Commemorated on the Chatham Naval Memorial, Kent, England (10). *J/18808 on ADM.

J/27121 Boy 1st Class **BENJAMIN EDGAR SELL** - Aged 16 years and 9 months. Native of East Ham, London. Son of Benjamin and Charlotte Eliza Sell of 42, Kensington Avenue, Manor Park, London. Commemorated on the Chatham Naval Memorial, Kent, England (10).

K/17386 Stoker 1st Class **ARTHUR JAMES SELLIS** - Aged 19. Born Wainscott, Kent. Son of William Thomas Sellis. Commemorated on the Chatham Naval Memorial, Kent, England (12).

Assistant Paymaster (RNR) **SIDNEY JAMES SETON** - Aged 22. Native of Clapham, London. Eldest son of Alice and the late James Henry Seton of 5, Upland Road, Eastbourne. Commemorated on the Chatham Naval Memorial, Kent, England (13).

CH/17675 Private (RMLI) **MAXWELL HERBERT BUCHANAN SEXTON** - Aged 24. Born Brixton, London. Son of Mr and Mrs Thomas Sexton of 8, Rydon Crescent, London. Commemorated on the Chatham Naval Memorial, Kent, England (13).

J/29526 Boy 1st Class **ALBERT SHAW** - Commemorated on the Plymouth Naval Memorial, Devon, England (6).

Tyneside I/82 (RNVR) Able Seaman **ROBERT SHEA** - Aged 24. Son of John and Janet Shea of 29, Herbert Street, Newcastle-upon-Tyne. Commemorated on the Chatham Naval Memorial, Kent, England (15).

J/6846 Signalman **EDWARD SHELDRAKE** - Aged 21. Son of Herbert and Elizabeth Sheldrake of 2, Bell Lane, Bell Street, Henley-on-Thames. Commemorated on the Chatham Naval Memorial, Kent, England (10).

271006 Engine Room Artificer 2nd Class **SYDNEY SHIEL** - Aged 33. Son of the late Walter and Jane Shiel of Sunderland and husband of Charlotte Shiel of 122, Livingstone Road, Gillingham, Kent. Commemorated on the Chatham Naval Memorial, Kent, England (11).

1318S (RNR) Stoker **JACOB SHIELDS** - Aged 30. Son of William and Elizabeth Shields of Middlesbrough. Commemorated on the Chatham Naval Memorial, Kent, England (14).

Sub Lieutenant (RNR) **HERBERT FORSYTH CRAIG SHINNIE** - Born Aberdeen July 21, 1892. Son of Robert and Anne Taylor Shinnie of 150, Bon Accord Street, Aberdeen. Attended Aberdeen Grammar School (1902-7) and joined the Navy League in 1906. Indentured as an apprentice in seamanship to the Adam Line. Served for four years on SS *Aberlour* and sailed around the world three times during this spell. Gazetted as a Midshipman, Royal Naval Reserve, on April 1, 1911. After serving on HMS Africa, he joined the British India Company and served aboard SS *Ekma,* SS *Ellenga,* RMS *Kaurthala and* SS *Chakrata*. He passed his First Officer's Certificate in June 1914 and was notified by the Admiralty to join the Home Fleet. He was despatched to HMS *Formidable*, and during his first three months aboard, was twice mentioned for commendable service, which led to his promotion to Sub-Lieutenant. During the sinking, a fellow Petty Officer, who was with Shinnie on the quarterdeck wrote; '*I had no time to exchange words with my officers, but Sub-Lieut. Shinnie superintended the lowering of the quarterdeck boats and ordered Petty Officers to take charge of them as they were mostly married men. He remained perfectly cool and calm to the very end and when the order came from the Captain to look out for ourselves, the Sub-Lieut. went to see that each of the men near him had something that would float. As far as I know, he went down with the ship.'* Commemorated on the Chatham Naval Memorial, Kent, England (13).

J/29547 Boy 1st Class **JESSE JAMES SHOESMITH** - Aged 17. Native of Walworth, London. Son of Jesse and Susan Shoesmith of 10, Clarence Street, Brunel Road, Rotherhithe. Commemorated on the Chatham Naval Memorial, Kent, England (10).

288844 (RFR/CH/B/6701) Leading Stoker **EDWIN SHUTTLEWORTH** - Aged 39. Native of Manchester. Son of Richard and Ann Shuttleworth. Commemorated on the Chatham Naval Memorial, Kent, England (11).

279875 Mechanician **ALFRED SIDELL** - Commemorated on the Chatham Naval Memorial, Kent, England (11).

SS/4904 Ordinary Seaman **JOHN JOSEPH SIMS** - Aged 23. Son of Catherine and the late James Sims of 97, Park View Cottages, Ringsend, County Dublin. Commemorated on the Chatham Naval Memorial, Kent, England (10).

K/20661* Stoker 1st Class **ALBERT WILLIAM SKEATES** - Commemorated on the Chatham Naval Memorial, Kent, England (12). *K/20651 on CWGC.

SS/114579 Stoker 1st Class **JAMES SKINNER** - Commemorated on the Chatham Naval Memorial, Kent, England (12).

Sub Lieutenant **PHILIP JOHN LANCELOT SKINNER** - Born The Chantry, Ipswich, January 23, 1894. Son of Major Charles Lancelot (late of the 4th Hussars) and Sarah Kathleen Skinner (nee Ponsonby) of 57, Eccleston Square, who was the daughter of Walter William Brabazon, 7th Earl of Bessborough. Educated at St. Andrews, Eastbourne and Osborne and Dartmouth Royal Naval Colleges where he was a cadet captain. H.R.H. the Prince of Wales at one time was under his charge. Joined HMS *Hercules* as a Midshipman in 1911 and then served on HMS *King George V*. Appointed Sub Lieut. on HMS *Formidable* on July 29, 1914. Commemorated on the Chatham Naval Memorial, Kent, England (8).

K/14626 Stoker 1st Class **CHARLES HENRY SLATER** - Aged 32. Born Ladywell, London. Son of Mr C. H. and Sarah Slater and husband of Mary Tucker (formerly Slater) of 64, Porthcawl Road, Lower Sydenham, London. Commemorated on the Chatham Naval Memorial, Kent, England (12).

CH/17141 Private (RMLI) **JOHN SLATTIE** - Aged 20. Born Edinburgh. Son of John and Janet Slattie of 23, South Street, James Street, Edinburgh. Commemorated on the Chatham Naval Memorial, Kent, England (13).

Midshipman **JOHN SLINGSBY** - Aged 16. Son of The Reverend C. and Mrs Slingsby of Scriven Park, Knaresborough, Yorkshire. Commemorated on the Chatham Naval Memorial, Kent, England (8).

201965 (RFR/CH/IC/977) Stoker 1st Class **ALBERT EDWARD SMITH** - Commemorated on the Chatham Naval Memorial, Kent, England (12).

J/29915 Ordinary Seaman **CHARLES FREDERICK SMITH** - Commemorated on the Plymouth Naval Memorial, Devon, England (6).

J/1884 Able Seaman **CHARLES WILLIAM SMITH** - Native of Poplar, London. Son of Charles and Florence Smith of 27, Clever Road, Custom House, London. Commemorated on the Chatham Naval Memorial, Kent, England (10).

K/1501 Petty Officer Stoker **GEORGE THOMAS SMITH** - Aged 27. Native of Wouldham. Husband of Elsie Catherine Smith of 9, Providence Place, Wouldham, Rochester, Kent. Commemorated on the Chatham Naval Memorial, Kent, England (11).

J/29893 Ordinary Seaman **HORACE SMITH** - Aged 18. Son of Charles and Jane Smith of Chelmarsh, Bridgnorth, Shropshire. Commemorated on the Plymouth Naval Memorial, Devon, England (6).

SS/110583 Stoker 1st Class **JOSIAH JOHN SMITH*** - Aged 24. Son of Thomas and Cecilia Smith of 64, Thurston Road, Lewisham, London. Commemorated on the Chatham Naval Memorial, Kent, England (12). *JOSEPH (not JOSIAH) on CWGC.

K/18529 Stoker 1st Class **ROBERT SMITH** - Aged 22. Native of Lambeth, London. Son of the late Frederick Smith. Commemorated on the Chatham Naval Memorial, Kent, England (12).

194682 Chief Yeoman of Signals **SYDNEY RICHARD SMITH** - Aged 33. Son of Richard and Emma Smith of Beltinge, Herne Bay. Commemorated on the Chatham Naval Memorial, Kent, England (10).

CH/17800 Private (RMLI) **FRANK SMITHIES** - Aged 20. Son of Charles and Edith Smithies of 44, Rand Street, Bradford, Yorkshire. Commemorated on the Chatham Naval Memorial, Kent, England (13).

K/6537 Stoker 1st Class **ROBERT SMITHSON** - Aged 22. Son of William Major and Harriet Smithson of 56, Tindall Street, Scarborough. Commemorated on the Chatham Naval Memorial, Kent, England (12).

J/23725 Boy 1st Class **BERNARD ARTHUR de PLUMLEY SMYTHE*** - Aged 17. Son of Reginald and Emily Smythe* of "Berwyn," 53, Silversea Drive, Westcliffe-on-Sea. Buried Lyme Regis Cemetery, Dorset, England (D. 14/17). *SMYTH on CWGC and ADM. Spelling taken from grave inscription.

3029T (RNR) JAMES **WHITE SNADEN** - Commemorated on the Chatham Naval Memorial, Kent, England (14).

341095 Chief Armourer **WILLIAM JOHN SNEDDEN** - Aged 38. Husband of Lizzie Gertrude Snedden of 87, Smithfield Bank, Brook, Chatham, Kent. Commemorated on the Chatham Naval Memorial, Kent, England (12).

Midshipman (RNR) **FRANK BOUSFIELD SOMERVILLE** - Aged 17. Son of Michael Bousfield and Mary Elizabeth Somerville of 3, Carlton Gardens, Stanwix, Carlisle. Commemorated on the Chatham Naval Memorial, Kent, England (13).

2373S* (RNR) Stoker **HENRY SOUTER** - Aged 27. Son of Jane Souter of 25, Melville Road, Stonebridge Park, London. Buried Lyme Regis Cemetery, Dorset, England (D. 14/17). *23735 on CWGC.

173372 Chief Armourer **WALTER SPARROW** - Commemorated on the Chatham Naval Memorial, Kent, England (12).

277613 Stoker 1st Class **ALFRED SPENCER** - Aged 40. Son of the late Mr and Mrs William Spencer and husband of Alice Louisa Spencer of 9, Lea Road, Beckenham, Kent. Commemorated on the Chatham Naval Memorial, Kent, England (12).

J/29917 Ordinary Seaman **WILLIAM SPOORS** - Aged 18. Son of John and Florence Elizabeth Spoors of Heaton, Newcastle-upon-Tyne. Commemorated on the Plymouth Naval Memorial, Devon, England (6).

179143 Chief Petty Officer **FREDERICK STEPHENS** - Aged 37. Son of John and Sarah Ann Stephens of 8, East Bridge Road, Newhaven, Sussex. Commemorated on the Chatham Naval Memorial, Kent, England (9).

J/28378 Boy 1st Class **FRANK HENRY STEPTOE** - Commemorated on the Chatham Naval Memorial, Kent, England (10).

227578 Able Seaman **HARRY STEVENS** - Aged 27. Son of Kitty and the late George Lewis Stevens of 4, South Terrace, Halton, Hastings. Commemorated on the Chatham Naval Memorial, Kent, England (10).

CH/15057 Private (RMLI) **WALTER WILLIAM STIGGANTS** - Aged 30. Son of Mrs Brett of Niton Terrace, North Wall Road and husband of Mrs D. Hill (formerly Stiggants) of 27, Foundry Lane, Freemantle, Southampton. Had served in the Royal Marines for around eleven years, the first four years as a bugler. Served on HMS *Berwick* and had been onboard HMS *Formidable* about two years. Commemorated on the Chatham Naval Memorial, Kent, England (13).

187811 Petty Officer 1st Class **JAMES STOBO** - Aged 35. Son of the late William Stobo of Glasgow. Commemorated on the Chatham Naval Memorial, Kent, England (9).

Lieutenant Commander **HENRY LAYARD STREET** - Commemorated on the Chatham Naval Memorial, Kent, England (8).

187215 Petty Officer 1st Class **ALBERT STRUDWICK** - Aged 34. Son of Henry and Rebecca Strudwick of Amberley, Sussex and husband of Charlotte Lucy Strudwick of 45, Milford Road, Fratton, Portsmouth. Commemorated on the Chatham Naval Memorial, Kent, England (9).

214859 Petty Officer **HENRY JOHN STUBBS** - Aged 30. Son of Frederick and the late Florence Caroline Stubbs of 49, Raymond Road, Upton Park, London. Commemorated on the Chatham Naval Memorial, Kent, England (9).

CH/10877 Sergeant (RMLI) **ALFRED MARK SUTTON*** - Aged 35. Husband of G. M. Sutton of 3, Tennyson Road, Gillingham. Commemorated on the Chatham Naval Memorial, Kent, England (13). *ALBERT (not ALFRED) on CWGC.

312044 Leading Stoker **CHARLES SWABY** - Aged 33. Son of Mr and Mrs Swaby of 6, Sydney Terrace, Folkestone Road, Dover. Commemorated on the Chatham Naval Memorial, Kent, England (11).

J/29543 Boy 1st Class **WILLIAM EDWARD SWAIN** - Commemorated on the Chatham Naval Memorial, Kent, England (10).

SS/4917 ALFRED **ARTHUR SWIFT** - Aged 21. Son of Mrs M. A. Swift of 52, Lurgan Avenue, Fulham, London. Commemorated on the Chatham Naval Memorial, Kent, England (10).

K/555 Stoker 1st Class **ERNEST TARRANT** - Commemorated on the Chatham Naval Memorial, Kent, England (12).

Lieutenant **TREVOR HODGSON STANLEY TATHAM** - Born November 16, 1887, Newcastle-on-Tyne. Eldest son of Stanley and Frances Emma Constance Tatham of Montana, Burton Road, Branksome Park, Bournemouth. Became a Midshipman on February 15, 1904 and a Sub-Lieut. on April 15, 1907, followed by promotion to Lieutenant on July 15, 1908. Served six years on HMS *Formidable*, *Duncan* and *Barham* and was A.D.C. to Captain Walker while a Midshipman on *Formidable*. Took part in the Somaliland Expedition in 1909 (medal) and was re-appointed to HMS *Formidable* on August 9, 1913. His mother awoke as the bells rung in the 1915 New Year and saw Lieutenant Tatham at the end of her bed, so knew he wouldn't be coming home. Trevor's younger brother Second Lieutenant Lawrence Castell Stanley Tatham of No.5 Squadron, Royal Flying Corps, was killed in action on January 10, 1918 over Vimy Ridge, when his aircraft was shot down by a shell. Commemorated on the Chatham Naval Memorial, Kent, England (8).

Midshipman (RNR) **DONALD STEWART TATTERSALL** - Son of Arthur and Louisa Tattersall of "Oakenrod," 3, Blackpool Road, Lytham, Blackpool. Commemorated on the Chatham Naval Memorial, Kent, England (13).

Fleet Surgeon **GODFREY TAYLOR** - Aged 42. Son of Godfrey Lovelace and Dorothea Marie Taylor of Grangeville, Fethard, County Wexford. Commemorated on the Chatham Naval Memorial, Kent, England (9).

CH/17955 Private (RMLI) **JAMES HENRY THACKER** - Aged 18. Native of Camberwell, London. Son of Mr W. J. and Mrs L. J. Thacker of 3, Lestock Place, East Street, Walworth, London. Commemorated on the Chatham Naval Memorial, Kent, England (13).

J/29212 Boy 1st Class **WILLIAM GEORGE THOMAS** - Aged 16. Son of Henry Cameron and Eliza Thomas of 75, Milton Avenue, East Ham, London. Commemorated on the Chatham Naval Memorial, Kent, England (10).

K/1063 Stoker 1st Class **JAMES GEORGE LONSDALE THOMSON** - Commemorated on the Chatham Naval Memorial, Kent, England (12).

CH/14928 Corporal (RMLI) **JOHN WILLIAM THORPE** - Aged 29. Native of Gillingham, Kent. Son of Henry and Elizabeth Thorpe of 26, Thorne Street, White Hart Lane, Barnes, London. Commemorated on the Chatham Naval Memorial, Kent, England (13).

J/10402 Able Seaman **OLIVER TIDY** - Aged 20. Son of James and Rita Tidy of 7, Coneyhurst Lane, Ewhurst, Surrey. Commemorated on the Chatham Naval Memorial, Kent, England (10).

168300 Chief Petty Officer **WILLIAM GILBERT TILL** - Aged 38. Son of Joseph and S. S. Till of Wimbleton and husband of Jennie Till of 31, George Street, Ramsgate. Commemorated on the Chatham Naval Memorial, Kent, England (9).

165546 Petty Officer 1st Class **WILLIAM TILTON** - Aged 37. Son of the late Alfred and Elizabeth Tilton of Camberwell, London and husband of Annie Frances Tilton of 13, Strode

Road, Forest Gate, London. Awarded Messina Medal and Long Service and Good Conduct Medal. Commemorated on the Chatham Naval Memorial, Kent, England (9).

K/15852 Stoker 1st Class **WILLIAM GEORGE TITMUSS** - Aged 23. Son of Walter George and Elizabeth Titmuss of 18, Helder Street, South Croydon, Surrey. Commemorated on the Chatham Naval Memorial, Kent, England (12).

CH/16728 Private (RMLI) **HERBERT CHARLES TORAH** - Commemorated on the Chatham Naval Memorial, Kent, England (13).

201836 Leading Seaman **SAMUEL TORRENCE** - Aged 32. Son of Edmund and Mary Torrence of Preston, Lancashire. Commemorated on the Chatham Naval Memorial, Kent, England (9).

344808 Shipwright 2nd Class **ROBERT TOSH** - Commemorated on the Chatham Naval Memorial, Kent, England (12).

CH/17920 Private (RMLI) **ARTHUR JOHN TUNGATE** - Aged 19. Son of James and Louisa Tungate of 5, Stone Row, Bebside Furnace, Northumberland. Commemorated on the Chatham Naval Memorial, Kent, England (13).

CH/17274 Private (RMLI) **ALFRED JAMES TURNER** - Aged 21. Son of Alfred James and Alice Turner of 40, Holly Cottages, Charlton, Middlesex. Commemorated on the Chatham Naval Memorial, Kent, England (13).

K/16303 Stoker 1st Class **GEORGE JAMES TURNER** - Aged 20. Son of John Arthur and Hannah Sarah Turner of 65, Stebondale Street, Cubitt Town, Poplar, London. Commemorated on the Chatham Naval Memorial, Kent, England (12).

SS/112450 Stoker 1st Class **SIDNEY TURNER** - Aged 23. Son of Mr and Mrs Turner of Middle Street, Nazeing, Essex. Commemorated on the Chatham Naval Memorial, Kent, England (12).

J/26250 Ordinary Seaman **WILLIE JAMES TURPIN** - Commemorated on the Plymouth Naval Memorial, Devon, England (6).

J/15578 Ordinary Signalman **GEORGE TYLER** - Commemorated on the Chatham Naval Memorial, Kent, England (10).

SS/107088 (RFR/CH/B/9482) Stoker 1st Class **SAMUEL WALLACE UNDERHILL** - Aged 23. Son of Joseph William and Annie Underhill of Stourport, Worcestershire. Commemorated on the Chatham Naval Memorial, Kent, England (12).

M/7963 Armourer's Crew **ALBERT HENRY UPTON** - Aged 18. Son of Frederick and Mary Ann Upton of 23, Barbara Street, Barnsbury, London. Commemorated on the Chatham Naval Memorial, Kent, England (12).

M/5992* Sick Berth Attendant **REGINALD GODFREY VENNILS** - Aged 21. Son of Charles and T. J. Vennils of 94, Mayplace Road, Bexley Heath, Kent. Commemorated on the Chatham Naval Memorial, Kent, England (12) *M/8992 on CWGC.

M/10984 Senior Reserve Attendant **HENRI VILLIERS RUSSELL** - Aged 29. Son of Isabelina and the late Benjamin Villiers Russell of 17, Audley Street, Crewe, Cheshire. A member of the Royal Naval Auxiliary Sick Berth Reserve and formerly employed in Crewe Works. His twin brother John died in the same incident. Buried Coppenhall (St. Michael) Churchyard, Crewe, Cheshire (south-east corner).

M/10985 Senior Reserve Attendant **JOHN VILLIERS RUSSELL** - Aged 29. Son of Isabelina and the late Benjamin Villiers Russell of 17, Audley Street, Crewe, Cheshire. A member of the Royal Naval Auxiliary Sick Berth Reserve and formerly employed in Crewe Works. His twin brother Henri died in the same incident. Buried Coppenhall (St. Michael) Churchyard, Crewe, Cheshire (south-east corner).

J/29903 Ordinary Seaman **MARTIN WALSH** - Aged 18. Son of Philip and Alice Walsh of St. Hellens Street, Galway. Commemorated on the Plymouth Naval Memorial, Devon, England (6).

CH/17219 Private (RMLI) **JAMES WARBURTON** - Aged 20. Son of Kate Warburton of Seamons Road, Dunham Massey, Altrincham, Cheshire. Commemorated on the Chatham Naval Memorial, Kent, England (13).

2046U (RNR) **JOSEPH WARD** - Commemorated on the Portsmouth Naval Memorial, Hampshire, England (10).

293138 Mechanician **GEORGE ALBERT ALFRED WARN** - Commemorated on the Chatham Naval Memorial, Kent, England (11).

SS/109366 Stoker 1st Class **JOHN HENRY WARREN** - Commemorated on the Chatham Naval Memorial, Kent, England (12).

176004 Chief Stoker **JOHN WATERMAN** - Commemorated on the Chatham Naval Memorial, Kent, England (11).

Engineer Lieutenant **WILLIAM WATERS** - Aged 29. Son of the late William and Annie Waters of Caerphilly, Glamorgan and husband of Jessie Rhena Waters of 34, Royal Park, Clifton, Bristol. Commemorated on the Chatham Naval Memorial, Kent, England (8).

291436 (RFR/CH/B/7405) Stoker 1st Class **CHARLES EDWARD WATKINS** - Commemorated on the Chatham Naval Memorial, Kent, England (12).

CH/16890 Private (RMLI) **REGINALD JOHN WATKINS** - Commemorated on the Chatham Naval Memorial, Kent, England (13).

284894 Mechanician **HENRY JAMES WATSON** - Resided at Third Avenue, Chatham. Commemorated on the Chatham Naval Memorial, Kent, England (11).

312171 Leading Stoker **JOSEPH ALBERT WELLER** - Aged 25. Son of the late Joseph and Mary Weller. Commemorated on the Chatham Naval Memorial, Kent, England (11).

M/6769 Cook's Mate 2nd Class **ARTHUR EDWIN WELLS** - Aged 19. Son of Albert and Lucy Wells of 22, Baches Street, Hoxton, London. Commemorated on the Chatham Naval Memorial, Kent, England (12).

159303 Ship's Corporal 1st Class **CHARLES WILLIAM WEST** - Aged 38. Husband of Ellen West of 46, Sidney Road, Gillingham, Kent. Commemorated on the Chatham Naval Memorial, Kent, England (12).

344901 Shipwright 2nd Class **GEORGE WEST** - Commemorated on the Chatham Naval Memorial, Kent, England (12).

CH/13788 Private (RMLI) **HENRY WILLIAM WESTON** - Commemorated on the Chatham Naval Memorial, Kent, England (13).

K/2155 Stoker 1st Class **WILLIAM WHIDDETT** - Aged 22. Son of Alfred Whiddett of Church Street, St. Mary, Sandwich and husband of Ethel Simmons (formerly Whiddett) of 7, Broadway, Swanspool, Wellingborough, Northamptonshire. Two other brothers also served during the war. Commemorated on the Chatham Naval Memorial, Kent, England (12).

K/20995 Stoker 1st Class **BENJAMIN JAMES WHITE** - Aged 19. Son of Alice White of 6, New Park Street, Colchester. Commemorated on the Chatham Naval Memorial, Kent, England (12).

341051 Plumber **HENRY BURBRIDGE WHITE*** - Aged 47. Husband of Blanche White of 52, Chaucer Road, Gillingham, Kent. Commemorated on the Chatham Naval Memorial, Kent, England (12). *served as HENRY RUCK.

CH/9383 Sergeant (RMLI) **THOMAS HENRY WHITE** - Resided at 19, Jeyes Street, Chatham. Commemorated on the Chatham Naval Memorial, Kent, England (13).

J/29911 Boy 1st Class **WILLIAM WHITE** - Aged 18. Son of William and Mary White of 30, English Street, Dumfries. Commemorated on the Plymouth Naval Memorial, Devon, England (6).

210652 Stoker 1st Class **ALBERT WHITING** - Aged 32. Son of Mrs Whiting of 47, St. George's Road, Hastings, Sussex. Commemorated on the Chatham Naval Memorial, Kent, England (12).

344568 Carpenter's Crew **JAMES WIGNALL** - Commemorated on the Chatham Naval Memorial, Kent, England (12).

J/26578 Boy 1st Class **JOHN ALBERT WILKINS** - Aged 17. Son of John and Ada Matilda Wilkins of 18, Wansey Street, Walworth Road, Walworth, London. Commemorated on the Chatham Naval Memorial, Kent, England (10).

CH/13156 Private (RMLI) **WILLIAM GEORGE WILKINS** - Commemorated on the Chatham Naval Memorial, Kent, England (13).

1222S (RNR) Stoker **JOHN WILSON** - Aged 27. Son of the late Thomas and Elizabeth Wilson of Teesdale Street, Thornaby-on-Tees. Commemorated on the Chatham Naval Memorial, Kent, England (14).

296945 (RFR/CH/A/2005) Petty Officer Stoker **GEORGE WILLIAM WIMBLE** - Aged 44. Son of George William and the late Elizabeth Wimble of Grimsby and husband of Lily Alice Wimble of 44, Britton Street, Gillingham, Kent. Commemorated on the Chatham Naval Memorial, Kent, England (11).

Midshipman **GEORGE STEPHENSON WINGROVE** - Aged 16. Born Banstead. Son of Stephen and Eleanor Sarah Wingrove of Buff House, Banstead, Surrey. Commemorated on the Chatham Naval Memorial, Kent, England (8).

195251 Able Seaman **JOHN CLARK WINYARD** - Commemorated on the Chatham Naval Memorial, Kent, England (10).

K/12042 Stoker 1st Class **CHARLES FREDERICK WOOD** - Aged 24. Son of John and Elizabeth Wood of 12, Blenheim Road, Penge, London. Commemorated on the Chatham Naval Memorial, Kent, England (12).

CH/17519 Private (RMLI) **ROLAND WALTER WOODS** - Resided in Wokingham, Berkshire and was the eldest of six children. Joined the Royal Marines Light Infantry aged 17. Commemorated on the Chatham Naval Memorial, Kent, England (13).

236037 Leading Seaman **ALEXANDER JAMES WOOLDRIDGE** - Aged 24. Son of Frederick George and Harriet Wooldridge of 25, Hinton Road, Herne Hill, London. Commemorated on the Chatham Naval Memorial, Kent, England (9).

J/5531 Able Seaman **PERCY JOHN WRAIGHT** - Commemorated on the Chatham Naval Memorial, Kent, England (10).

CH/17864 Private (RMLI) **VICTOR HERBERT WRIGHT** - Aged 17. Native of Brixton, London. Son of Edward Phillip and Amy Wright of The Corner House, High Street, Leatherhead, Surrey. Commemorated on the Chatham Naval Memorial, Kent, England (13).

270041 Engine Room Artificer 1st Class **LOUIS FRED WYERS** - Commemorated on the Chatham Naval Memorial, Kent, England (11).

CH/16853 Private (RMLI) **ALBERT PERCY YORKE** - Aged 22. Son of Henry and Jane Yorke of 99, Winsover Road, Spalding. Commemorated on the Chatham Naval Memorial, Kent, England (13).

EPILOGUE

A total of thirteen British battleships were sunk during the war (11 pre-dreadnought's), of which five were sunk by U-boat torpedoes. In 1914 the Royal Navy lost HMS *Audacious* (mine) and HMS *Bulwark* (internal explosion) as explained in earlier notes. The year of 1915 however would be the most costly with six battleships lost. After the *Formidable*, five were sunk during the disastrous Dardanelles campaign. On March 18, HMS *Irresistible* and HMS *Ocean* were sunk. HMS *Goliath* was lost on May 13 - torpedoed by a Turkish torpedo boat - and *U-21* sunk HMS *Triumph* on May 25 and HMS *Majestic*,

Pictures of the Fallen.

Private (RMLI) Albert Douce.

| **Stoker** | **ERA** | **Private (RMLI)** |
| **Ernest Tarrant** | **John Charlesworth** | **George Faulkner** |

Lieutenant Trevor Hodgson Stanley Tatham.

HMS *Formidable* Gunroom c1905. Trevor Tatham is standing second on the right. (Below) Trevor Tatham posing with the HMS *Barham* 2nd XI football team c1909.

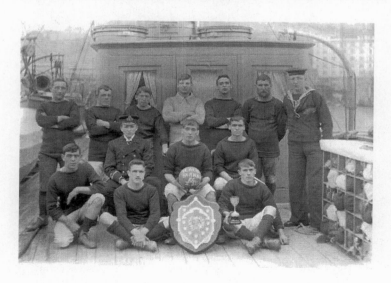

Private (RMLI) Harry Wright Ostick.

**Able Seaman
Albert Botley**

**Leading Stoker
James Early**

**Chief Petty Officer
Walter Horton**

**Sergeant (RMLI)
John Reed**

**Commander
Charles Ballard**

**Stoker
John Forward**

**Ship's Chief Cook
Charles Bryant**

**Corporal (RMLI)
George Fuggles**

**Private (RMLI)
Ernest Booth**

**Gunner
Percival Hallett**

**Private (RMLI)
Henry May**

**Plumber
Henry White (Ruck)**

**Blacksmith's Mate
Albert Nicholls**

**Sergeant (RMLI)
Thomas White**

**Private (RMLI)
William Bennett**

**Private (RMLI)
Walter Stiggants**

**Petty Officer
William Denham**

**Chief Armourer
William Snedden**

**Ship's Corporal
Henry Croxson**

**Private (RMLI)
Herbert Phillips**

**Boy 1st Class
Bernard Smythe**

**Surgeon
Septimus Hibbert**

**Cook's Mate
John Kerswell**

**Sub Lieutenant
Philip Skinner**

**Private (RMLI)
Robert Kemp**

**Leading Stoker
William Howland**

**Lieutenant
George Hathorn**

**Blacksmith
Sydney Eyres**

**Private (RMLI)
Frank Royes**

**Petty Officer
Samuel Colville**

Private (RMLI) Roland Woods

**Mechanician
Henry Watson**

**Ship's Corporal
Jack Cripps**

**Surgeon
William Mearns**

two days later, both off Gaba Tepe. In 1916, the mine would claim two more battleships, when on January 6, HMS *King Edward VII* was sunk off the Scottish coast and on April 27, HMS *Russell* struck a mine off Malta. Two more were lost in 1917. HMS *Cornwallis* was torpedoed by *U-32* on January 29, again off the Maltese coast and on July 9, HMS *Vanguard* suffered a similar fate as the *Bulwark,* when she blew up at anchor at Scapa Flow. The final battleship loss of the war occurred just two days before the Armistice, when *UB-50* sank HMS *Brittania* off Cape Trafalgar.

On the eve of the First World War, the art of submarine warfare was barely a decade old. None of the super naval powers had submarine-qualified officers serving at senior staff level or had developed any positive method of dealing with and destroying what would become "the dreaded underwater scourge." The submarine did not rate highly in the structures of the world's navies. Bigger, faster and better armed battleships were top of the list, in terms of importance. By the end of the war however, submarines had changed naval warfare forever. On the German side, a total of 373 U-boats saw service during the Great War, accounting for nearly 6,500 merchant ships - a staggering 11,000,000 tonnes of shipping. Also 100 enemy warships were sunk and countless thousands of crew members paid the price of their superiors ignorance towards the initial threat of the submarine as a potential weapon of war. Of all the operational U-boats of the war, nearly half (178) were lost, with many sunk in British coastal waters. The draw of lucrative pickings in the English Channel would prove too tempting for the U-boat commanders and many would be sunk attempting to pass through the heavily-protected Dover Straits and in the killing grounds of the English Channel. This stretch of water would become the final resting place of many a U-boat crew, and the graveyard for all of their victims. Among them, as we have read, were 547 crew members of the old British battleship HMS *Formidable.*

Today the *Formidable* lies in around 60 metres of water, after the wreck was officially identified in 1981. A Devon salvage team led by Captain Silas Oates, salvage master for a salvage company at Yealhampton, Devon, had hoped to salvage the wreck after locating her after a two year survey. She had been identified by divers from brass plates bearing her name. The wreck had been described as in good condition and surrounded by trawling nets. The heavy salvage vessel *Salvos 1* was prepared in the hope that the battleship could be salvaged and sold for scrap, but thankfully they were refused permission on the grounds that it was a tomb to the men who had gone down on her. After that it became a favourite dive for amateur and professional divers alike, until the site was designated a war grave. The official wreck position is 50-13-12 N, 03-03-58 W. She lies completely upside down and there is a split in her hull forward of the foremost funnel and forward gun barbette some twenty feet wide. There is also large evidence of looting. One propeller has been removed in unauthorised salvage and another has been blown off but lies nearby still attached to the shaft. The protection of Military Remains Act was passed in 1986, but the application to wrecks and sea graves was not enforced. In November 2001, greater protection was given to military wrecks and maritime graves, following rising concerns over disturbance and trophy hunting by an irresponsible minority of divers. Sixteen wrecks in waters under United Kingdom jurisdiction were designated as Controlled Sites. Included among the WW1 ships are HMS *Bulwark, Hampshire, Vanguard* and *Formidable*. Thankfully diving on these sixteen wrecks is now prohibited unless a specific licence is obtained. We will never forget their contribution to winning the freedom of our forbearers and moulding the world today that we live in.

In December 1915, nearly one year after the sinking, the capsized cutter of the *Formidable* still lay on the Chesil Beach, half buried in the sand and forgotten - just like the sinking of HMS *Formidable* is forgotten today. We hope that this book brings to the forefront this most tragic of episodes during the Great War of 1914-19.

THE LOSS OF THE FORMIDABLE ON NEW YEAR'S MORN.
By F. Wood

"The" New Year's morn, had but awoke-
When on our ears great sorrow broke,
For sighted, in the Channel, lay,
Just at the early dawn of day,
A ship, her New Year's banner scarce unfurled,
When she, the great "Formidable" was hurled,
Lying like a lion with its prey,
Then leaped into space; mid the ocean spray,
Into the unfathomable Abyss.
O mystery of great mysteries, this
And Oh, her brave and gallant crew
Their duty anxious each to do,
"But Ah!" many sank to a watery grave,
So few the number, could be saved,
Their Captain, stalwart and so true,
"At his post" when the last blast blew,
May they be piloted to that shore
Where there is "Peace for evermore,"
For a noble honour is it to live
The wrong to right, their life to give.
Tho' their bodies, in the Ocean lie,
Yet in our memory ne'er will die,
Their "Epitaph" is but the wave,
No other stone to mark their grave,
Their voyage on this earth is done.
But the wreaths of laurels, surely won,
And, may the saved and rescued few,
Just live their lives to Him anew,
For sure a Providential Hand,
Had brought them safely to the land,
No other compass but His guide,
Their own long drifted from their side,

Thoughts to their hearts may rise like this,
"Why was I saved and my comrades missed."

When half the good folk of Lyme Regis lie sleeping,
A few anxious watchers, an outlook was keeping,
And what is that speck, near a mile from the bay,
"Why sure 'tis a boat" the good Coastguard does say,
"I've watched her she's coming, she's on her track,
Now boys to be ready, sure our help she do lack,
And soon all astir, for the news went afloat,
That nearing the bay, was the incoming boat,
In her fifty poor souls, well nigh beat,
Tossed hours on rough seas, and not a morsel to eat,
Perishing cold, and many weary and sad,
And many indeed were but scantily clad,
From that ill-fated ship, long hours had been,
Oft crying for help, and none could be seen,
At times they seemed doomed, yet their hearts did not fail,
But took their boots out the water to bale,
And a light hearted comrade oft cheered the crew,
With "pull up" boys "pull" we shall surely get through,
At last came sound of the breakers, with joy, well nigh cried,
For sure these brave men had been bitterly tried.
At length the old shingle, in touch with their keel,
Ne'er so thankful before in their life did they feel,
And a kind hearted crowd, just gave of their best,
To help the poor sufferer's to comfort and rest.
But both joy and sorrow, did mingle the throng,
In that boat, a few souls had passed to that "Land Beyond,"
No need of our love, nay, even the best,
God grant, had called them to His "Haven of Rest."
And the good folk of Lyme Regis, that quaint little spot,
Holds, that night in the year, will ne'er be forgot.
Meanwhile from Brixham Bay, a captain brave,
Put out to sea, that he might save,

With his stalwart little crew,
Ready, so ready, their best to do,
Thinking not of what the cost,
Should they, and their little skiff be lost,
So, on and on, and on they went,
In the well fought little "Provident,"
Their only thought to reach their goal,
E'en to save one perishing soul.
So for hours rode on an angry sea,
For three times, oft repelled they be,
Yet their courage did not fail,
On they went, through the blinding gale,
For waves, rose high, full thirty feet,
But at last, a gleam their eye did meet,
And they were nearing human cries,
Which, my poor pen, can n'er descry.
What hopes were hovering round that boat,
Could they but keep her still afloat,
Ah! Yes, Good Pillar was not made of salt,
But must be sure of granite, wrought,
For at last with Oh, such wondrous skill,
The line was cast, the boat they fill,
With seventy perishing souls, or more,
And land them safely to Brixham shore.
And from many a heart arose a prayer,
For the safety of those they held most dear,
A gathering crowd, so welcomed them back,
And no need of comfort, did the sufferer's lack,
But all were most anxious their best to bestow,
That they in their hearts, might their gratitude show,
And blithe little Dan, the life of the crew,
Just nimbled about, that he might his part do,
Aud voices rang out with "Auld Lang Syne,"
Near to the hour of the midnight chime,
But their voices rose higher with right good cheer,
To the "Provident's" heroes, "The first of the year.

BIBLIOGRAPHY

CONWAY'S ALL THE WORLD'S FIGHTING SHIPS 1906-1921 *by Conway Maritime Press*
CONWAY'S ALL THE WORLD'S FIGHTING SHIPS 1860-1905 *by Conway Maritime Press*
JANE'S FIGHTING SHIPS OF WORLD WAR ONE *by Jane's Publishing Company*
THE NAVAL WHO'S WHO 1917
BRITISH BATTLESHIPS *by Commander Randolph Pears*
THE MACMILLAN DICTIONARY OF THE FIRST WORLD WAR *by Stephen Pope and Elizabeth-Anne Wheal*
BRIXHAM OF YESTERYEAR PART III *by Chips Barber*
DEAR MRS JONES - THE GREAT WAR DEAD OF CREWE & NANTWICH *by Mark Potts and Joy Bratherton*
DEAR MRS JONES - THE NEXT GENERATION *by Mark Potts and Tony Marks*
CAPTAIN LOXLEY'S LITTLE DOG *Anon*
BRIXHAM AND ITS PEOPLE *by Arthur C. Ellis*
THE BLINDFOLD GAME *by Ewart Oakeshott*
BRITISH VESSELS LOST AT SEA 1914-18 *by HMSO*
THE SAILORS WAR 1914-18 *by Peter H. Liddle*
PROVIDENT AND THE STORY OF THE BRIXHAM SMACKS *by John Corin*
NAVAL OPERATIONS, VOLUME ONE *by Sir Julian S. Corbett*
NAVAL OPERATIONS, VOLUME TWO *by Sir Julian S. Corbett*
BRITISH BATTLESHIPS *by Oscar Parkes*
BRITISH BATTLESHIPS 1889-1904 *by R. A. Burt*
WARRIOR TO DREADNOUGHT *by D. K. Brown*
THE GRAND FLEET *by Admiral Viscount Jellicoe*
PULL TOGETHER *by Admiral Sir Lewis Bayly*
BRIDPORT AND THE GREAT WAR *by J. W. Rowson*
FIND AND DESTROY *by Dwight R. Messimer*
THE DAY THE EAST COAST BLED *by Mark Marsay*
DEEDS OF A GREAT RAILWAY by *G. R. S. Darroch*

INDEX

Printed in Great Britain by
Amazon.co.uk, Ltd.,
Marston Gate.